THE OF

CHECK LIST
AND
RECORD BOOK OF UNITED STATES PAPER MONEY

THE OFFICIAL RED BOOK®

CHECK LIST
AND
RECORD BOOK OF
UNITED STATES
PAPER MONEY

THE OFFICIAL RED BOOK is a trademark of Whitman Publishing, LLC.
ISBN 0794845177

© 2017 Whitman Publishing, LLC
1960 Chandalar Drive • Suite E • Pelham, AL 35124

WHITMAN®

For a complete listing of numismatic reference
books, supplies, and storage products,
visit us at www.whitman.com

Printed in the United States of America.

CONTENTS

HOW TO USE THIS BOOK

The *Check List and Record Book of United States Paper Money* is a valuable resource for keeping track of your collection. It covers all federal series from $1 to $10,000, as well as error notes, Postage and Fractional Currency, and Encased Postage. In addition to "star" notes (notes issued to replace previously destroyed notes with the same serial number), the *Check List* also includes mule notes—unusual combinations of face and back plates—along with many new discoveries not documented elsewhere!

Federal series are presented first, in denomination order; other specialties are located toward the back of the book (see the table of contents). Within each denomination, the notes are organized by Friedberg numbers so they can be located easily; updated printages and rarities, based on the latest research available as of press time, are included. Beside each note-number is a generous area for recording details—where and when you obtained the note, its grade, the price, and any other information you want to jot down.

In addition its Friedberg number, each note is cross-referenced to its Whitman number. Both can be used to look up your notes and study them in-depth in references such as the *Whitman Encyclopedia of U.S. Paper Money*.

Letters in the Friedberg/Whitman numbers representing the issuing Federal Reserve banks are as follows:

A	Boston	G	Chicago
B	New York	H	St. Louis
C	Philadelphia	I	Minneapolis
D	Cleveland	J	Kansas City
E	Richmond	K	Dallas
F	Atlanta	L	San Francisco

Notes that are not known to exist have been omitted from this checklist. Check boxes are black for notes known to exist only in institutional collections.

LARGE-SIZE

$1 Legal Tender Notes

F-No. (W-No.) • Printage *(rarity)*	Grade	Comments
Series of 1862		
❑ F-16 (W-5) • est. 813,224 *(150–180)*		
❑ F-16 (W-6) • est. 5,850,776 *(500–700)*		
❑ F-16 (W-9) • 4,946,000 *(800–1,000)*		
❑ F-16a (W-8) • est. 150,000 *(60–65)*		
❑ F-17 (W-1) • est. 5,000 *(5 known)*		
❑ F-17a (W-4) • est. 16,512,000 *(450–600)*		
❑ F-17a (W-7) • est. 50,000 *(20–25)*		
❑ F-17b (W-2) • est. 7,000 *(6 known)*		
❑ F-17b (W-3) • est. 12,000 *(1 known)*		
Series of 1869		
❑ F-18 (W-11) • 41,868,000 *(1,000–1,400)*		
Series of 1874		
❑ F-19 (W-14) • 18,988,000 *(225–250)*		
Series of 1875		
❑ F-20 (W-20) • 9,000,000 *(225–250)*		
❑ F-21 (W-15) • 1,000,000 *(30–35)*		
❑ F-22 (W-16) • 1,000,000 *(26–32)*		
❑ F-23 (W-17) • 1,000,000 *(42–46)*		
❑ F-24 (W-18) • 1,000,000 *(18–20)*		
❑ F-25 (W-19) • 1,000,000 *(26–30)*		
❑ F-26 (W-21) • 12,212,000 *(450–550)*		

F-No. (W-No.) • Printage (rarity)	Grade	Comments
Series of 1878		
❑ F-27 (W-22) • 12,512,000 (350–400)		
Series of 1880		
❑ F-28 (W-23a, Back Style 1) • est. 2,000,000 (5–10)		
❑ F-28 (W-23b, Back Style 2) • est. 17,964,000 (250–290)		
❑ F-29 (W-24) • est. 17,036,000 (250–290)		
❑ F-30 (W-25) • est. 18,208,000 (600–700)		
❑ F-31 (W-27) • est. 704,000 (140–150)		
❑ F-32 (W-28) • est. 432,000 (70–80)		
❑ F-33 (W-29) • est. 56,000 (35–38)		
❑ F-34 (W-30) • est. 1,488,000 (120–140)		
❑ F-35 (W-31) • est. 1,996,000 (170–185)		
Series of 1917		
❑ F-36 (W-33) • est. 269,684,000 (2,000–2,500)		
❑ F-36★ (W-33★) • (200–250)		
❑ F-37 (W-34) • est. 299,032,000 (3,000–4,000)		
❑ F-37★ (W-34★) • (275–325)		
❑ F-37a (W-35) • est. 100,000 (130–160)		
❑ F-38 (W-36) • est. 20,000,000 (200–300)		
❑ F-38★ (W-36★) • (80–90)		
❑ F-38 (W-36 Mule) • est. 81,876,000 (650–800)		
❑ F-38★ (W-36 Mule★) • (65–70)		
❑ F-39 (W-37) • est. 289,376,000 (5,000–8,000)		
❑ F-39★ (W-37★) • (300–325)		
❑ F-39 (W-37 Mule) • est. 7,000,000 (90–120)		
❑ F-39★ (W-37 Mule★) • (20–25)		
Series of 1923		
❑ F-40 (W-38) • 81,872,000 (3,500–5,000)		
❑ F-40★ (W-38★) • (180–220)		

$1 National Bank Notes

F-No. (W-No.) • Printage (rarity)	Grade	Comments
Original Series ("First Charter Period")		
❑ F-380 (W-40) • (2,500–3,000)		
❑ F-381 (W-41) • (9–10)		
❑ F-382 (W-42) • (800–1,000)		

F-No. (W-No.) • Printage *(rarity)*	Grade	Comments
Series of 1875 ("First Charter Period")		
❏ F-383 (W-43) • *(500–600)*		
❏ F-384 (W-44) • *(475–550)*		
❏ F-385 (W-45) • *(200–225)*		
❏ F-386 (W-46) • *(80–90)*		

$1 Silver Certificates

F-No. (W-No.) • Printage *(rarity)*	Grade	Comments
Series of 1886		
❏ F-215 (W-50) • est. 13,660,000 *(650–800)*		
❏ F-216 (W-51) • est. 7,380,000 *(250–300)*		
❏ F-217 (W-52) • est. 18,780,000 *(500–600)*		
❏ F-218 (W-53) • est. 13,760,000 *(275–325)*		
❏ F-219 (W-54) • est. 10,300,000 *(325–375)*		
❏ F-220 (W-55) • est. 4,400,000 *(150–165)*		
❏ F-221 (W-56) • est. 4,204,000 *(145–175)*		
Series of 1891		
❏ F-222 (W-57) • est. 13,320,000 *(250–300)*		
❏ F-223 (W-58) • est. 52,088,000 *(1,100–1,400)*		
Series of 1896		
❏ F-224 (W-59) • est. 33,952,000 *(3,500–5,000)*		
❏ F-225 (W-60) • est. 23,392,000 *(1,500–2,000)*		
Series of 1899		
❏ F-226 (W-61) • 100,000,000 *(425–475)*		
❏ F-226a (W-62) • est. 350,900,000 *(900–1,100)*		
❏ F-227 (W-63) • est. 108,900,000 *(300–350)*		
❏ F-228 (W-64) • est. 374,199,600 *(1,000–1,200)*		
❏ F-229 (W-65) • est. 224,792,000 *(700–850)*		
❏ F-229★ (W-65★) • *(35–40)*		
❏ F-229a (W-66) • est. 26,612,000 *(150–165)*		
❏ F-229a★ (W-66★) • *(2 known)*		
❏ F-230 (W-67) • est. 469,020,000 *(1,300–1,600)*		
❏ F-230★ (W-67★) • *(45–48)*		
❏ F-231 (W-68) • 6,740,000 *(150–160)*		
❏ F-232 (W-69) • est. 354,268,000 *(1,200–1,400)*		
❏ F-232★ (W-69★) • *(53–55)*		

F-No. (W-No.) • Printage *(rarity)*	Grade	Comments
Series of 1899 *(continued)*		
❑ F-233 (W-70) • est. 790,444,000 *(5,000–7,000)*		
❑ F-233★ (W-70★) • *(185–200)*		
❑ F-234 (W-71) • est. 60,320,000 *(1,000–1,200)*		
❑ F-234★ (W-71★) • *(55–60)*		
❑ F-234 (W-71 Mule) • est. 2,000,000 *(55–65)*		
❑ F-234★ (W-71 Mule★) • *(9–11)*		
❑ F-235 (W-72) • est. 174,460,000 *(1,600–2,000)*		
❑ F-235★ (W-72★) • *(150–200)*		
❑ F-235 (W-72 Mule) • est. 58,000,000 *(500–600)*		
❑ F-235★ (W-72 Mule★) • *(30–35)*		
❑ F-236 (W-73) • est. 588,200,000 *(6,000–9,000)*		
❑ F-236★ (W-73★) • *(225–235)*		
❑ F-236 (W-73 Mule) • est. 5,000,000 *(60–90)*		
❑ F-236★ (W-73 Mule★) • *(6 known)*		
Series of 1923		
❑ F-237 (W-74) • est. 2,431,800,000 *(16,000–22,000)*		
❑ F-237★ (W-74★) • *(1,400–1,500)*		
❑ F-238 (W-75) • est. 223,496,000 *(5,000–6,000)*		
❑ F-238★ (W-75★) • *(425–450)*		
❑ F-239 (W-76) • est. 4,700,000 *(400–450)*		
❑ F-239★ (W-76★) • *(12–14)*		

$1 Treasury or Coin Notes

F-No. (W-No.) • Printage *(rarity)*	Grade	Comments
Series of 1890		
❑ F-347 (W-80) • est. 4,288,000 *(400–500)*		
❑ F-348 (W-81) • est. 552,000 *(50–55)*		
❑ F-349 (W-82) • est. 2,320,000 *(160–180)*		
Series of 1891		
❑ F-350 (W-83) • 13,160,000 *(325–375)*		
❑ F-351 (W-84) • est. 35,940,000 *(1,200–1,400)*		
❑ F-352 (W-85) • est. 8,444,000 *(500–750)*		

$1 Federal Reserve Bank Notes

F-No. (W-No.) • Printage *(rarity)*	Grade	Comments
Series of 1918		
❑ F-708 (W-100A) • est. 14,776,000 *(est. 300–375)*		
❑ F-708★ (W-100A★) • *(est. 12–14)*		
❑ F-709 (W-101A) • est. 4,924,000 *(est. 80–90)*		
❑ F-710 (W-102A) • est. 19,900,000 *(est. 500–600)*		
❑ F-710★ (W-102A★) • *(est. 19–21)*		
❑ F-711 (W-104B) • est. 8,616,000 *(est. 300–350)*		
❑ F-711★ (W-104B★) • *(est. 11–13)*		
❑ F-712 (W-105B) • est. 60,528,000 *(est. 800–950)*		
❑ F-712★ (W-105B★) • *(est. 28–32)*		
❑ F-713 (W-106B) • est. 37,580,000 *(est. 600–700)*		
❑ F-713★ (W-106B★) • *(est. 37–42)*		
❑ F-714 (W-107C) • est. 2,504,000 *(est. 120–135)*		
❑ F-714★ (W-107C★) • *(est. 9–10)*		
❑ F-715 (W-108C) • est. 19,364,000 *(est. 325–375)*		
❑ F-715★ (W-108C★) • *(est. 16–18)*		
❑ F-716 (W-109C) • est. 9,696,000 *(est. 85–90)*		
❑ F-716★ (W-109C★) • *(2 known)*		
❑ F-717 (W-110C) • est. 19,492,000 *(est. 450–550)*		
❑ F-717★ (W-110C★) • *(est. 28–30)*		
❑ F-718 (W-111D) • est. 8,828,000 *(est. 400–500)*		
❑ F-718★ (W-111D★) • *(est. 15–17)*		
❑ F-719 (W-112D) • est. 11,448,000 *(est. 150–165)*		
❑ F-719★ (W-112D★) • *(7 known)*		
❑ F-720 (W-113D) • est. 22,608,000 *(est. 350–400)*		
❑ F-720★ (W-113D★) • *(est. 18–20)*		
❑ F-721 (W-114E) • est. 14,040,000 *(est. 250–300)*		
❑ F-721★ (W-114E★) • *(est. 9–10)*		
❑ F-722 (W-115E) • est. 14,344,000 *(est. 160–180)*		
❑ F-722★ (W-115E★) • *(est. 9–10)*		
❑ F-723 (W-116F) • est. 8,204,000 *(est. 175–190)*		
❑ F-723★ (W-116F★) • *(2 known)*		
❑ F-724 (W-117F) • est. 2,656,000 *(est. 35–40)*		

F-No. (W-No.) • Printage (rarity)	Grade	Comments
Series of 1918 (continued)		
❑ F-724★ (W-117F★) • (4 known)		
❑ F-725 (W-118F) • est. 5,240,000 (est. 50–60)		
❑ F-725★ (W-118F★) • (3 known)		
❑ F-726 (W-119F) • est. 18,524,000 (est. 150–165)		
❑ F-726★ (W-119F★) • (4 known)		
❑ F-727 (W-120G) • est. 22,300,000 (est. 500–700)		
❑ F-727★ (W-120G★) • (est. 22–24)		
❑ F-728 (W-121G) • est. 13,388,000 (est. 140–150)		
❑ F-728★ (W-121G★) • (5 known)		
❑ F-729 (W-122G) • est. 28,744,000 (est. 550–700)		
❑ F-729★ (W-122G★) • (est. 17–19)		
❑ F-730 (W-123H) • est. 9,728,000 (est. 160–170)		
❑ F-730★ (W-123H★) • (est. 10–12)		
❑ F-731 (W-124H) • est. 4,472,000 (est. 60–70)		
❑ F-731★ (W-124H★) • (5 known)		
❑ F-732 (W-125H) • est. 5,100,000 (est. 55–65)		
❑ F-732★ (W-125H★) • (1 known)		
❑ F-733 (W-126H) • est. 8,608,000 (est. 115–130)		
❑ F-733★ (W-126H★) • (5 known)		
❑ F-734 (W-127I) • est. 9,120,000 (est. 150–165)		
❑ F-734★ (W-127I★) • (5 known)		
❑ F-735 (W-128I) • est. 600,000 (est. 55–65)		
❑ F-735★ (W-128I★) • (3 known)		
❑ F-736 (W-129I) • est. 7,092,000 (est. 150–160)		
❑ F-736★ (W-129I★) • (6 known)		
❑ F-737 (W-130J) • est. 12,000,000 (est. 225–275)		
❑ F-737★ (W-130J★) • (est. 9–10)		
❑ F-738 (W-131J) • est. 2,700,000 (est. 220–240)		
❑ F-738★ (W-131J★) • (6 known)		
❑ F-739 (W-132J) • est. 10,120,000 (est. 220–240)		
❑ F-739★ (W-132J★) • (5 known)		
❑ F-740 (W-133K) • est. 8,600,000 (est. 180–200)		
❑ F-740★ (W-133K★) • (est. 10–12)		

F-No. (W-No.) • Printage *(rarity)*	Grade	Comments
❑ F-741 (W-134K) • est. 2,632,000 *(est. 55–60)*		
❑ F-741★ (W-134K★) • *(5 known)*		
❑ F-742 (W-135K) • est. 6,632,000 *(est. 115–130)*		
❑ F-742★ (W-135K★) • *(est. 10–12)*		
❑ F-743 (W-136L) • est. 12,260,000 *(est. 275–325)*		
❑ F-743★ (W-136L★) • *(est. 15–17)*		
❑ F-744 (W-137L) • est. 2,140,000 *(est. 45–50)*		
❑ F-744★ (W-137L★) • *(3 known)*		
❑ F-745 (W-138L) • est. 3,376,000 *(est. 60–70)*		
❑ F-745★ (W-138L★) • *(4 known)*		
❑ F-746 (W-139L) • est. 6,008,000 *(est. 130–150)*		
❑ F-746★ (W-139L★) • *(2 known)*		

SMALL-SIZE

$1 Legal Tender Notes

F-No. (W-No.) • Printage *(rarity)*	Grade	Comments
Series of 1928		
❑ F-1500 (W-140) • 1,872,012		
❑ F-1500★ (W-140★) • 8,000		

$1 Silver Certificates

F-No. (W-No.) • Printage *(rarity)*	Grade	Comments
Series of 1928–1928-E		
❑ F-1600 (W-141) • 638,296,908		
❑ F-1600★ (W-141★)		
❑ F-1601 (W-142) • 2,267,809,500		

F-No. (W-No.) • Printage *(rarity)*	Grade	Comments
Series of 1928–1928-E *(continued)*		
❏ F-1601★ (W-142★)		
❏ F-unlisted (W-143)		
❏ F-unlisted (W-144)		
❏ F-unlisted (W-145)		
❏ F-1602 (W-146) • 674,597,808		
❏ F-1602★ (W-146★)		
❏ F-unlisted (W-147)		
❏ F-unlisted (W-148)		
❏ F-unlisted (W-149)		
❏ F-1603 (W-150) • 5,364,348		
❏ F-1603★ (W-150★) • *(12–16)*		
❏ F-1604 (W-151) • 14,451,372		
❏ F-1604★ (W-151★) • *(12–16)*		
❏ F-1605 (W-152) • 3,519,324		
❏ F-1605★ (W-152★) • *(9–11)*		
Series of 1934		
❏ F-1606 (W-153) • 682,176,000		
❏ F-1606★ (W-153★) • 7,680,000		
Series of 1935		
❏ F-1607 (W-154) • 1,681,552,000		
❏ F-1607★ (W-154★)		
❏ F-1607 (W-154 Mule)		
❏ F-1607★ (W-154 Mule★)		
Series of 1935-A, Blue Seal		
❏ F-1608 (W-158) • 6,111,832,000		
❏ F-1608★ (W-158★)		
❏ F-1608 (W-158 Mule)		
❏ F-1608★ (W-158 Mule★)		
❏ F-1609 (W-159) • 1,184,000		
❏ F-1609★ (W-159★) • 12,000		
❏ F-1610 (W-160) • 1,184,000		
❏ F-1610★ (W-160★) • 12,000		
Series of 1935-A, Brown Seal, HAWAII Overprint		
❏ F-2300 (W-161) • 35,052,000		
❏ F-2300★ (W-161★) • 204,000		

F-No. (W-No.) • Printage *(rarity)*	Grade	Comments
Series of 1935-A, Yellow Seal for North Africa		
❑ F-2306 (W-162) • 26,916,000		
❑ F-2306★ (W-162★) • 144,000		
Series of 1935-B and 1935-C		
❑ F-1611 (W-163) • 806,612,000		
❑ F-1611★ (W-163★)		
❑ F-1612 (W-164) • 3,088,108,000		
❑ F-1612★ (W-164★)		
Series of 1935-D, Wide Back		
❑ F-1613W (W-165) • 4,656,968,000		
❑ F-1613W★ (W-165★)		
Series of 1935-D, Narrow Back		
❑ F-1613N (W-166) • incl. in F-1613W		
❑ F-1613N★ (W-166★)		
Series of 1935-E and 1935-F		
❑ F-1614 (W-167) • 5,134,056,000		
❑ F-1614★ (W-167★) • est. 225,000,000		
❑ F-1615 (W-168) • 1,173,360,000		
❑ F-1615★ (W-168★) • 53,200,000		
Series of 1935-G, No Motto		
❑ F-1616 (W-169) • 194,600,000		
❑ F-1616★ (W-169★) • 8,640,000		
Series of 1935-G and 1935-H, With Motto		
❑ F-1617 (W-170) • 31,320,000		
❑ F-1617★ (W-170★) • 1,080,000		
❑ F-1618 (W-171) • 30,520,000		
❑ F-1618★ (W-171★) • 1,436,000		
Series of 1957–1957-B		
❑ F-1619 (W-172) • 2,609,600,000		
❑ F-1619★ (W-172★) • 307,640,000		
❑ F-1620 (W-173) • 1,594,080,000		
❑ F-1620★ (W-173★) • 94,720,000		
❑ F-1621 (W-174) • 718,400,000		
❑ F-1621★ (W-174★) • 49,280,000		

$1 Federal Reserve Notes

F-No. (W-No.) • Printage (rarity)	Grade	Comments
Series of 1963–1963-B		
❑ F-1900A (W-175A) • 87,680,000		
❑ F-1900A★ (W-175A★) • 6,400,000		
❑ F-1900B (W-175B) • 219,200,000		
❑ F-1900B★ (W-175B★) • 15,360,000		
❑ F-1900C (W-175C) • 123,680,000		
❑ F-1900C★ (W-175C★) • 10,880,000		
❑ F-1900D (W-175D) • 108,320,000		
❑ F-1900D★ (W-175D★) • 8,320,000		
❑ F-1900E (W-175E) • 159,520,000		
❑ F-1900E★ (W-175E★) • 12,160,000		
❑ F-1900F (W-175F) • 221,120,000		
❑ F-1900F★ (W-175F★) • 19,200,000		
❑ F-1900G (W-175G) • 279,360,000		
❑ F-1900G★ (W-175G★) • 19,840,000		
❑ F-1900H (W-175H) • 99,840,000		
❑ F-1900H★ (W-175H★) • 9,600,000		
❑ F-1900I (W-175I) • 44,800,000		
❑ F-1900I★ (W-175I★) • 5,120,000		
❑ F-1900J (W-175J) • 88,960,000		
❑ F-1900J★ (W-175J★) • 8,960,000		
❑ F-1900K (W-175K) • 85,760,000		
❑ F-1900K★ (W-175K★) • 8,960,000		
❑ F-1900L (W-175L) • 1,999,999,999		
❑ F-1900L★ (W-175L★) • 14,720,000		
❑ F-1901A (W-176A) • 319,840,000		
❑ F-1901A★ (W-176A★) • 19,840,000		
❑ F-1901B (W-176B) • 657,600,000		
❑ F-1901B★ (W-176B★) • 47,680,000		
❑ F-1901C (W-176C) • 375,520,000		
❑ F-1901C★ (W-176C★) • 26,240,000		
❑ F-1901D (W-176D) • 337,120,000		
❑ F-1901D★ (W-176D★) • 21,120,000		

F-No. (W-No.) • Printage *(rarity)*	Grade	Comments
❑ F-1901E (W-176E) • 532,000,000		
❑ F-1901E★ (W-176E★) • 41,600,000		
❑ F-1901F (W-176F) • 636,480,000		
❑ F-1901F★ (W-176F★) • 40,960,000		
❑ F-1901G (W-176G) • 784,480,000		
❑ F-1901G★ (W-176G★) • 52,640,000		
❑ F-1901H (W-176H) • 264,000,000		
❑ F-1901H★ (W-176H★) • 17,920,000		
❑ F-1901I (W-176I) • 112,160,000		
❑ F-1901I★ (W-176I★) • 7,040,000		
❑ F-1901J (W-176J) • 219,200,000		
❑ F-1901J★ (W-176J★) • 14,720,000		
❑ F-1901K (W-176K) • 288,960,000		
❑ F-1901K★ (W-176K★) • 19,184,000		
❑ F-1901L (W-176L) • 576,800,000		
❑ F-1901L★ (W-176L★) • 43,040,000		
❑ F-1902B (W-177B) • 123,040,000		
❑ F-1902B★ (W-177B★) • 3,680,000		
❑ F-1902E (W-177E) • 93,600,000		
❑ F-1902E★ (W-177E★) • 3,200,000		
❑ F-1902G (W-177G) • 91,040,000		
❑ F-1902G★ (W-177G★) • 2,400,000		
❑ F-1902J (W-177J) • 44,800,000		
❑ F-1902L (W-177L) • 106,400,000		
❑ F-1902L★ (W-177L★) • 3,040,000		
Series of 1969–1969-D		
❑ F-1903A (W-178A) • 99,200,000		
❑ F-1903A★ (W-178A★) • 5,120,000		
❑ F-1903B (W-178B) • 269,120,000		
❑ F-1903B★ (W-178B★) • 14,080,000		
❑ F-1903C (W-178C) • 68,480,000		
❑ F-1903C★ (W-178C★) • 3,776,000		
❑ F-1903D (W-178D) • 120,480,000		
❑ F-1903D★ (W-178D★) • 5,760,000		

F-No. (W-No.) • Printage *(rarity)*	Grade	Comments
Series of 1969–1969-D *(continued)*		
❑ F-1903E (W-178E) • 250,560,000		
❑ F-1903E★ (W-178E★) • 10,880,000		
❑ F-1903F (W-178F) • 185,120,000		
❑ F-1903F★ (W-178F★) • 7,680,000		
❑ F-1903G (W-178G) • 359,520,000		
❑ F-1903G★ (W-178G★) • 12,160,000		
❑ F-1903H (W-178H) • 74,880,000		
❑ F-1903H★ (W-178H★) • 3,840,000		
❑ F-1903I (W-178I) • 48,000,000		
❑ F-1903I★ (W-178I★) • 1,920,000		
❑ F-1903J (W-178J) • 95,360,000		
❑ F-1903J★ (W-178J★) • 5,760,000		
❑ F-1903K (W-178K) • 113,440,000		
❑ F-1903K★ (W-178K★) • 5,120,000		
❑ F-1903L (W-178L) • 226,240,000		
❑ F-1903L★ (W-178L★) • 9,600,000		
❑ F-1904A (W-179A) • 40,480,000		
❑ F-1904A★ (W-179A★) • 1,120,000		
❑ F-1904B (W-179B) • 122,400,000		
❑ F-1904B★ (W-179B★) • 6,240,000		
❑ F-1904C (W-179C) • 44,960,000		
❑ F-1904C★ (W-179C★) • 1,760,000		
❑ F-1904D (W-179D) • 30,080,000		
❑ F-1904D★ (W-179D★) • 1,280,000		
❑ F-1904E (W-179E) • 66,080,000		
❑ F-1904E★ (W-179E★) • 3,200,000		
❑ F-1904F (W-179F) • 70,560,000		
❑ F-1904F★ (W-179F★) • 2,400,000		
❑ F-1904G (W-179G) • 75,680,000		
❑ F-1904G★ (W-179G★) • 4,480,000		
❑ F-1904H (W-179H) • 41,420,000		
❑ F-1904H★ (W-179H★) • 1,280,000		
❑ F-1904I (W-179I) • 21,760,000		

F-No. (W-No.) • Printage *(rarity)*	Grade	Comments
❑ F-1904I★ (W-179I★) • 640,000		
❑ F-1904J (W-179J) • 40,480,000		
❑ F-1904J★ (W-179J★) • 1,120,000		
❑ F-1904K (W-179K) • 27,520,000		
❑ F-1904L (W-179L) • 51,840,000		
❑ F-1904L★ (W-179L★) • 3,840,000		
❑ F-1905A (W-180A) • 94,720,000		
❑ F-1905A★ (W-180A★) • 1,920,000		
❑ F-1905B (W-180B) • 329,440,000		
❑ F-1905B★ (W-180B★) • 7,040,000		
❑ F-1905C (W-180C) • 133,280,000		
❑ F-1905C★ (W-180C★) • 3,200,000		
❑ F-1905D (W-180D) • 91,520,000		
❑ F-1905D★ (W-180D★) • 4,480,000		
❑ F-1905E (W-180E) • 180,000,000		
❑ F-1905E★ (W-180E★) • 3,480,000		
❑ F-1905F (W-180F) • 200,000,000		
❑ F-1905F★ (W-180F★) • 3,840,000		
❑ F-1905G (W-180G) • 204,480,000		
❑ F-1905G★ (W-180G★) • 4,480,000		
❑ F-1905H (W-180H) • 59,520,000		
❑ F-1905H★ (W-180H★) • 1,920,000		
❑ F-1905I (W-180I) • 33,920,000		
❑ F-1905I★ (W-180I★) • 640,000		
❑ F-1905J (W-180J) • 67,200,000		
❑ F-1905J★ (W-180J★) • 2,560,000		
❑ F-1905K (W-180K) • 116,640,000		
❑ F-1905K★ (W-180K★) • 5,120,000		
❑ F-1905L (W-180L) • 208,960,000		
❑ F-1905L★ (W-180L★) • 5,760,000		
❑ F-1906B (W-181B) • 49,920,000		
❑ F-1906D (W-181D) • 15,520,000		
❑ F-1906D★ (W-181D★) • 480,000		
❑ F-1906E (W-181E) • 61,600,000		

F-No. (W-No.) • Printage *(rarity)*	Grade	Comments
Series of 1969–1969-D *(continued)*		
❑ F-1906E★ (W-181E★) • 480,000		
❑ F-1906F (W-181F) • 60,960,000		
❑ F-1906F★ (W-181F★) • 3,680,000		
❑ F-1906G (W-181G) • 137,120,000		
❑ F-1906G★ (W-181G★) • 1,748,000		
❑ F-1906H (W-181H) • 23,680,000		
❑ F-1906H★ (W-181H★) • 640,000		
❑ F-1906I (W-181I) • 25,600,000		
❑ F-1906I★ (W-181I★) • 640,000		
❑ F-1906J (W-181J) • 38,560,000		
❑ F-1906J★ (W-181J★) • 1,120,000		
❑ F-1906K (W-181K) • 29,440,000		
❑ F-1906K★ (W-181K★) • 640,000		
❑ F-1906L (W-181L) • 101,280,000		
❑ F-1906L★ (W-181L★) • 2,400,000		
❑ F-1907A (W-182A) • 187,040,000		
❑ F-1907A★ (W-182A★) • 1,120,000		
❑ F-1907B (W-182B) • 468,480,000		
❑ F-1907B★ (W-182B★) • 4,480,000		
❑ F-1907C (W-182C) • 218,560,000		
❑ F-1907C★ (W-182C★) • 4,320,000		
❑ F-1907D (W-182D) • 161,440,000		
❑ F-1907D★ (W-182D★) • 2,400,000		
❑ F-1907E (W-182E) • 374,240,000		
❑ F-1907E★ (W-182E★) • 8,480,000		
❑ F-1907F (W-182F) • 377,440,000		
❑ F-1907F★ (W-182F★) • 5,280,000		
❑ F-1907G (W-182G) • 378,080,000		
❑ F-1907G★ (W-182G★) • 5,270,000		
❑ F-1907H (W-182H) • 168,480,000		
❑ F-1907H★ (W-182H★) • 1,760,000		
❑ F-1907I (W-182I) • 83,200,000		
❑ F-1907J (W-182J) • 185,760,000		

F-No. (W-No.) • Printage *(rarity)*	Grade	Comments
❑ F-1907J★ (W-182J★) • 3,040,000		
❑ F-1907K (W-182K) • 158,240,000		
❑ F-1907K★ (W-182K★) • 6,240,000		
❑ F-1907L (W-182L) • 400,640,000		
❑ F-1907L★ (W-182L★) • 6,400,000		
Series of 1974		
❑ F-1908A (W-183A) • 269,760,000		
❑ F-1908A★ (W-183A★) • 2,400,000		
❑ F-1908B (W-183B) • 740,320,000		
❑ F-1908B★ (W-183B★) • 8,800,000		
❑ F-1908C (W-183C) • 308,800,000		
❑ F-1908C★ (W-183C★) • 1,600,000		
❑ F-1908D (W-183D) • 240,960,000		
❑ F-1908D★ (W-183D★) • 960,000		
❑ F-1908E (W-183E) • 644,000,000		
❑ F-1908E★ (W-183E★) • 4,960,000		
❑ F-1908F (W-183F) • 599,680,000		
❑ F-1908F★ (W-183F★) • 5,632,000		
❑ F-1908G (W-183G) • 473,600,000		
❑ F-1908G★ (W-183G★) • 4,992,000		
❑ F-1908H (W-183H) • 291,520,000		
❑ F-1908H★ (W-183H★) • 2,880,000		
❑ F-1908I (W-183I) • 144,160,000		
❑ F-1908I★ (W-183I★) • 480,000		
❑ F-1908J (W-183J) • 223,520,000		
❑ F-1908J★ (W-183J★) • 2,144,000		
❑ F-1908K (W-183K) • 330,560,000		
❑ F-1908K★ (W-183K★) • 1,216,000		
❑ F-1908L (W-183L) • 736,960,000		
❑ F-1908L★ (W-183L★) • 3,520,000		
Series of 1977 and 1977-A		
❑ F-1909A (W-184A) • 188,160,000		
❑ F-1909A★ (W-184A★) • 3,072,000		
❑ F-1909B (W-184B) • 635,520,000		

F-No. (W-No.) • Printage *(rarity)*	Grade	Comments
Series of 1977 and 1977-A *(continued)*		
❏ F-1909B★ (W-184B★) • 10,112,000		
❏ F-1909C (W-184C) • 216,960,000		
❏ F-1909C★ (W-184C★) • 4,480,000		
❏ F-1909D (W-184D) • 213,120,000		
❏ F-1909D★ (W-184D★) • 3,328,000		
❏ F-1909E (W-184E) • 418,560,000		
❏ F-1909E★ (W-184E★) • 640,000		
❏ F-1909F (W-184F) • 565,120,000		
❏ F-1909F★ (W-184F★) • 8,960,000		
❏ F-1909G (W-184G) • 615,680,000		
❏ F-1909G★ (W-184G★) • 9,472,000		
❏ F-1909H (W-184H) • 199,680,000		
❏ F-1909H★ (W-184H★) • 2,048,000		
❏ F-1909I (W-184I) • 115,200,000		
❏ F-1909I★ (W-184I★) • 2,944,000		
❏ F-1909J (W-184J) • 223,360,000		
❏ F-1909J★ (W-184J★) • 3,840,000		
❏ F-1909K (W-184K) • 289,280,000		
❏ F-1909K★ (W-184K★) • 4,608,000		
❏ F-1909L (W-184L) • 516,480,000		
❏ F-1909L★ (W-184L★) • 8,320,000		
❏ F-1910A (W-185A) • 204,800,000		
❏ F-1910A★ (W-185A★) • 2,432,000		
❏ F-1910B (W-185B) • 592,000,000		
❏ F-1910B★ (W-185B★) • 9,472,000		
❏ F-1910C (W-185C) • 196,480,000		
❏ F-1910C★ (W-185C★) • 2,688,000		
❏ F-1910D (W-185D) • 174,720,000		
❏ F-1910D★ (W-185D★) • 2,560,000		
❏ F-1910E (W-185E) • 377,600,000		
❏ F-1910E★ (W-185E★) • 6,400,000		
❏ F-1910F (W-185F) • 396,160,000		
❏ F-1910F★ (W-185F★) • 5,376,000		

F-No. (W-No.) • Printage *(rarity)*	Grade	Comments
❑ F-1910G (W-185G) • 250,680,000		
❑ F-1910G★ (W-185G★) • 2,560,000		
❑ F-1910H (W-185H) • 103,680,000		
❑ F-1910H★ (W-185H★) • 1,664,000		
❑ F-1910I (W-185I) • 38,400,000		
❑ F-1910I★ (W-185I★) • 384,000		
❑ F-1910J (W-185J) • 266,880,000		
❑ F-1910J★ (W-185J★) • 4,864,000		
❑ F-1910K (W-185K) • 313,600,000		
❑ F-1910K★ (W-185K★) • 6,016,000		
❑ F-1910L (W-185L) • 432,280,000		
❑ F-1910L★ (W-185L★) • 5,888,000		
Series of 1981 and 1981-A		
❑ F-1911A (W-186A) • 308,480,000		
❑ F-1911A★ (W-186A★) • 3,200,000		
❑ F-1911B (W-186B) • 963,840,000		
❑ F-1911B★ (W-186B★) • 11,776,000		
❑ F-1911C (W-186C) • 359,680,000		
❑ F-1911C★ (W-186C★) • 1,536,000		
❑ F-1911D (W-186D) • 295,680,000		
❑ F-1911D★ (W-186D★) • 1,792,000		
❑ F-1911E (W-186E) • 603,520,000		
❑ F-1911E★ (W-186E★) • 3,840,000		
❑ F-1911F (W-186F) • 741,760,000		
❑ F-1911F★ (W-186F★) • 3,200,000		
❑ F-1911G (W-186G) • 629,760,000		
❑ F-1911G★ (W-186G★) • 5,184,000		
❑ F-1911H (W-186H) • 163,840,000		
❑ F-1911H★ (W-186H★) • 1,056,000		
❑ F-1911I (W-186I) • 105,600,000		
❑ F-1911I★ (W-186I★) • 1,152,000		
❑ F-1911J (W-186J) • 302,080,000		
❑ F-1911J★ (W-186J★) • 3,216,000		
❑ F-1911K (W-186K) • 385,920,000		

F-No. (W-No.) • Printage *(rarity)*	Grade	Comments
Series of 1981 and 1981-A *(continued)*		
❏ F-1911K★ (W-186K★) • 1,920,000		
❏ F-1911L (W-186L) • 677,760,000		
❏ F-1911L★ (W-186L★) • 4,992,000		
❏ F-1912A (W-187A) • 204,800,000		
❏ F-1912B (W-187B) • 537,600,000		
❏ F-1912B★ (W-187B★) • 9,216,000		
❏ F-1912C (W-187C) • 99,200,000		
❏ F-1912D (W-187D) • 188,800,000		
❏ F-1912E (W-187E) • 441,600,000		
❏ F-1912E★ (W-187E★) • 6,400,000		
❏ F-1912F (W-187F) • 483,200,000		
❏ F-1912G (W-187G) • 482,000,000		
❏ F-1912G★ (W-187G★) • 3,200,000		
❏ F-1912H (W-187H) • 182,400,000		
❏ F-1912I (W-187I) • 122,400,000		
❏ F-1912J (W-187J) • 176,000,000		
❏ F-1912K (W-187K) • 188,800,000		
❏ F-1912K★ (W-187K★) • 3,200,000		
❏ F-1912L (W-187L) • 659,000,000		
❏ F-1912L★ (W-187L★) • 3,200,000		
Series of 1985		
❏ F-1913A (W-188A) • 553,600,000		
❏ F-1913B (W-188B) • 1,795,200,000		
❏ F-1913C (W-188C) • 422,400,000		
❏ F-1913D (W-188D) • 636,800,000		
❏ F-1913E (W-188E) • 1,190,400,000		
❏ F-1913E★ (W-188E★) • 6,400,000		
❏ F-1913F (W-188F) • 1,414,400,000		
❏ F-1913G (W-188G) • 1,190,400,000		
❏ F-1913G★ (W-188G★) • 5,120,000		
❏ F-1913H (W-188H) • 400,000,000		
❏ F-1913H★ (W-188H★) • 640,000		
❏ F-1913I (W-188I) • 246,400,000		

F-No. (W-No.) • Printage *(rarity)*	Grade	Comments
❏ F-1913I★ (W-188I★) • 3,200,000		
❏ F-1913J (W-188J) • 390,400,000		
❏ F-1913K (W-188K) • 697,600,000		
❏ F-1913K★ (W-188K★) • 3,200,000		
❏ F-1913L (W-188L) • 1,881,600,000		
❏ F-1913L★ (W-188L★) • 9,600,000		
Series of 1988 and 1988-A		
❏ F-1914A (W-189A) • 214,400,000		
❏ F-1914A★ (W-189A★) • 3,200,000		
❏ F-1914B (W-189B) • 921,600,000		
❏ F-1914B★ (W-189B★) • 2,560,000		
❏ F-1914C (W-189C) • 96,000,000		
❏ F-1914D (W-189D) • 195,200,000		
❏ F-1914E (W-189E) • 728,800,000		
❏ F-1914E★ (W-189E★) • 2,688,000		
❏ F-1914F (W-189F) • 390,400,000		
❏ F-1914F★ (W-189F★) • 3,840,000		
❏ F-1914G (W-189G) • 416,400,000		
❏ F-1914H (W-189H) • 396,800,000		
❏ F-1914I (W-189I) • 246,400,000		
❏ F-1914J (W-189J) • 390,400,000		
❏ F-1914J★ (W-189J★) • 3,200,000		
❏ F-1914K (W-189K) • 80,000,000		
❏ F-1914K★ (W-189K★) • 1,248,000		
❏ F-1914L (W-189L) • 585,600,000		
❏ F-1914L★ (W-189L★) • 3,200,000		
❏ F-1915A (W-190A) • 582,400,000		
❏ F-1915B (W-190B) • 2,161,344,000		
❏ F-1915B★ (W-190B★) • 12,800,000		
❏ F-1915C (W-190C) • 472,320,000		
❏ F-1915D (W-190D) • 454,400,000		
❏ F-1915D★ (W-190D★) • 6,400,000		
❏ F-1915E (W-190E) • 1,593,600,000		
❏ F-1915E★ (W-190E★) • 10,880,000		

F-No. (W-No.) • Printage *(rarity)*	Grade	Comments
Series of 1988 and 1988-A *(continued)*		
❑ F-1915F (W-190F) • 1,747,200,000		
❑ F-1915F★ (W-190F★) • 12,800,000		
❑ F-1915G (W-190G) • 1,728,000,000		
❑ F-1915G★ (W-190G★) • 19,200,000		
❑ F-1915H (W-190H) • 410,400,000		
❑ F-1915H★ (W-190H★) • 3,200,000		
❑ F-1915I (W-190I) • 76,800,000		
❑ F-1915I★ (W-190I★) • 5,760,000		
❑ F-1915J (W-190J) • 96,000,000		
❑ F-1915K (W-190K) • 211,200,000		
❑ F-1915L (W-190L) • 280,600,000		
❑ F-1916F (W-192F) • 533,000,000		
❑ F-1916G (W-192G) • 748,800,000		
❑ F-1916G★ (W-192G★) • 6,400,000		
❑ F-1916H (W-192H) • 326,400,000		
❑ F-1916I (W-192I) • 844,800,000		
❑ F-1916I★ (W-192I★) • 7,680,000		
❑ F-1916J (W-192J) • 300,800,000		
❑ F-1916K (W-192K) • 761,000,000		
❑ F-1916K★ (W-192K★) • 3,200,000		
❑ F-1916L (W-192L) • 2,009,600,000		
❑ F-1916L★ (W-192L★) • 19,200,000		
❑ F-1917A (W-191A) • 64,000,000		
❑ F-1917B (W-191B) • 1,920,000		
❑ F-1917C (W-191C) • 12,800,000		
❑ F-1917E (W-191E) • 38,400,000		
❑ F-1917F (W-191F) • 89,600,000		
❑ F-1917F★ (W-191F★) • 640,000		
❑ F-1917G (W-191G) • 19,200,000		
Series of 1993		
❑ F-1918A (W-193A) • 140,800,000		
❑ F-1918B (W-193B) • 716,800,000		
❑ F-1918B★ (W-193B★) • 2,240,000		

F-No. (W-No.) • Printage *(rarity)*	Grade	Comments
❑ F-1918C (W-193C) • 70,400,000		
❑ F-1918C★ (W-193C★) • 640,000		
❑ F-1918D (W-193D) • 108,800,000		
❑ F-1918E (W-193E) • 524,800,000		
❑ F-1918F (W-193F) • 787,200,000		
❑ F-1918F★ (W-193F★) • 16,000,000		
❑ F-1918G (W-193G) • 96,000,000		
❑ F-1918L (W-193L) • 128,000,000		
❑ F-1919G (W-195G) • 646,400,000		
❑ F-1919G★ (W-195G★) • 8,960,000		
❑ F-1919H (W-195H) • 121,600,000		
❑ F-1919I (W-195I) • 25,600,000		
❑ F-1919K (W-195K) • 620,800,000		
❑ F-1919K★ (W-195K★) • 19,200,000		
❑ F-1919L (W-195L) • 1,171,200,000		
❑ F-1920B (W-194B) • 12,800,000		
❑ F-1920C (W-194C) • 12,800,000		
Series of 1995		
❑ F-1921A (W-196A) • 1,134,745,600		
❑ F-1921A★ (W-196A★) • 12,160,000		
❑ F-1921B (W-196B) • 2,062,080,000		
❑ F-1921B★ (W-196B★) • 9,600,000		
❑ F-1921C (W-196C) • 428,800,000		
❑ F-1921C★ (W-196C★) • 9,600,000		
❑ F-1921D (W-196D) • 1,452,800,000		
❑ F-1921D★ (W-196D★) • 7,040,000		
❑ F-1921E (W-196E) • 1,831,400,000		
❑ F-1921E★ (W-196E★) • 7,040,000		
❑ F-1921F (W-196F) • 1,279,360,000		
❑ F-1921F★ (W-196F★) • 19,840,000		
❑ F-1921G (W-196G) • 38,400,000		
❑ F-1921I (W-196I) • 76,800,000		
❑ F-1921J (W-196J) • 83,200,000		
❑ F-1921L (W-196L) • 44,800,000		

F-No. (W-No.) • Printage *(rarity)*	Grade	Comments
Series of 1995 *(continued)*		
❑ F-1922C (W-198C) • 76,800,000		
❑ F-1922C★ (W-198C★) • 3,200,000		
❑ F-1922D (W-198D) • 134,400,000		
❑ F-1922F (W-198F) • 452,480,000		
❑ F-1922F★ (W-198F★) • 3,584,000		
❑ F-1922G (W-198G) • 1,459,200,000		
❑ F-1922G★ (W-198G★) • 10,240,000		
❑ F-1922H (W-198H) • 921,600,000		
❑ F-1922I (W-198I) • 1,310,720,000		
❑ F-1922I★ (W-198I★) • 14,080,000		
❑ F-1922J (W-198J) • 262,400,000		
❑ F-1922J★ (W-198J★) • 6,400,000		
❑ F-1922K (W-198K) • 1,273,600,000		
❑ F-1922K★ (W-198K★) • 1,440,000		
❑ F-1922L (W-198L) • 2,252,800,000		
❑ F-1922L★ (W-198L★) • 6,400,000		
❑ F-1923A (W-197A) • 18,560,000		
❑ F-1923B (W-197B) • 12,800,000		
❑ F-1923D (W-197D) • 6,400,000		
❑ F-1923F (W-197F) • 12,800,000		
Series of 1999		
❑ F-1924A (W-199A) • 556,800,000		
❑ F-1924A★ (W-199A★) • 3,840,000		
❑ F-1924B (W-199B) • 1,497,600,000		
❑ F-1924B★ (W-199B★) • 9,600,000		
❑ F-1924C (W-199C) • 1,062,400,000		
❑ F-1924C★ (W-199C★) • 13,760,000		
❑ F-1924D (W-199D) • 268,800,000		
❑ F-1924D★ (W-199D★) • 640,000		
❑ F-1924E (W-199E) • 748,800,000		
❑ F-1924E★ (W-199E★) • 7,040,000		
❑ F-1924F (W-199F) • 780,800,000		
❑ F-1925F (W-200F) • 1,062,400,000		

F-No. (W-No.) • Printage *(rarity)*	Grade	Comments
❑ F-1925F★ (W-200F★) • 640,000		
❑ F-1925G (W-200G) • 864,400,000		
❑ F-1925H (W-200H) • 89,600,000		
❑ F-1925H★ (W-200H★) • 7,040,000		
❑ F-1925I (W-200I) • 12,800,000		
❑ F-1925J (W-200J) • 339,200,000		
❑ F-1925K (W-200K) • 934,400,000		
❑ F-1925L (W-200L) • 1,920,000,000		
❑ F-1925L★ (W-200L★) • 19,840,000		
Series of 2001		
❑ F-1926A (W-201A) • 448,000,000		
❑ F-1926A★ (W-201A★) • 3,520,000		
❑ F-1926B (W-201B) • 678,400,000		
❑ F-1926C (W-201C) • 550,400,000		
❑ F-1926C★ (W-201C★) • 6,400,000		
❑ F-1926D (W-201D) • 307,200,000		
❑ F-1926E (W-201E) • 70,400,000		
❑ F-1926F (W-201F) • 499,200,000		
❑ F-1926F★ (W-201F★) • 3,520,000		
❑ F-1926H (W-201H) • 147,200,000		
❑ F-1926H★ (W-201H★) • 640,000		
❑ F-1926I (W-201I) • 6,400,000		
❑ F-1926J (W-201J) • 19,200,000		
❑ F-1927F★ (W-202F★) • 3,840,000		
❑ F-1927G (W-202G) • 358,400,000		
❑ F-1927G★ (W-202G★) • 4,480,000		
❑ F-1927H (W-202H) • 128,000,000		
❑ F-1927I (W-202I) • 57,600,000		
❑ F-1927J (W-202J) • 160,000,000		
❑ F-1927K (W-202K) • 300,800,000		
❑ F-1927K★ (W-202K★) • 3,200,000		
❑ F-1927L (W-202L) • 1,152,000,000		
❑ F-1927L★ (W-202L★) • 3,200,000		

F-No. (W-No.) • Printage *(rarity)*	Grade	Comments
Series of 2003 and 2003-A		
❏ F-1928A (W-203A) • 384,000,000		
❏ F-1928A★ (W-203A★) • 3,200,000		
❏ F-1928B (W-203B) • 610,600,000		
❏ F-1928B★ (W-203B★) • 5,760,000		
❏ F-1928C (W-203C) • 460,800,000		
❏ F-1928D (W-203D) • 326,400,000		
❏ F-1928D★ (W-203D★) • 320,000		
❏ F-1928E (W-203E) • 953,600,000		
❏ F-1928E★ (W-203E★) • 6,880,000		
❏ F-1928F (W-203F) • 153,600,000		
❏ F-1928F★ (W-203F★) • 320,000		
❏ F-1929F (W-204F) • 140,800,000		
❏ F-1929F★ (W-204F★) • 3,200,000		
❏ F-1929G (W-204G) • 742,400,000		
❏ F-1929G★ (W-204G★) • 10,240,000		
❏ F-1929H (W-204H) • 268,800,000		
❏ F-1929I (W-204I) • 147,200,000		
❏ F-1929J (W-204J) • 179,200,000		
❏ F-1929K (W-204K) • 704,000,000		
❏ F-1929K★ (W-204K★) • 3,200,000		
❏ F-1929L (W-204L) • 1,267,200,000		
❏ F-1929L★ (W-204L★) • 3,200,000		
❏ F-1930A (W-205A) • 300,800,000		
❏ F-1930B (W-205B) • 966,400,000		
❏ F-1930B★ (W-205B★) • 7,360,000		
❏ F-1930C (W-205C) • 224,000,000		
❏ F-1930C★ (W-205C★) • 4,128,000		
❏ F-1930D (W-205D) • 390,400,000		
❏ F-1930E (W-205E) • 742,400,000		
❏ F-1930E★ (W-205E★) • 3,520,000		
❏ F-1930F (W-205F) • 723,200,000		
❏ F-1930F★ (W-205F★) • 7,040,000		
❏ F-1931F (W-206F) • 691,200,000		

F-No. (W-No.) • Printage *(rarity)*	Grade	Comments
❑ F-1931F★ (W-206F★) • 7,040,000		
❑ F-1931G (W-206G) • 851,200,000		
❑ F-1931H (W-206H) • 166,400,000		
❑ F-1931I (W-206I) • 76,800,000		
❑ F-1931J (W-206J) • 448,000,000		
❑ F-1931J★ (W-206J★) • 3,200,000		
❑ F-1931K (W-206K) • 678,400,000		
❑ F-1931K★ (W-206K★) • 1,280,000		
❑ F-1931L (W-206L) • 1,516,800,000		
Series of 2006 and 2006-A		
❑ F-1932A (W-207A) • 428,800,000		
❑ F-1932B (W-207B) • 7,424,000,000		
❑ F-1932B★ (W-207B★) • 7,680,000		
❑ F-1932C (W-207C) • 371,200,000		
❑ F-1932D (W-207D)		
❑ F-1932E (W-207E)		
❑ F-1932F (W-207F)		
❑ F-1932F★ (W-207F★)		
❑ F-1933A (W-208) • 243,200,000		
❑ F-1933B (W-208B) • 382,400,000		
❑ F-1933B★ (W-208★)		
❑ F-1933C (W-208C) • 128,000,000		
❑ F-1933D (W-208D) • 313,600,000		
❑ F-1933D★ (W-208D★) • 640,000		
❑ F-1933E (W-208E) • 345,600,000		
❑ F-1933F (W-208F) • 1,606,400,000		
❑ F-1933F★ (W-208F★) • 1,280,000		
❑ F-1933G (W-208G) • 716,800,000		
❑ F-1933G★ (W-208G★) • 6,912,000		
❑ F-1933H (W-208H) • 377,600,000		
❑ F-1933I (W-208I) • 204,000,000		
❑ F-1933J (W-208J) • 262,400,000		
❑ F-1933J★ (W-208J★) • 3,840,000		
❑ F-1933K (W-208K) • 596,600,000		

F-No. (W-No.) • Printage *(rarity)*	Grade	Comments
Series of 2006 and 2006-A *(continued)*		
❏ F-1933K★ (W-208K★) • 3,200,000		
❏ F-1933L (W-208L) • 1,184,000,000		
❏ F-1933L★ (W-208L★) • 3,840,000		
Series of 2009 and 2009-A		
❏ F-1934A (W-209A) • 6,400,000		
❏ F-1934B (W-209B) • 102,400,000		
❏ F-1934B★ (W-209B★) • 1,280,000		
❏ F-1934C (W-209C) • 166,400,000		
❏ F-1934D (W-209D) • 416,000,000		
❏ F-1934E (W-209E) • 83,200,000		
❏ F-1934F (W-209F) • 864,000,000		
❏ F-1934F★ (W-209F★) • 6,400,000		
❏ F-1934G (W-209G) • 889,600,000		
❏ F-1934G★ (W-209G★) • 1,280,000		
❏ F-1934H (W-209H) • 358,400,000		
❏ F-1934H★ (W-209H★) • 320,000		
❏ F-1934I (W-209I) • 121,600,000		
❏ F-1934J (W-209J) • 268,800,000		
❏ F-1934J★ (W-209J★) • 1,280,000		
❏ F-1934K (W-209K) • 902,400,000		
❏ F-1934K★ (W-209K★) • 640,000		
❏ F-1934L (W-209L) • 2,124,800,000		
❏ F-1934L★ (W-209L★) • 640,000		
❏ F-3000A • 339,156,000		
❏ F-3000A★ • 6,080,000		
❏ F-3000B • 10,649,600,000		
❏ F-3000B★ • 88,712,000		
❏ F-3000C • 160,000,000		
❏ F-3000D • 51,200,000		
❏ F-3000D★ • 3,200,000		
❏ F-3000E • 646,400,000		
❏ F-3000F • 518,400,000		
❏ F-3000I • 32,000,000		

F-No. (W-No.) • Printage *(rarity)*	Grade	Comments
Series of 2013		
❑ F-3001A		
❑ F-3001C		
❑ F-3001D		
❑ F-3001E		
❑ F-3001F		
❑ F-3001F★		
❑ F-3001G		
❑ F-3001G★		
❑ F-3001H		
❑ F-3001I		
❑ F-3001J		
❑ F-3001K		
❑ F-3001K★		
❑ F-3001L		
❑ F-3001L★		
❑ F-3002A		
❑ F-3002B		
❑ F-3002B★		
❑ F-3002C		
❑ F-3002F		
❑ F-3002F★		
❑		
❑		
Series of 2017		
❑		
❑		
❑		
❑		
❑		
❑		
❑		
❑		
❑		

LARGE-SIZE

$2 Legal Tender Notes

F-No. (W-No.) • Printage *(rarity)*	Grade	Comments
Series of 1862		
❑ F-41 (W-305) • est. 8,318,800 *(700–900)*		
❑ F-41a (W-301) • est. 10,000 *(6 known)*		
❑ F-41a (W-302) • est. 178,000 *(5 known)*		
❑ F-41a (W-303) • est. 12,000 *(3 known)*		
❑ F-41a (W-304) • est. 8,511,160 *(225–275)*		
Series of 1869		
❑ F-42 (W-310) • 24,796,000 *(600–750)*		
Series of 1874		
❑ F-43 (W-311) • 8,260,000 *(125–150)*		
Series of 1875		
❑ F-44 (W-314) • 4,160,000 *(75–85)*		
❑ F-45 (W-312) • 1,000,000 *(30–40)*		
❑ F-46 (W-313) • 1,000,000 *(40–50)*		
❑ F-47 (W-315) • 5,358,000 *(90–120)*		
Series of 1878		
❑ F-48 (W-316) • est. 4,576,000 *(190–225)*		
❑ F-49 (W-317) • est. 100,000 *(16–18)*		
Series of 1880		
❑ F-50 (W-318) • est. 8,400,000 *(135–160)*		
❑ F-51 (W-319) • est. 7,540,000 *(155–175)*		
❑ F-52 (W-320a, Back Style 1) • est. 520,000 *(3 known)*		

F-No. (W-No.) • Printage *(rarity)*	Grade	Comments
❑ F-52 (W-320b, Back Style 2) • est. 8,064,000 *(240–280)*		
❑ F-53 (W-323) • est. 348,000 *(55–65)*		
❑ F-54 (W-324) • est. 316,000 *(25–30)*		
❑ F-55 (W-325) • est. 740,000 *(60–70)*		
❑ F-56 (W-326) • est. 1,232,000 *(220–250)*		
Series of 1917		
❑ F-57 (W-327) • est. 69,072,000 *(700–850)*		
❑ F-57★ (W-327★) • *(63–67)*		
❑ F-58 (W-328) • est. 47,246,000 *(425–525)*		
❑ F-58★ (W-328★) • *(50–55)*		
❑ F-58 (W-328 Mule) • est. 50,000 *(3 known)*		
❑ F-59 (W-329) • est. 14,060,000 *(350–500)*		
❑ F-59★ (W-329★) • *(20–24)*		
❑ F-59 (W-329 Mule) • est. 10,000,000 *(70–80)*		
❑ F-59★ (W-329 Mule★) • *(16–18)*		
❑ F-60 (W-330) • est. 175,388,000 *(6,000–8,000)*		
❑ F-60★ (W-330★) • *(300–320)*		
❑ F-60 (W-330 Mule) • est. 1,600,000 *(28–32)*		

$2 National Bank Notes

F-No. (W-No.) • Printage *(rarity)*	Grade	Comments
Original Series ("First Charter Period")		
❑ F-387 (W-340) • *(1,000–1,100)*		
❑ F-388 (W-341) • *(5 known)*		
❑ F-389 (W-342) • *(320–350)*		
Series of 1875 ("First Charter Period")		
❑ F-390 (W-343) • *(220–240)*		
❑ F-391 (W-344) • *(290–320)*		
❑ F-392 (W-345) • *(70–85)*		
❑ F-393 (W-346) • *(50–55)*		

$2 Silver Certificates

F-No. (W-No.) • Printage *(rarity)*	Grade	Comments
Series of 1886		
❑ F-240 (W-360) • est. 4,280,000 *(170–190)*		
❑ F-241 (W-361) • est. 2,020,000 *(115–130)*		

F-No. (W-No.) • Printage *(rarity)*	Grade	Comments
Series of 1886 *(continued)*		
❑ F-242 (W-362) • est. 6,960,000 *(475–600)*		
❑ F-243 (W-363) • est. 4,480,000 *(130–150)*		
❑ F-244 (W-364) • est. 3,260,000 *(165–195)*		
Series of 1891		
❑ F-245 (W-365) • est. 6,560,000 *(330–340)*		
❑ F-246 (W-366) • est. 14,428,000 *(450–550)*		
Series of 1896		
❑ F-247 (W-367) • est. 9,400,000 *(1,000–1,200)*		
❑ F-248 (W-368) • est. 11,252,000 *(900–1,100)*		
Series of 1899		
❑ F-249 (W-369) • est. 111,000,000 *(400–450)*		
❑ F-250 (W-370) • est. 20,000,000 *(110–130)*		
❑ F-251 (W-371) • est. 76,326,000 *(380–450)*		
❑ F-252 (W-372) • 45,852,000 *(225–275)*		
❑ F-252★ (W-372★) • *(12–14)*		
❑ F-253 (W-373) • 78,936,000 *(450–550)*		
❑ F-253★ (W-373★) • *(11–13)*		
❑ F-254 (W-374) • 1,816,000 *(95–120)*		
❑ F-255 (W-375) • 61,600,000 *(600–800)*		
❑ F-255★ (W-375★) • *(8 known)*		
❑ F-256 (W-376) • 91,816,000 *(800–1,000)*		
❑ F-256★ (W-376★) • *(45–50)*		
❑ F-257 (W-377) • est. 4,488,000 *(210–230)*		
❑ F-257★ (W-377★) • *(18–20)*		
❑ F-257 (W-377 Mule) • est. 500,000 *(20–25)*		
❑ F-257★ (W-377 Mule★) • *(3 known)*		
❑ F-258 (W-378) • est. 41,800,000 *(1,400–1,700)*		
❑ F-258★ (W-378★) • *(50–55)*		
❑ F-258 (W-378 Mule) • est. 4,600,000 *(65–75)*		
❑ F-258★ (W-378 Mule★) • *(2 known)*		

$2 Treasury or Coin Notes

F-No. (W-No.) • Printage *(rarity)*	Grade	Comments
Series of 1890		
❑ F-353 (W-390) • est. 2,600,000 *(190–210)*		

F-No. (W-No.) • Printage *(rarity)*	Grade	Comments
❑ F-354 (W-391) • est. 500,000 *(40–45)*		
❑ F-355 (W-392) • est. 1,832,000 *(90–100)*		
Series of 1891		
❑ F-356 (W-393) • est. 4,660,000 *(125–150)*		
❑ F-357 (W-394) • est. 12,300,000 *(500–650)*		
❑ F-358 (W-395) • 3,012,000 *(150–165)*		

$2 Federal Reserve Bank Notes

F-No. (W-No.) • Printage *(rarity)*	Grade	Comments
Series of 1918		
❑ F-747 (W-400A) • est. 4,012,000 *(125–140)*		
❑ F-747★ (W-400A★) • *(3 known)*		
❑ F-748 (W-401A) • est. 2,388,000 *(40–50)*		
❑ F-748★ (W-401A★) • *(2 known)*		
❑ F-749 (W-402A) • est. 6,068,000 *(220–240)*		
❑ F-749★ (W-402A★) • *(10–12)*		
❑ F-750 (W-403B) • est. 1,400,000 *(125–150)*		
❑ F-750★ (W-403B★) • *(6 known)*		
❑ F-751 (W-404B) • est. 7,800,000 *(140–160)*		
❑ F-751★ (W-404B★) • *(4 known)*		
❑ F-752 (W-405B) • est. 6,016,000 *(210–230)*		
❑ F-752★ (W-405B★) • *(1 known)*		
❑ F-753 (W-406C) • est. 284,000 *(90–100)*		
❑ F-753★ (W-406C★) • *(1 known)*		
❑ F-754 (W-407C) • est. 3,356,000 *(100–110)*		
❑ F-755 (W-408C) • est. 660,000 *(20–24)*		
❑ F-756 (W-409C) • est. 3,704,000 *(125–140)*		
❑ F-756★ (W-409C★) • *(9–10)*		
❑ F-757 (W-410D) • est. 1,420,000 *(340–380)*		
❑ F-757★ (W-410D★) • *(4 known)*		
❑ F-758 (W-411D) • est. 1,156,000 *(45–55)*		
❑ F-758★ (W-411D★) • *(1 known)*		
❑ F-759 (W-412D) • est. 2,072,000 *(90–100)*		
❑ F-759★ (W-412D★) • *(1 known)*		
❑ F-760 (W-413E) • est. 1,700,000 *(50–60)*		

F-No. (W-No.) • Printage *(rarity)*	Grade	Comments
Series of 1918 *(continued)*		
❑ F-760★ (W-413E★) • *(5 known)*		
❑ F-761 (W-414E) • est. 2,036,000 *(58–62)*		
❑ F-762 (W-415F) • est. 780,000 *(70–80)*		
❑ F-763 (W-416F) • est. 1,276,000 *(40–45)*		
❑ F-763★ (W-416F★) • *(1 known)*		
❑ F-764 (W-417F) • est. 1,212,000 *(35–40)*		
❑ F-765 (W-418G) • est. 2,400,000 *(135–150)*		
❑ F-765★ (W-418G★) • *(5 known)*		
❑ F-766 (W-419G) • est. 2,200,000 *(50–60)*		
❑ F-767 (W-420G) • est. 4,928,000 *(160–180)*		
❑ F-767★ (W-420G★) • *(3 known)*		
❑ F-768 (W-421H) • est. 1,160,000 *(60–70)*		
❑ F-769 (W-422H) • est. 660,000 *(20–24)*		
❑ F-770 (W-423H) • est. 560,000 *(27–32)*		
❑ F-771 (W-424H) • est. 920,000 *(38–47)*		
❑ F-772 (W-425I) • est. 1,236,000 *(140–160)*		
❑ F-772★ (W-425I★) • *(2 known)*		
❑ F-773 (W-426I) • est. 440,000 *(60–70)*		
❑ F-774 (W-427J) • est. 1,460,000 *(120–140)*		
❑ F-774★ (W-427J★) • *(3 known)*		
❑ F-775 (W-428J) • est. 1,192,000 *(70–90)*		
❑ F-776 (W-429K) • est. 1,100,000 *(120–140)*		
❑ F-776★ (W-429K★) • *(2 known)*		
❑ F-777 (W-431K) • est. 112,000 *(38–47)*		
❑ F-778 (W-432L) • est. 1,812,000 *(62–66)*		
❑ F-778★ (W-432L★) • *(1 known)*		
❑ F-779 (W-433L) • est. 572,000 *(38–47)*		
❑ F-779★ (W-433L★) • *(7 known)*		
❑ F-780 (W-434L) • est. 804,000 *(60–70)*		

SMALL-SIZE

$2 Legal Tender Notes

F-No. (W-No.) • Printage *(rarity)*	Grade	Comments
Series of 1928–1928-G		
❏ F-1501 (W-500) • 55,889,424		
❏ F-1501★ (W-500★)		
❏ F-1502 (W-501) • 46,859,136		
❏ F-1502★ (W-501★)		
❏ F-1503 (W-502) • 9,001,632		
❏ F-1503★ (W-502★)		
❏ F-1504 (W-503) • 86,584,008		
❏ F-1504★ (W-503★)		
❏ F-1504 (W-503 Mule)		
❏ F-1505 (W-504) • 146,381,364		
❏ F-1505★ (W-504★)		
❏ F-1505 (W-504 Mule)		
❏ F-1505★ (W-504 Mule★)		
❏ F-1506 (W-505) • 5,261,016		
❏ F-1506★ (W-505★)		
❏ F-1507 (W-506) • 43,349,292		
❏ F-1507★ (W-506★)		
❏ F-1508 (W-507) • 52,208,000		
❏ F-1508★ (W-507★)		
Series of 1953–1953-C		
❏ F-1509 (W-508) • 45,360,000		
❏ F-1509★ (W-508★) • 2,160,000		
❏ F-1510 (W-509) • 18,000,000		

F-No. (W-No.) • Printage *(rarity)*	Grade	Comments
Series of 1953–1953-C *(continued)*		
❏ F-1510★ (W-509★) • 720,000		
❏ F-1511 (W-510) • 10,800,000		
❏ F-1511★ (W-510★) • 720,000		
❏ F-1512 (W-511) • 5,760,000		
❏ F-1512★ (W-511★) • 360,000		
Series of 1963 and 1963-A		
❏ F-1513 (W-512) • 15,360,000		
❏ F-1513★ (W-512★) • 640,000		
❏ F-1514 (W-513) • 3,200,000		
❏ F-1514★ (W-513★) • 640,000		

$2 Federal Reserve Notes

F-No. (W-No.) • Printage *(rarity)*	Grade	Comments
Series of 1976		
❏ F-1935A (W-550A) • 29,440,000		
❏ F-1935A★ (W-550A★) • 1,280,000		
❏ F-1935B (W-550B) • 67,200,000		
❏ F-1935B★ (W-550B★) • 2,560,000		
❏ F-1935C (W-550C) • 33,280,000		
❏ F-1935C★ (W-550C★) • 1,280,000		
❏ F-1935D (W-550D) • 31,360,000		
❏ F-1935D★ (W-550D★) • 1,280,000		
❏ F-1935E (W-550E) • 56,960,000		
❏ F-1935E★ (W-550E★) • 640,000		
❏ F-1935F (W-550F) • 60,800,000		
❏ F-1935F★ (W-550F★) • 1,280,000		
❏ F-1935G (W-550G) • 84,480,000		
❏ F-1935G★ (W-550G★) • 1,280,000		
❏ F-1935H (W-550H) • 39,040,000		
❏ F-1935H★ (W-550H★) • 1,280,000		
❏ F-1935I (W-550I) • 23,680,000		
❏ F-1935I★ (W-550I★) • 640,000		
❏ F-1935J (W-550J) • 24,960,000		
❏ F-1935J★ (W-550J★) • 640,000		

F-No. (W-No.) • Printage *(rarity)*	Grade	Comments
❏ F-1935K (W-550K) • 41,600,000		
❏ F-1935K★ (W-550K★) • 1,280,000		
❏ F-1935L (W-550L) • 82,560,000		
❏ F-1935L★ (W-550L★) • 1,920,000		
Series of 1995		
❏ F-1936A★ (W-551A★) • 9,999		
❏ F-1936B★ (W-551B★) • 9,999		
❏ F-1936C★ (W-551C★) • 9,999		
❏ F-1936D★ (W-551D★) • 9,999		
❏ F-1936E★ (W-551E★) • 9,999		
❏ F-1936F (W-551F) • 153,600,000		
❏ F-1936F★ (W-551F★) • 9,999 Plus 1,280,000 sold as part of sheets.		
❏ F-1936G★ (W-551G★) • 9,999		
❏ F-1936H★ (W-551H★) • 9,999		
❏ F-1936I★ (W-551I★) • 9,999		
❏ F-1936J★ (W-551J★) • 9,999		
❏ F-1936K★ (W-551K★) • 9,999		
❏ F-1936L★ (W-551L★) • 9,999		
Series of 2003 and 2003-A		
❏ F-1937A★ (W-552A★) • 16,000‡		
❏ F-1937B★ (W-552B★) • 16,000‡		
❏ F-1937C★ (W-552C★) • 16,000‡		
❏ F-1937D★ (W-552D★) • 16,000‡		
❏ F-1937E★ (W-552E★) • 16,000‡		
❏ F-1937F★ (W-552F★) • 16,000‡		
❏ F-1937G★ (W-552G★) • 16,000‡		
❏ F-1937H★ (W-552H★) • 16,000‡		
❏ F-1937I (W-553I) • 121,600,000		
❏ F-1937I★ (W-552I★) • 16,000‡		
❏ F-1937I★ (W-553I★) • 3,840,000		
❏ F-1937J★ (W-552J★) • 16,000‡		
❏ F-1937K★ (W-552K★) • 16,000‡		
❏ F-1937L★ (W-552L★) • 16,000‡		

‡ Collector products issued by the Bureau of Engraving and Printing.

F-No. (W-No.) • Printage *(rarity)*	Grade	Comments
Series of 2003 and 2003-A *(continued)*		
❏ F-1938A (W-554A) • 12,800,000		
❏ F-1938B (W-554B) • 25,600,000		
❏ F-1938C (W-554C) • 6,400,000		
❏ F-1938D (W-554D) • 19,200,000		
❏ F-1938E (W-554E) • 190,200,000		
❏ F-1938F (W-554F) • 320,000		
❏ F-1938G (W-554G) • 25,600,000		
❏ F-1938H (W-554H) • 6,400,000		
❏ F-1938I (W-554I) • 6,400,000		
❏ F-1938J (W-554J) • 12,800,000		
❏ F-1938K (W-554K) • 12,800,000		
❏ F-1938L (W-554L) • 64,000,000		
❏ F-1938L★ (W-554L★) • 384,400		
Series of 2009		
❏ F-1939A • 12,800,000		
❏ F-1939B • 32,000,000		
❏ F-1939B★ • 128,000		
❏ F-1939D • 12,800,000		
❏ F-1939F • 12,800,000		
❏ F-1939G • 12,800,000		
❏ F-1939K • 12,800,000		
❏ F-1939K★ • 512,000		
❏ F-1939L • 38,400,000		
❏ F-1939L★ • 128,000		
Series of 2013		
❏ F-1940B		
❏ F-1940E		
❏ F-1940F		
❏ F-1940F★		
❏ F-1940K		
❏ F-1940L		
❏		
❏		
❏		

F-No. (W-No.) • Printage *(rarity)*	Grade	Comments
❑		
❑		
❑		
❑		
Series of 2017		
❑		
❑		
❑		
❑		
❑		
❑		
❑		
❑		
❑		
❑		
❑		
❑		
❑		
❑		
❑		
❑		
❑		
❑		
❑		
❑		
❑		
❑		
❑		
❑		
❑		
❑		
❑		
❑		

LARGE-SIZE

$5 Demand Notes

F-No. (W-No.) • Printage *(rarity)*	Grade	Comments
Series of 1861		
❏ F-1 (W-607) • est. 90,000 *(8–12)*		
❏ F-1 (W-608) • 1,400,000 *(120–130)*		
❏ F-1a (W-606) • est. 10,000 *(9 known)*		
❏ F-2 (W-609) • 100,000 *(8–12)*		
❏ F-2 (W-610) • 1,300,000 *(120–130)*		
❏ F-3 (W-602) • est. 98,000 *(7–9)*		
❏ F-3 (W-603) • 1,240,000 *(105–115)*		
❏ F-3a (W-601) • est. 2,000 *(1 known)*		
❏ F-4 (W-605) • est. 43,000 *(5 known)*		
❏ F-5 (W-612) • est. 75,000 *(9–10)*		

$5 Legal Tender Notes

F-No. (W-No.) • Printage *(rarity)*	Grade	Comments
Series of 1862, First Obligation		
❏ F-61 (W-631) • 100,000 *(10 known)*		
❏ F-61a (W-632) • est. 5,750,000 *(400–500)*		
❏ F-61a (W-633) • est. 1,350,000 *(50–100)*		
❏ F-61a (W-634) • 4,700,000 *(300–400)*		
Series of 1862, Second Obligation		
❏ F-62 (W-635) • 2,300,000 *(70–80)*		

F-No. (W-No.) • Printage *(rarity)*	Grade	Comments
Series of 1863		
❏ F-63 (W-636) • 4,032,764 *(190–210)*		
❏ F-63a (W-637) • 1,000,000 *(180–200)*		
❏ F-63b (W-638) • 867,236 *(130–150)*		
Series of 1869		
❏ F-64 (W-650) • 10,068,000 *(700–900)*		
Series of 1875		
❏ F-65 (W-653) • 3,800,000 *(70–80)*		
❏ F-66 (W-651) • 1,000,000 *(35–40)*		
❏ F-67 (W-652) • 1,000,000 *(135–150)*		
❏ F-68 (W-654) • 3,436,000 *(140–160)*		
Series of 1878		
❏ F-69 (W-655) • 6,032,000 *(165–180)*		
Series of 1880		
❏ F-70 (W-656) • est. 4,100,000 *(100–140)*		
❏ F-71 (W-657) • est. 7,400,000 *(115–125)*		
❏ F-72 (W-658) • est. 7,760,000 *(145–160)*		
❏ F-73 (W-659) • est. 2,504,000 *(220–235)*		
❏ F-74 (W-660) • est. 6,196,000 *(148–155)*		
❏ F-75 (W-661) • est. 1,508,000 *(32–36)*		
❏ F-76 (W-662) • est. 4,592,000 *(75–85)*		
❏ F-77 (W-663) • est. 4,200,000 *(90–100)*		
❏ F-78 (W-664) • est. 700,000 *(45–55)*		
❏ F-79 (W-665) • est. 7,000,000 *(105–120)*		
❏ F-80 (W-666) • est. 16,400,000 *(325–425)*		
❏ F-81 (W-667) • est. 6,100,000 *(125–150)*		
❏ F-82 (W-668) • est. 4,532,000 *(60–70)*		
Series of 1907		
❏ F-83 (W-669) • 36,010,000 *(165–180)*		
❏ F-84 (W-670) • 32,120,000 *(140–170)*		
❏ F-84★ (W-670★) • *(5 known)*		
❏ F-85 (W-671) • 54,004,000 *(325–425)*		
❏ F-86 (W-672) • 1,596,000 *(75–85)*		
❏ F-87 (W-673) • 47,116,000 *(350–425)*		
❏ F-87★ (W-673★) • *(8 known)*		
❏ F-88 (W-674) • est. 97,268,000 *(550–600)*		

F-No. (W-No.) • Printage *(rarity)*	Grade	Comments
Series of 1907 *(continued)*		
❏ F-88★ (W-674★) • *(52–55)*		
❏ F-89 (W-675) • est. 2,300,000 *(80–90)*		
❏ F-89★ (W-675★) • *(11–13)*		
❏ F-89 (W-675 Mule) • est. 240,000 *(6 known)*		
❏ F-89★ (W-675 Mule★) • *(1 known)*		
❏ F-90 (W-676) • est. 13,000,000 *(250–325)*		
❏ F-90★ (W-676★) • *(11–13)*		
❏ F-90 (W-676 Mule) • est. 3,228,000 *(23–26)*		
❏ F-90★ (W-676 Mule★) • *(5 known)*		
❏ F-91 (W-677) • est. 160,160,000 *(4,000–5,500)*		
❏ F-91★ (W-677★) • *(155–170)*		
❏ F-91 (W-677 Mule) • est. 100,000 *(6–8)*		
❏ F-91★ (W-677 Mule★) • *(1 known)*		
❏ F-92 (W-678) • est. 14,892,000 *(200–230)*		
❏ F-92★ (W-678★) • *(6 known)*		

$5 National Bank Notes

F-No. (W-No.) • Printage *(rarity)*	Grade	Comments
Original Series ("First Charter Period")		
❏ F-394 (W-680) • *(200–225)*		
❏ F-397 (W-681) • *(360–420)*		
❏ F-398 (W-682) • *(11–13)*		
❏ F-399 (W-683) • *(205–220)*		
Series of 1875 ("First Charter Period")		
❏ F-401 (W-698) • *(800–1,200)*		
❏ F-402 (W-699) • *(170–190)*		
❏ F-403 (W-700) • *(135–150)*		
❏ F-404 (W-701) • *(450–550)*		
❏ F-405 (W-702) • *(300–400)*		
❏ F-406 (W-703) • *(4 known)*		
❏ F-406a (W-704) • *(4 known)*		
❏ F-407 (W-706) • *(36–42)*		
❏ F-408 (W-705) • *(7 known)*		
❏ F-408a (W-707) • *(2 known)*		
❏ F-408b (W-708) • *(2 known)*		

F-No. (W-No.) • Printage *(rarity)*	Grade	Comments
Series of 1882, Brown Back ("Second Charter Period")		
❑ F-466 (W-710) • *(600–900)*		
❑ F-467 (W-711) • *(1,600–2,200)*		
❑ F-468 (W-712) • *(350–500)*		
❑ F-469 (W-713) • *(800–950)*		
❑ F-470 (W-714) • *(300–350)*		
❑ F-471 (W-715) • *(700–800)*		
❑ F-472 (W-716) • *(600–700)*		
❑ F-473 (W-717) • *(23–26)*		
❑ F-474 (W-718) • *(650–750)*		
❑ F-475 (W-719) • *(125–140)*		
❑ F-476 (W-720) • *(60–70)*		
❑ F-477 (W-721) • *(15–18)*		
❑ F-478 (W-723) • *(7 known)*		
Series of 1882, Date Back ("Second Charter Period")		
❑ F-532 (W-730) • *(48–55)*		
❑ F-533 (W-731) • *(120–130)*		
❑ F-533a (W-732) • *(3 known)*		
❑ F-534 (W-733) • *(325–400)*		
❑ F-535 (W-734) • *(36–42)*		
❑ F-536 (W-735) • *(28–32)*		
❑ F-537 (W-736) • *(1,100–1,250)*		
❑ F-538 (W-737) • *(32–36)*		
❑ F-538b (W-739) • *(7 known)*		
Series of 1882, Value Back ("Second Charter Period")		
❑ F-573 (W-745) • *(10–12)*		
❑ F-573a (W-746) • *(6 known)*		
❑ F-574 (W-748) • *(800–900)*		
❑ F-574a (W-747) • *(8 or 9 known)*		
❑ F-575 (W-750) • *(28–32)*		
❑ F-575a (W-751) • *(11–13)*		
❑ F-575b (W-752) • *(6 known)*		
Series of 1902, Red Seal ("Third Charter Period")		
❑ F-587 (W-755) • *(1,400–1,550)*		
❑ F-588 (W-756) • *(155–165)*		

F-No. (W-No.) • Printage *(rarity)*	Grade	Comments
Series of 1902, Red Seal ("Third Charter Period") *(continued)*		
❑ F-589 (W-757) • *(185–205)*		
Series of 1902, Blue Seal, Date Back ("Third Charter Period")		
❑ F-590 (W-760) • *(1,650–1,900)*		
❑ F-591 (W-761) • *(250–300)*		
❑ F-592 (W-762) • *(700–900)*		
❑ F-593 (W-763) • *(600–750)*		
❑ F-594 (W-764) • *(240–280)*		
❑ F-595 (W-765) • *(52–60)*		
❑ F-596 (W-766) • *(34–40)*		
❑ F-597 (W-767) • *(70–85)*		
❑ F-597a (W-768) • *(1 known)*		
Series of 1902, Blue Seal, Plain Back ("Third Charter Period")		
❑ F-598 (W-770) • *(10,000–12,000)*		
❑ F-599 (W-771) • *(1,300–1,600)*		
❑ F-600 (W-772) • *(3,800–4,500)*		
❑ F-601 (W-773) • *(2,600–3,200)*		
❑ F-602 (W-774) • *(1,900–2,400)*		
❑ F-603 (W-775) • *(350–425)*		
❑ F-604 (W-776) • *(250–300)*		
❑ F-605 (W-777) • *(900–1,100)*		
❑ F-606 (W-778) • *(3,800–4,500)*		
❑ F-607 (W-779) • *(2,800–3,500)*		
❑ F-608 (W-780) • *(1,200–1,400)*		
❑ F-609 (W-781) • *(3,000–3,800)*		
❑ F-610 (W-782) • *(120–130)*		
❑ F-611 (W-783) • *(185–205)*		
❑ F-612 (W-784) • *(24–28)*		

$5 National Gold Bank Notes

F-No. (W-No.) • Printage *(rarity)*	Grade	Comments
❑ F-1136 (W-690) • 33,000 *(400–600)*		
❑ F-1137 (W-692) • 17,840 *(9–10)*		
❑ F-1138 (W-691) • 7,960 *(42–46)*		
❑ F-1139 (W-693) • 4,000 *(10–12)*		

F-No. (W-No.) • Printage *(rarity)*	Grade	Comments
❑ F-1140 (W-694) • 2,000 *(15–17)*		
❑ F-1141 (W-695) • 8,028 *(50–60)*		

$5 Silver Certificates

F-No. (W-No.) • Printage *(rarity)*	Grade	Comments
Series of 1886		
❑ F-259 (W-790) • est. 1,500,000 *(40–50)*		
❑ F-260 (W-791) • est. 7,440,000 *(140–155)*		
❑ F-261 (W-792) • est. 12,172,000 *(240–275)*		
❑ F-262 (W-793) • est. 3,388,000 *(75–90)*		
❑ F-263 (W-794) • est. 6,800,000 *(310–360)*		
❑ F-264 (W-795) • est. 1,840,000 *(60–70)*		
❑ F-265 (W-796) • est. 740,000 *(36–42)*		
Series of 1891		
❑ F-266 (W-797) • est. 7,100,000 *(75–85)*		
❑ F-267 (W-798) • est. 24,456,000 *(330–360)*		
Series of 1896		
❑ F-268 (W-799) • est. 17,300,000 *(800–1,000)*		
❑ F-269 (W-800) • est. 10,700,000 *(500–650)*		
❑ F-270 (W-801) • est. 6,932,000 *(300–350)*		
Series of 1899		
❑ F-271 (W-802) • est. 172,500,000 *(800–950)*		
❑ F-272 (W-803) • est. 29,500,000 *(225–275)*		
❑ F-273 (W-804) • est. 82,870,000 *(375–450)*		
❑ F-274 (W-805) • 46,020,000 *(225–275)*		
❑ F-274★ (W-805★) • *(11–13)*		
❑ F-275 (W-806) • 62,780,000 *(550–700)*		
❑ F-275★ (W-806★) • *(4 known)*		
❑ F-276 (W-807) • 2,324,000 *(60–70)*		
❑ F-277 (W-808) • 46,100,000 *(500–650)*		
❑ F-277★ (W-808★) • *(10–12)*		
❑ F-278 (W-809) • 42,276,000 *(500–650)*		
❑ F-278★ (W-809★) • *(16–18)*		
❑ F-279 (W-810) • est. 9,036,000 *(275–350)*		
❑ F-279★ (W-810★) • *(18–20)*		
❑ F-280 (W-811) • est. 2,500,000 *(100–120)*		

F-No. (W-No.) • Printage (rarity)	Grade	Comments
Series of 1899 (continued)		
❑ F-280 (W-811 Mule) • est. 24,568,00 (800–1,200)		
❑ F-280★ (W-811 Mule★) • (32–36)		
❑ F-281 (W-812) • est. 41,080,000 (1,200–1,500)		
❑ F-281★ (W-812★) • (9–10)		
❑ F-281 (W-812 Mule) • 4,500,000 (45–50)		
Series of 1923		
❑ F-282 (W-813) • 6,316,000 (1,300–1,600)		
❑ F-282★ (W-813★) • (43–45)		

$5 Treasury or Coin Notes

F-No. (W-No.) • Printage (rarity)	Grade	Comments
Series of 1890		
❑ F-359 (W-820) • est. 3,520,000 (130–145)		
❑ F-360 (W-821) • est. 280,000 (15–17)		
❑ F-361 (W-822) • est. 3,400,000 (140–155)		
Series of 1891		
❑ F-362 (W-823) • est. 2,800,000 (145–160)		
❑ F-363 (W-824) • est. 11,840,000 (275–350)		
❑ F-364 (W-825) • est. 1,920,000 (165–180)		
❑ F-365 (W-826) • est. 700,000 (30–40)		

$5 Federal Reserve Notes

F-No. (W-No.) • Printage (rarity)	Grade	Comments
Series of 1914, Red Seal		
❑ F-832A (W-830A-a) • 1,300,000 (30–35)		
❑ F-832B (W-830A-b) • 2,300,000 (60–70)		
❑ F-833A (W-830B-a) • 5,200,000 (60–70)		
❑ F-833B (W-830B-b) • 16,392,000 (225–275)		
❑ F-834A (W-830C-a) • 780,000 (28–32)		
❑ F-834B (W-830C-b) • 3,220,000 (100–120)		
❑ F-835A (W-830D-a) • 520,000 (20–23)		
❑ F-835B (W-830D-b) • 3,016,000 (70–80)		
❑ F-836A (W-830E-a) • 520,000 (20–23)		
❑ F-836B (W-830E-b) • 1,480,000 (32–36)		
❑ F-837A (W-830F-a) • 520,000 (28–32)		

F-No. (W-No.) • Printage *(rarity)*	Grade	Comments
❑ F-837B (W-830F-b) • 1,080,000 *(46–52)*		
❑ F-838A (W-830G-a) • 1,300,000 *(70–80)*		
❑ F-838B (W-830G-b) • 3,500,000 *(135–145)*		
❑ F-839A (W-830H-a) • 780,000 *(40–45)*		
❑ F-839B (W-830H-b) • 1,612,000 *(135–145)*		
❑ F-840A (W-830I-a) • 520,000 *(35–40)*		
❑ F-840B (W-830I-b) • 1,088,000 *(60–70)*		
❑ F-841A (W-830J-a) • 520,000 *(38–47)*		
❑ F-841B (W-830J-b) • 1,080,000 *(34–40)*		
❑ F-842A (W-830K-a) • 520,000 *(6 known)*		
❑ F-842B (W-830K-b) • 1,080,000 *(36–42)*		
❑ F-843A (W-830L-a) • 520,000 *(11–13)*		
❑ F-843B (W-830L-b) • 2,280,000 *(40–45)*		
Series of 1914, Blue Seal		
❑ F-844 (W-840A-b) • est. 10,000,000 *(60–70)*		
❑ F-844★ (W-840A-b★) • *(4 known)*		
❑ F-845 (W-841A-b) • est. 9,000,000 *(65–75)*		
❑ F-845★ (W-841A-b★) • *(4 known)*		
❑ F-846 (W-842A-b) • est. 14,376,000 *(120–130)*		
❑ F-846★ (W-842A-b★) • *(10–12)*		
❑ F-847A (W-843A-b) • est. 48,024,000 *(475–550)*		
❑ F-847A★ (W-843A-b★) • *(25–30)*		
❑ F-847B (W-843A-c) • est. 5,716,000 *(70–80)*		
❑ F-848 (W-844B-b) • est. 50,140,000 *(175–190)*		
❑ F-848★ (W-844B-b★) • *(6 known)*		
❑ F-849 (W-845B-b) • est. 17,268,000 *(95–105)*		
❑ F-849★ (W-845B-b★) • *(5 known)*		
❑ F-850 (W-846B-b) • est. 37,012,000 *(280–340)*		
❑ F-850★ (W-846B-b★) • *(30–35)*		
❑ F-851A (W-847B-b) • est. 130,760,000 *(1,100–1,300)*		
❑ F-851A★ (W-847B-b★) • *(90–95)*		
❑ F-851B (W-847B-c) • est. 16,568,000 *(115–125)*		
❑ F-851B★ (W-847B-c★) • *(5 known)*		
❑ F-851C (W-847B-d) • est. 24,512,000 *(325–375)*		

F-No. (W-No.) • Printage *(rarity)*	Grade	Comments
Series of 1914, Blue Seal *(continued)*		
❑ F-851C★ (W-847B-d★) • *(19–22)*		
❑ F-852 (W-848C-b) • est. 8,808,000 *(60–70)*		
❑ F-852★ (W-848C-b★) • *(5 known)*		
❑ F-853 (W-849C-b) • est. 8,316,000 *(70–80)*		
❑ F-853★ (W-849C-b★) • *(1 known)*		
❑ F-854 (W-850C-b) • est. 14,168,000 *(120–135)*		
❑ F-854★ (W-850C-b★) • *(11–13)*		
❑ F-855A (W-851C-b) • est. 55,160,000 *(750–900)*		
❑ F-855A★ (W-851C-b★) • *(55–65)*		
❑ F-855B (W-851C-c) • est. 8,088,000 *(75–85)*		
❑ F-855B★ (W-851C-c★) • *(3 known)*		
❑ F-855C (W-851C-d) • est. 5,284,000 *(225–275)*		
❑ F-855C★ (W-851C-d★) • *(7 known)*		
❑ F-856 (W-852D-b) • est. 6,324,000 *(60–70)*		
❑ F-856★ (W-852D-b★) • *(2 known)*		
❑ F-857 (W-853D-b) • est. 3,340,000 *(42–46)*		
❑ F-857★ (W-853D-b★) • *(3 known)*		
❑ F-858 (W-854D-b) • est. 12,296,000 *(100–110)*		
❑ F-858★ (W-854D-b★) • *(11–13)*		
❑ F-859A (W-855D-b) • est. 36,184,000 *(350–425)*		
❑ F-859A★ (W-855D-b★) • *(30–35)*		
❑ F-859B (W-855D-c) • est. 4,432,000 *(90–95)*		
❑ F-859B★ (W-855D-c★) • *(2 known)*		
❑ F-859C (W-855D-d) • est. 7,104,000 *(185–200)*		
❑ F-859C★ (W-855D-d★) • *(5 known)*		
❑ F-860 (W-856E-b) • est. 6,684,000 *(60–70)*		
❑ F-861 (W-857E-b) • est. 4,616,000 *(35–40)*		
❑ F-862 (W-858E-b) • est. 11,452,000 *(105–120)*		
❑ F-862★ (W-858E-b★) • *(12–14)*		
❑ F-863A (W-859E-b) • est. 20,140,000 *(275–300)*		
❑ F-863A★ (W-859E-b★) • *(10–12)*		
❑ F-863B (W-859E-c) • est. 3,316,000 *(4 known)*		
❑ F-864 (W-860F-b) • est. 8,700,000 *(60–65)*		

F-No. (W-No.) • Printage *(rarity)*	Grade	Comments
❏ F-864★ (W-860F-b★) • *(1 known)*		
❏ F-865 (W-861F-b) • est. 5,200,000 *(40–45)*		
❏ F-865★ (W-861F-b★) • *(1 known)*		
❏ F-866 (W-862F-b) • est. 9,200,000 *(62–66)*		
❏ F-866★ (W-862F-b★) • *(11–13)*		
❏ F-867A (W-863F-b) • est. 28,092,000 *(215–230)*		
❏ F-867A★ (W-863F-b★) • *(11–13)*		
❏ F-867B (W-863F-c) • est. 2,112,000 *(9–10)*		
❏ F-868 (W-864G-b) • est. 19,020,000 *(110–130)*		
❏ F-868★ (W-864G-b★) • *(2 known)*		
❏ F-869 (W-865G-b) • est. 10,380,000 *(95–105)*		
❏ F-869★ (W-865G-b★) • *(6 known)*		
❏ F-870 (W-866G-b) • est. 17,484,000 *(180–200)*		
❏ F-870★ (W-866G-b★) • *(25–28)*		
❏ F-871A (W-867G-b) • est. 90,376,000 *(800–1,000)*		
❏ F-871A★ (W-867G-b★) • *(70–80)*		
❏ F-871B (W-867G-c) • est. 16,472,000 *(300–400)*		
❏ F-871B★ (W-867G-c★) • *(2 known)*		
❏ F-871C (W-867G-d) • est. 6,344,000 *(145–155)*		
❏ F-871C★ (W-867G-d★) • *(4 known)*		
❏ F-872 (W-868H-b) • est. 7,356,000 *(85–95)*		
❏ F-872★ (W-868H-b★) • *(4 known)*		
❏ F-873 (W-869H-b) • est. 6,552,000 *(75–85)*		
❏ F-873★ (W-869H-b★) • *(9–10)*		
❏ F-874 (W-870H-b) • est. 15,500,000 *(165–180)*		
❏ F-874★ (W-870H-b★) • *(14–16)*		
❏ F-875A (W-871H-b) • est. 8,060,000 *(155–165)*		
❏ F-857A★ (W-871H-b★) • *(5 known)*		
❏ F-875B (W-871H-c) • est. 1,844,000 *(75–85)*		
❏ F-876 (W-872I-b) • est. 7,612,000 *(95–105)*		
❏ F-876★ (W-872I-b★) • *(1 known)*		
❏ F-877 (W-873I-b) • est. 3,080,000 *(55–65)*		

F-No. (W-No.) • Printage (rarity)	Grade	Comments
Series of 1914, Blue Seal (continued)		
❑ F-877★ (W-873I-b★) • (3 known)		
❑ F-878 (W-874I-b) • est. 3,640,000 (58–64)		
❑ F-878★ (W-874I-b★) • (11–13)		
❑ F-879A (W-875I-b) • est. 14,068,000 (350–425)		
❑ F-879A★ (W-875I-b★) • (10–12)		
❑ F-880 (W-876J-b) • est. 11,108,000 (100–115)		
❑ F-880★ (W-876J-b★) • (2 known)		
❑ F-881 (W-877J-b) • est. 5,192,000 (46–52)		
❑ F-881★ (W-877J-b★) • (3 known)		
❑ F-882 (W-878J-b) • est. 2,888,000 (130–150)		
❑ F-882★ (W-878J-b★) • (10–12)		
❑ F-883A (W-879J-b) • est. 22,728,000 (375–450)		
❑ F-883A★ (W-879J-b★) • (15–17)		
❑ F-883B (W-879J-c) • est. 880,000 (23–27)		
❑ F-884 (W-880K-b) • est. 4,500,000 (36–42)		
❑ F-885 (W-881K-b) • est. 4,700,000 (35–40)		
❑ F-885★ (W-881K-b★) • (2 known)		
❑ F-886 (W-882K-b) • est. 3,904,000 (48–54)		
❑ F-886★ (W-882K-b★) • (4 known)		
❑ F-887A (W-883K-b) • est. 12,996,000 (185–205)		
❑ F-887A★ (W-883K-b★) • (8 known)		
❑ F-887B (W-883K-c) • est. 1,544,000 (30–35)		
❑ F-888 (W-884L-b) • est. 10,600,000 (55–65)		
❑ F-888★ (W-884L-b★) • (1 known)		
❑ F-889 (W-885L-b) • est. 4,200,000 (18–20)		
❑ F-890 (W-886L-b) • est. 12,628,000 (55–65)		
❑ F-890★ (W-886L-b★) • (4 known)		
❑ F-891A (W-887L-b) • est. 54,596,000 (300–350)		
❑ F-891A★ (W-887L-b★) • (23–26)		
❑ F-891B (W-887L-c) • est. 5,576,000 (65–70)		
❑ F-891B★ (W-887L-c★) • (1 known)		
❑ F-891C (W-887L-d) • est. 1,768,000 (24–28)		

$5 Federal Reserve Bank Notes

F-No. (W-No.) • Printage (rarity)	Grade	Comments
Series of 1915		
❏ F-788 (W-901F) • est. 68,000 *(16–18)*		
❏ F-788a (W-898F) • *(1 known)*		
❏ F-789 (W-896F) • est. 60,000 *(32–36)*		
❏ F-793 (W-902G) • 320,000 *(40–45)*		
❏ F-800 (W-904J) • est. 688,000 *(70–80)*		
❏ F-801 (W-903J) • est. 160,000 *(12–14)*		
❏ F-802 (W-905J) • est. 24,000 *(5 known)*		
❏ F-805 (W-906K) • est. 208,000 *(20–24)*		
❏ F-806 (W-907K) • est. 120,000 *(13–15)*		
❏ F-808 (W-908L) • 336,000 *(35–40)*		
Series of 1918		
❏ F-781 (W-909A) • 440,000 *(40–55)*		
❏ F-781★ (W-909A★) • *(2 known)*		
❏ F-782 (W-910B) • 6,400,000 *(185–220)*		
❏ F-782★ (W-910B★) • *(3 known)*		
❏ F-783 (W-911C) • est. 516,000 *(48–54)*		
❏ F-784 (W-912C) • est. 1,084,000 *(40–45)*		
❏ F-785 (W-913D) • est. 1,376,000 *(275–350)*		
❏ F-785★ (W-913D★) • *(3 known)*		
❏ F-786 (W-914D) • est. 376,000 *(19–22)*		
❏ F-787 (W-915D) • est. 848,000 *(54–58)*		
❏ F-790 (W-916F) • est. 832,000 *(70–80)*		
❏ F-791 (W-917F) • est. 200,000 *(19–22)*		
❏ F-792 (W-918F) • est. 168,000 *(13–15)*		
❏ F-794 (W-919G) • est. 2,848,000 *(190–210)*		
❏ F-794★ (W-919G★) • *(3 known)*		
❏ F-795 (W-920G) • est. 152,000 *(9–10)*		
❏ F-796 (W-921H) • est. 920,000 *(100–110)*		
❏ F-797 (W-922H) • est. 272,000 *(35–40)*		
❏ F-798 (W-923H) • est. 332,000 *(30–35)*		
❏ F-799 (W-924I) • 828,000 *(70–80)*		
❏ F-803 (W-925J) • est. 1,660,000 *(65–75)*		
❏ F-803★ (W-925J★) • *(2 known)*		

F-No. (W-No.) • Printage *(rarity)*	Grade	Comments
Series of 1918 *(continued)*		
❏ F-804 (W-926J) • est. 2,340,000 *(120–130)*		
❏ F-807 (W-927K) • 500,000 *(28–33)*		
❏ F-809 (W-929L) • est. 896,000 *(19–22)*		
❏ F-809a (W-928L) • est. 300,000 *(23–28)*		

SMALL-SIZE

$5 Legal Tender Notes

F-No. (W-No.) • Printage *(rarity)*	Grade	Comments
Series of 1928–1928-E		
❏ F-1525 (W-1000) • 267,209,616		
❏ F-1525★ (W-1000★) • est. 3,150,000		
❏ F-1526 (W-1002) • 58,194,600		
❏ F-1526★ (W-1002★)		
❏ F-1527 (W-1004) • 147,827,340		
❏ F-1527★ (W-1004★) • est. 1,600,000		
❏ F-1527 (W-1004 Mule)		
❏ F-1527★ (W-1004 Mule★)		
❏ F-1528 (W-1006) • 214,735,765		
❏ F-1528★ (W-1006★) • est. 2,050,000		
❏ F-1528 (W-1006 Mule)		
❏ F-1528★ (W-1006 Mule★)		
❏ F-1529 (W-1008) • 9,297,120		
❏ F-1529★ (W-1008★)		
❏ F-1529 (W-1008 Mule)		
❏ F-1530 (W-1010) • 109,952,760		

F-No. (W-No.) • Printage *(rarity)*	Grade	Comments
❑ F-1530★ (W-1010★) • est. 1,550,000		
❑ F-1530 (W-1010 Mule)		
❑ F-1530★ (W-1010 Mule★) • *(1 known)*		
Series of 1928-F, Wide Back 1		
❑ F-1531 (W-1012) • 104,194,704		
❑ F-1531★ (W-1012★) • est. 1,250,000		
Series of 1928-F, Narrow Back		
❑ F-1531 (W-1013) • incl. in F-1531/W-1012		
❑ F-1531★ (W-1013★)		
Series of 1928-F, Wide Back 2		
❑ F-1531 (W-1014) • incl. in F-1531/W-1012		
❑ F-1531★ (W-1014★)		
Series of 1953–1953-C		
❑ F-1532 (W-1016) • 120,880,000		
❑ F-1532★ (W-1016★) • 5,760,000		
❑ F-1533 (W-1018) • 90,280,000		
❑ F-1533★ (W-1018★) • 5,400,000		
❑ F-1534 (W-1020) • 44,640,000		
❑ F-1534★ (W-1020★) • 2,160,000		
❑ F-1535 (W-1022) • 8,640,000		
❑ F-1535★ (W-1022★) • 320,000		
Series of 1963		
❑ F-1536 (W-1030) • 63,360,000		
❑ F-1536★ (W-1030★) • 3,840,000		

$5 National Bank Notes

F-No. (W-No.) • Printage *(rarity)*	Grade	Comments
Series of 1929, Type 1		
❑ F-1800-1 (W-1046) • *(28,000–30,000)*		
Series of 1929, Type 2		
❑ F-1800-2 (W-1048) • *(15,000–17,000)*		

$5 Silver Certificates

F-No. (W-No.) • Printage *(rarity)*	Grade	Comments
Series of 1934 and 1934-A, Blue Seal		
❑ F-1650 (W-1078) • 393,088,368		
❑ F-1650★ (W-1078★) • est. 3,960,000		

F-No. (W-No.) • Printage *(rarity)*	Grade	Comments
Series of 1934 and 1934-A, Blue Seal *(continued)*		
❏ F-1650 (W-1078 Mule)		
❏ F-1651 (W-1083) • 656,265,948		
❏ F-1651★ (W-1083★) • est. 7,320,000		
❏ F-1651 (W-1083 Mule)		
❏ F-1651★ (W-1083 Mule★)		
Series of 1934-A, Yellow Seal for North Africa		
❏ F-2307 (W-1086) • 16,710,000		
❏ F-2307★ (W-1086★) • 100,000		
Series of 1934-B		
❏ F-1652 (W-1090) • 59,128,500		
❏ F-1652★ (W-1090★) • est. 700,000		
❏ F-1652 (W-1090 Mule)		
❏ F-1652★ (W-1090 Mule★)		
Series of 1934-C, Wide Face		
❏ F-1653 (W-1100) • 403,146,148		
❏ F-1653★ (W-1100★) • est. 5,210,000		
❏ F-1653 (W-1110 Mule)		
❏ F-1653★ (W-1110 Mule★)		
Series of 1934-C, Narrow Face		
❏ F-1653 (W-1102) • incl. in F-1653/W-1100		
❏ F-1653★ (W-1102★) • *(2 known)*		
❏ F-1653 (W-1102 Mule)		
❏ F-1653★ (W-1102 Mule★) • *(1 known)*		
Series of 1934-D, Wide Back		
❏ F-1654 (W-1104) • 486,146,148		
❏ F-1654★ (W-1104★) • est. 5,800,000		
Series of 1934-D, Narrow Back		
❏ F-1654 (W-1105) • incl. in F-1654/W-1104		
❏ F-1654★ (W-1105★)		
Series of 1953–1953-C		
❏ F-1655 (W-1106) • 339,600,000		
❏ F-1655★ (W-1106★) • 15,120,000		
❏ F-1656 (W-1108) • 232,400,000		
❏ F-1656★ (W-1108★) • 12,960,000		
❏ F-1657 (W-1110) • 73,000,000		
❏ F-1657★ (W-1110★) • 3,240,000		

$5 Federal Reserve Bank Notes

F-No. (W-No.) • Printage (rarity)	Grade	Comments
Series of 1929		
❑ F-1850A (W-1050A) • 3,180,000		
❑ F-1850A★ (W-1050A★)		
❑ F-1850B (W-1050B) • 2,100,000		
❑ F-1850B★ (W-1050B★)		
❑ F-1850C (W-1050C) • 3,096,000		
❑ F-1850C★ (W-1050C★)		
❑ F-1850D (W-1050D) • 4,236,000		
❑ F-1850D★ (W-1050D★)		
❑ F-1850F (W-1050F) • 1,884,000		
❑ F-1850F★ (W-1050F★)		
❑ F-1850G (W-1050G) • 5,988,000		
❑ F-1850G★ (W-1050G★)		
❑ F-1850H (W-1050H) • 276,000		
❑ F-1850H★ (W-1050H★)		
❑ F-1850I (W-1050I) • 684,000		
❑ F-1850I★ (W-1050I★)		
❑ F-1850J (W-1050J) • 2,460,000		
❑ F-1850J★ (W-1050J★)		
❑ F-1850K (W-1050K) • 996,000		
❑ F-1850K★ (W-1050K★)		
❑ F-1850L (W-1050L) • 360,000		

$5 Federal Reserve Notes

F-No. (W-No.) • Printage (rarity)	Grade	Comments
Series of 1928 and 1928-A		
❑ F-1950A (W-1118A) • 8,025,300		
❑ F-1950A★ (W-1118A★)		
❑ F-1950B (W-1118B) • 14,701,884		
❑ F-1950B★ (W-1118B★)		
❑ F-1950C (W-1118C) • 11,819,712		
❑ F-1950C★ (W-1118C★)		
❑ F-1950D (W-1118D) • 9,049,500		
❑ F-1950D★ (W-1118D★)		

F-No. (W-No.) • Printage *(rarity)*	Grade	Comments
Series of 1928 and 1928-A *(continued)*		
❑ F-1950E (W-1118E) • 6,027,600		
❑ F-1950E★ (W-1118E★)		
❑ F-1950F (W-1118F) • 10,964,400		
❑ F-1950F★ (W-1118F★)		
❑ F-1950G (W-1118G) • 12,320,052		
❑ F-1950G★ (W-1118G★)		
❑ F-1950H (W-1118H) • 4,675,200		
❑ F-1950H★ (W-1118H★)		
❑ F-1950I (W-1118I) • 4,284,300		
❑ F-1950I★ (W-1118I★)		
❑ F-1950J (W-1118J) • 4,480,800		
❑ F-1950J★ (W-1118J★)		
❑ F-1950K (W-1118K) • 8,137,824		
❑ F-1950K★ (W-1118K★)		
❑ F-1950L (W-1118L) • 9,792,000		
❑ F-1950L★ (W-1118L★)		
❑ F-1951A (W-1120A) • 9,404,352		
❑ F-1951A★ (W-1120A★)		
❑ F-1951B (W-1120B) • 42,878,196		
❑ F-1951B★ (W-1120B★)		
❑ F-1951C (W-1120C) • 10,806,012		
❑ F-1951C★ (W-1120C★)		
❑ F-1951D (W-1120D) • 6,822,000		
❑ F-1951D★ (W-1120D★)		
❑ F-1951E (W-1120E) • 2,409,900		
❑ F-1951E★ (W-1120E★)		
❑ F-1951F (W-1120F) • 3,537,600		
❑ F-1951F★ (W-1120F★)		
❑ F-1951G (W-1120G) • 37,882,176		
❑ F-1951G★ (W-1120G★)		
❑ F-1951H (W-1120H) • 2,731,824		
❑ F-1951H★ (W-1120H★)		
❑ F-1951I (W-1120I) • 652,800		

F-No. (W-No.) • Printage *(rarity)*	Grade	Comments
❑ F-1951J (W-1120J) • 3,572,400		
❑ F-1951K (W-1120K) • 2,564,400		
❑ F-1951K★ (W-1120K★)		
❑ F-1951L (W-1120L) • 6,565,500		
❑ F-1951L★ (W-1120L★)		
Series of 1928-B, Green Seal		
❑ F-1952A (W-1122A) • 28,430,724		
❑ F-1952A★ (W-1122A★)		
❑ F-1952B (W-1122B) • 51,157,536		
❑ F-1952B★ (W-1122B★)		
❑ F-1952C (W-1122C) • 25,698,396		
❑ F-1952C★ (W-1122C★)		
❑ F-1952D (W-1122D) • 24,874,272		
❑ F-1952D★ (W-1122D★)		
❑ F-1952E (W-1122E) • 15,151,932		
❑ F-1952E★ (W-1122E★)		
❑ F-1952F (W-1122F) • 13,386,420		
❑ F-1952F★ (W-1122F★)		
❑ F-1952G (W-1122G) • 17,157,036		
❑ F-1952G★ (W-1122G★)		
❑ F-1952H (W-1122H) • 20,251,716		
❑ F-1952H★ (W-1122H★)		
❑ F-1952I (W-1122I) • 6,954,060		
❑ F-1952I★ (W-1122I★)		
❑ F-1952J (W-1122J) • 10,677,636		
❑ F-1952K (W-1122K) • 4,334,400		
❑ F-1952L (W-1122L) • 28,840,000		
❑ F-1952L★ (W-1122L★)		
Series of 1928-B, Light Yellow-Green Seal		
❑ F-1952A (W-1125A) • incl. in F-1952A/W-1122A		
❑ F-1952A★ (W-1125A★)		
❑ F-1952B (W-1125B) • incl. in F-1952B/W-1122B		
❑ F-1952B★ (W-1125B★)		
❑ F-1952C (W-1125C) • incl. in F-1952C/W-1122C		
❑ F-1952C★ (W-1125C★)		

F-No. (W-No.) • Printage *(rarity)*	Grade	Comments
Series of 1928-B, Light Yellow-Green Seal *(continued)*		
❑ F-1952D (W-1125D) • incl. in F-1952D/W-1122D		
❑ F-1952D★ (W-1125D★)		
❑ F-1952E (W-1125E) • incl. in F-1952E/W-1122E		
❑ F-1952E★ (W-1125E★)		
❑ F-1952F (W-1125F) • incl. in F-1952F/W-1122F		
❑ F-1952F★ (W-1125F★)		
❑ F-1952G (W-1125G) • incl. in F-1952G/W-1122G		
❑ F-1952G★ (W-1125G★)		
❑ F-1952H (W-1125H) • incl. in F-1952H/W-1122H		
❑ F-1952H★ (W-1125H★)		
❑ F-1952I (W-1125I) • incl. in F-1952I/W-1122I		
❑ F-1952I★ (W-1125I★)		
❑ F-1952J (W-1125J) • incl. in F-1952J/W-1122J		
❑ F-1952J★ (W-1125J★)		
❑ F-1952K (W-1125K) • incl. in F-1952K/W-1122K		
❑ F-1952K★ (W-1125K★)		
❑ F-1952L (W-1125L) • incl. in F-1952L/W-1122L		
❑ F-1952L★ (W-1125-L★)		
Series of 1928-C, Light Yellow-Green Seal		
❑ F-1953F (W-1128F) • 2,056,200		
Series of 1928-D, Green Seal		
❑ F-1954F (W-1131F) • 1,281,600		
Series of 1934, Light Yellow-Green Seal		
❑ F-1955A (W-1134A) • 30,510,036		
❑ F-1955A★ (W-1134A★)		
❑ F-1955B (W-1134B) • 47,888,760		
❑ F-1955B★ (W-1134B★)		
❑ F-1955C (W-1134C) • 47,327,760		
❑ F-1955C★ (W-1134C★)		
❑ F-1955D (W-1134D) • 62,273,508		
❑ F-1955D★ (W-1134D★)		
❑ F-1955E (W-1134E) • 62,128,452		
❑ F-1955E★ (W-1134E★)		
❑ F-1955F (W-1134F) • 50,548,608		

F-No. (W-No.) • Printage *(rarity)*	Grade	Comments
❏ F-1955F★ (W-1134F★)		
❏ F-1955G (W-1134G) • 31,299,156		
❏ F-1955G★ (W-1134G★)		
❏ F-1955H (W-1134H) • 48,737,280		
❏ F-1955H★ (W-1134H★)		
❏ F-1955I (W-1134I) • 16,795,392		
❏ F-1955I★ (W-1134I★)		
❏ F-1955J (W-1134J) • 31,854,432		
❏ F-1955J★ (W-1134J★)		
❏ F-1955K (W-1134K) • 33,332,208		
❏ F-1955K★ (W-1134K★)		
❏ F-1955L (W-1134L) • 39,324,168		
❏ F-1955L★ (W-1134L★)		
Series of 1934, Blue-Green Seal		
❏ F-1956A (W-1137A) • incl. in F-1955A/W-1134A		
❏ F-1956A★ (W-1137A★)		
❏ F-1956A (W-1137A Mule)		
❏ F-1956A★ (W-1137A Mule★)		
❏ F-1956B (W-1137B) • incl. in F-1955B/W-1134B		
❏ F-1956B★ (W-1137B★)		
❏ F-1956B (W-1137B Mule)		
❏ F-1956B★ (W-1137B Mule★)		
❏ F-1956C (W-1137C) • incl. in F-1955C/W-1134C		
❏ F-1956C★ (W-1137C★)		
❏ F-1956C (W-1137C Mule)		
❏ F-1956C★ (W-1137C Mule★)		
❏ F-1956D (W-1137D) • incl. in F-1955D/W-1134D		
❏ F-1956D★ (W-1137D★)		
❏ F-1956D (W-1137D Mule)		
❏ F-1956D★ (W-1137D Mule★)		
❏ F-1956E (W-1137E) • incl. in F-1955E/W-1134E		
❏ F-1956E★ (W-1137E★)		
❏ F-1956E (W-1137E Mule)		
❏ F-1956E★ (W-1137E Mule★)		

F-No. (W-No.) • Printage (rarity)	Grade	Comments
Series of 1934, Blue-Green Seal (continued)		
❏ F-1956F (W-1137F) • incl. in F-1955F/W-1134F		
❏ F-1956F★ (W-1137F★)		
❏ F-1956F (W-1137F Mule)		
❏ F-1956F★ (W-1137F Mule★)		
❏ F-1956G (W-1137G) • incl. in F-1955G/W-1134G		
❏ F-1956G★ (W-1137G★)		
❏ F-1956G (W-1137G Mule)		
❏ F-1956G★ (W-1137G Mule★)		
❏ F-1956H (W-1137H) • incl. in F-1955H/W-1134H		
❏ F-1956H★ (W-1137H★)		
❏ F-1956H (W-1137H Mule)		
❏ F-1956H★ (W-1137H Mule★)		
❏ F-1956I (W-1137I) • incl. in F-1955I/W-1134I		
❏ F-1956I★ (W-1137I★)		
❏ F-1956I (W-1137I Mule)		
❏ F-1956I★ (W-1137I Mule★)		
❏ F-1956J (W-1137J) • incl. in F-1955J/W-1134J		
❏ F-1956J★ (W-1137J★)		
❏ F-1956J (W-1137J Mule)		
❏ F-1956J★ (W-1137J Mule★) • *(2 known)*		
❏ F-1956K (W-1137K) • incl. in F-1955K/W-1134K		
❏ F-1956K★ (W-1137K★)		
❏ F-1956K (W-1137K Mule)		
❏ F-1956K★ (W-1137K Mule★)		
❏ F-1956L (W-1137L) • incl. in F-1955L/W-1134L		
❏ F-1956L★ (W-1137L★)		
❏ F-1956L (W-1137L Mule)		
❏ F-1956L★ (W-1137L Mule★)		
Series of 1934 and 1934-A, Brown Seal, HAWAII Overprint		
❏ F-2301 (W-1140L) • 9,416,000		
❏ F-2301★ (W-1140L★) • 80,000		
❏ F-2302 (W-1142L) • incl. in F-2301/W-1140L		
❏ F-2302★ (W-1142L★) • incl. in F-2301★/W-1140L★		

F-No. (W-No.) • Printage *(rarity)*	Grade	Comments
Series of 1934-A and 1934-B, Green Seal		
❑ F-1957A (W-1144A) • 23,231,568		
❑ F-1957A★ (W-1144A★)		
❑ F-1957B (W-1144B) • 143,199,336		
❑ F-1957B★ (W-1144B★)		
❑ F-1957B (W-1144B Mule)		
❑ F-1957C (W-1144C) • 30,691,632		
❑ F-1957C★ (W-1144C★)		
❑ F-1957C (W-1144C Mule)		
❑ F-1957D (W-1144D) • 1,610,676		
❑ F-1957D★ (W-1144D★)		
❑ F-1957E (W-1144E) • 6,555,168		
❑ F-1957E★ (W-1144E★)		
❑ F-1957F (W-1144F) • 22,811,916		
❑ F-1957F★ (W-1144F★)		
❑ F-1957G (W-1144G) • 88,376,376		
❑ F-1957G★ (W-1144G★)		
❑ F-1957G (W-1144G Mule)		
❑ F-1957G★ (W-1144G Mule★)		
❑ F-1957H (W-1144H) • 7,843,452		
❑ F-1957H★ (W-1144H★)		
❑ F-1957H (W-1144H Mule)		
❑ F-1957L (W-1144L) • 72,118,452		
❑ F-1957L★ (W-1144L★)		
❑ F-1957L (W-1144L Mule)		
❑ F-1957L★ (W-1144L Mule★)		
❑ F-1958A (W-1147A) • 3,457,800		
❑ F-1958A★ (W-1147A★)		
❑ F-1958A (W-1147A Mule)		
❑ F-1958B (W-1147B) • 14,099,580		
❑ F-1958B★ (W-1147B★)		
❑ F-1958B (W-1147B Mule)		
❑ F-1958C (W-1147C) • 8,306,820		
❑ F-1958C★ (W-1147C★)		

F-No. (W-No.) • Printage *(rarity)* Grade		Comments
Series of 1934-A and 1934-B, Green Seal *(continued)*		
❑ F-1958C (W-1147C Mule)		
❑ F-1958D (W-1147D) • 11,348,184		
❑ F-1958D★ (W-1147D★)		
❑ F-1958D (W-1147D Mule)		
❑ F-1958D★ (W-1147D Mule★)		
❑ F-1958E (W-1147E) • 5,902,848		
❑ F-1958E★ (W-1147E★)		
❑ F-1958F (W-1147F) • 4,314,048		
❑ F-1958F★ (W-1147F★)		
❑ F-1958G (W-1147G) • 9,070,932		
❑ F-1958G★ (W-1147G★)		
❑ F-1958G (W-1147G Mule)		
❑ F-1958H (W-1147H) • 4,307,712		
❑ F-1958H★ (W-1147H★)		
❑ F-1958H (W-1147H Mule)		
❑ F-1958I (W-1147I) • 2,482,500		
❑ F-1958I★ (W-1147I★)		
❑ F-1958I (W-1147I Mule)		
❑ F-1958J (W-1147J) • 73,800		
❑ F-1958L (W-1147L) • 9,910,296		
❑ F-1958L★ (W-1147L★)		
❑ F-1958L (W-1147L Mule)		
❑ F-1958L★ (W-1147L Mule★)		
Series of 1934-C, Wide Face		
❑ F-1959A (W-1150A) • 14,463,600		
❑ F-1959A★ (W-1150A★)		
❑ F-1959A (W-1150A Mule)		
❑ F-1959B (W-1150B) • 74,383,248		
❑ F-1959B★ (W-1150B★)		
❑ F-1959B (W-1150B Mule)		
❑ F-1959C (W-1150C) • 22,879,212		
❑ F-1959C★ (W-1150C★)		
❑ F-1959C (W-1150C Mule)		

F-No. (W-No.) • Printage *(rarity)*	Grade	Comments
❑ F-1959D (W-1150D) • 19,898,256		
❑ F-1959D★ (W-1150D★)		
❑ F-1959D (W-1150D Mule)		
❑ F-1959E (W-1150E) • 23,800,524		
❑ F-1959E★ (W-1150E★)		
❑ F-1959E (W-1150E Mule)		
❑ F-1959F (W-1150F) • 23,572,968		
❑ F-1959F★ (W-1150F★)		
❑ F-1959G (W-1150G) • 60,598,812		
❑ F-1959G★ (W-1150G★)		
❑ F-1959G (W-1150G Mule)		
❑ F-1959H (W-1150H) • 20,393,340		
❑ F-1959H★ (W-1150H★)		
❑ F-1959H (W-1150H Mule)		
❑ F-1959I (W-1150I) • 5,089,200		
❑ F-1959I★ (W-1150I★)		
❑ F-1959I (W-1150I Mule)		
❑ F-1959J (W-1150J) • 8,313,504		
❑ F-1959J★ (W-1150J★)		
❑ F-1959J (W-1150J Mule)		
❑ F-1959K (W-1150K) • 5,107,800		
❑ F-1959K★ (W-1150K★)		
❑ F-1959L (W-1150L) • 9,451,944		
❑ F-1959L★ (W-1150L★)		
❑ F-1959L (W-1150L Mule)		
Series of 1934-C, Narrow Face		
❑ F-1959B (W-1152B) • incl. in F-1959B/W-1150B		
❑ F-1959B★ (W-1152B★) • *(2 known)*		
Series of 1934-D		
❑ F-1960A (W-1155A) • 12,660,552		
❑ F-1960A★ (W-1155A★)		
❑ F-1960B (W-1155B) • 50,976,576		
❑ F-1960B★ (W-1155B★)		
❑ F-1960C (W-1155C) • 12,106,740		

F-No. (W-No.) • Printage *(rarity)*	Grade	Comments
Series of 1934-D *(continued)*		
❑ F-1960C★ (W-1155C★)		
❑ F-1960D (W-1155D) • 8,969,052		
❑ F-1960D★ (W-1155D★)		
❑ F-1960E (W-1155E) • 13,333,032		
❑ F-1960E★ (W-1155E★)		
❑ F-1960F (W-1155F) • 9,599,352		
❑ F-1960F★ (W-1155F★)		
❑ F-1960G (W-1155G) • 36,601,680		
❑ F-1960G★ (W-1155G★)		
❑ F-1960H (W-1155H) • 8,093,412		
❑ F-1960H★ (W-1155H★)		
❑ F-1960I (W-1155I) • 3,594,900		
❑ F-1960I★ (W-1155I★)		
❑ F-1960J (W-1155J) • 6,538,740		
❑ F-1960J★ (W-1155J★)		
❑ F-1960K (W-1155K) • 4,139,016		
❑ F-1960K★ (W-1155K★)		
❑ F-1960L (W-1155L) • 11,704,200		
❑ F-1960L★ (W-1155L★)		
Series of 1950, Wide Back 1		
❑ F-1961A (W-1157A) • 30,672,000		
❑ F-1961A★ (W-1157A★) • 408,000		
❑ F-1961B (W-1157B) • 106,768,000		
❑ F-1961B★ (W-1157B★) • 1,464,000		
❑ F-1961C (W-1157C) • 44,784,000		
❑ F-1961C★ (W-1157C★) • 600,000		
❑ F-1961D (W-1157D) • 54,000,000		
❑ F-1961D★ (W-1157D★) • 744,000		
❑ F-1961E (W-1157E) • 47,088,000		
❑ F-1961E★ (W-1157E★) • 684,000		
❑ F-1961F (W-1157F) • 52,416,000		
❑ F-1961F★ (W-1157F★) • 696,000		
❑ F-1961G (W-1157G) • 85,104,000		
❑ F-1961G★ (W-1157G★) • 1,176,000		

F-No. (W-No.) • Printage *(rarity)*	Grade	Comments
❑ F-1961H (W-1157H) • 36,864,000		
❑ F-1961H★ (W-1157H★) • 552,000		
❑ F-1961I (W-1157I★) • 11,796,000		
❑ F-1961I★ (W-1157I★) • 144,000		
❑ F-1961J (W-1157J) • 25,428,000		
❑ F-1961J★ (W-1157J★) • 360,000		
❑ F-1961K (W-1157K) • 22,848,000		
❑ F-1961K★ (W-1157K★) • 372,000		
❑ F-1961L (W-1157L) • 55,008,000		
❑ F-1961L★ (W-1157L★) • 744,000		
Series of 1950, Narrow Back		
❑ F-1961A (W-1159A) • incl. in F-1961A/W-1157A		
❑ F-1961B (W-1159B) • incl. in F-1961B/W-1157B		
❑ F-1961B★ (W-1159B★) • incl. in F-1961B★/W-1157B★		
❑ F-1961C (W-1159C) • incl. in F-1961C/W-1157C		
❑ F-1961C★ (W-1159C★) • incl. in F-1961C★/W-1157C★		
❑ F-1961D (W-1159D) • incl. in F-1961D/W-1157D		
❑ F-1961D★ (W-1159D★) • incl. in F-1961D★/W-1157D★		
❑ F-1961E (W-1159E) • incl. in F-1961E/W-1157E		
❑ F-1961E★ (W-1159E★) • incl. in F-1961E★/W-1157E★		
❑ F-1961F (W-1159F) • incl. in F-1961F/W-1157F		
❑ F-1961G (W-1159G) • incl. in F-1961G/W-1157G		
❑ F-1961G★ (W-1159G★) • incl. in F-1961G★/W-1157G★		
❑ F-1961H (W-1159H) • incl. in F-1961H/W-1157H		
❑ F-1961H★ (W-1159H★) • incl. in F-1961H★/W-1157H★		
❑ F-1961I (W-1159I) • incl. in F-1961I/W-1157I		
❑ F-1961J (W-1159J) • incl. in F-1961J/W-1157J		
❑ F-1961K (W-1159K) • incl. in F-1961K/W-1157K		
❑ F-1961L (W-1159L) • incl. in F-1961L/W-1157L		
❑ F-1961L★ (W-1159L★) • incl. in F-1961L★/W-1157L★		
Series of 1950, Wide Back 2		
❑ F-1961A (W-1160A) • incl. in F-1961A/W-1157A		
❑ F-1961B (W-1160B) • incl. in F-1961B/W-1157B		
❑ F-1961B★ (W-1160B★) • incl. in F-1961B★/W-1157B★		

F-No. (W-No.) • Printage *(rarity)*	Grade	Comments
Series of 1950, Wide Back 2 *(continued)*		
❏ F-1961C (W-1160C) • incl. in F-1961C/W-1157C		
❏ F-1961C★ (W-1160C★) • incl. in F-1961C★/W-1157C★		
❏ F-1961D (W-1160D) • incl. in F-1961D/W-1157D		
❏ F-1961D★ (W-1160D★) • incl. in F-1961D★/W-1157D★		
❏ F-1961E (W-1160E) • incl. in F-1961E/W-1157E		
❏ F-1961F (W-1160F) • incl. in F-1961F/W-1157F		
❏ F-1961G (W-1160G) • incl. in F-1961G/W-1157G		
❏ F-1961H (W-1160H) • incl. in F-1961H/W-1157H		
❏ F-1961I (W-1160I) • incl. in F-1961I/W-1157I		
❏ F-1961J (W-1160J) • incl. in F-1961J/W-1157J		
❏ F-1961K (W-1160K) • incl. in F-1961K/W-1157K		
❏ F-1961L (W-1160L) • incl. in F-1961L/W-1157L		
❏ F-1961L★ (W-1160L★) • incl. in F-1961L★/W-1157L★		
Series of 1950-A–1950-E		
❏ F-1962A (W-1161A) • 53,568,000		
❏ F-1962A★ (W-1161A★) • 2,808,000		
❏ F-1962B (W-1161B) • 186,472,000		
❏ F-1962B★ (W-1161B★) • 9,216,000		
❏ F-1962C (W-1161C) • 79,616,000		
❏ F-1962C★ (W-1161C★) • 4,320,000		
❏ F-1962D (W-1161D) • 45,360,000		
❏ F-1962D★ (W-1161D★) • 2,376,000		
❏ F-1962E (W-1161E) • 76,672,000		
❏ F-1962E★ (W-1161E★) • 5,400,000		
❏ F-1962F (W-1161F) • 86,464,000		
❏ F-1962F★ (W-1161F★) • 5,040,000		
❏ F-1962G (W-1161G) • 129,296,000		
❏ F-1962G★ (W-1161G★) • 6,284,000		
❏ F-1962H (W-1161H) • 54,936,000		
❏ F-1962H★ (W-1161H★) • 3,384,000		
❏ F-1962I (W-1161I) • 11,232,000		
❏ F-1962I★ (W-1161I★) • 864,000		
❏ F-1962J (W-1161J) • 29,952,000		

F-No. (W-No.) • Printage *(rarity)*	Grade	Comments
❑ F-1962J★ (W-1161J★) • 2,088,000		
❑ F-1962K (W-1161K) • 24,984,000		
❑ F-1962K★ (W-1161K★) • 1,368,000		
❑ F-1962L (W-1161L) • 90,712,000		
❑ F-1962L★ (W-1161L★) • 6,336,000		
❑ F-1963A (W-1163A) • 30,880,000		
❑ F-1963A★ (W-1163A★) • 2,520,000		
❑ F-1963B (W-1163B) • 85,960,000		
❑ F-1963B★ (W-1163B★) • 4,680,060		
❑ F-1963C (W-1163C) • 43,560,000		
❑ F-1963C★ (W-1163C★) • 2,880,000		
❑ F-1963D (W-1163D) • 38,800,000		
❑ F-1963D★ (W-1163D★) • 2,880,000		
❑ F-1963E (W-1163E) • 52,920,000		
❑ F-1963E★ (W-1163E★) • 2,080,000		
❑ F-1963F (W-1163F) • 80,560,000		
❑ F-1963F★ (W-1163F★) • 3,960,000		
❑ F-1963G (W-1163G) • 104,320,000		
❑ F-1963G★ (W-1163G★) • 6,120,000		
❑ F-1963H (W-1163H) • 25,840,000		
❑ F-1963H★ (W-1163H★) • 1,440,000		
❑ F-1963I (W-1163I) • 20,880,000		
❑ F-1963I★ (W-1163I★) • 792,000		
❑ F-1963J (W-1163J) • 32,400,000		
❑ F-1963J★ (W-1163J★) • 2,520,000		
❑ F-1963K (W-1163K) • 52,120,000		
❑ F-1963K★ (W-1163K★) • 3,240,000		
❑ F-1963L (W-1163L) • 56,080,000		
❑ F-1963L★ (W-1163L★) • 3,600,000		
❑ F-1964A (W-1165A) • 20,880,000		
❑ F-1964A★ (W-1165A★) • 720,000		
❑ F-1964B (W-1165B) • 47,440,000		
❑ F-1964B★ (W-1165B★) • 2,880,000		
❑ F-1964C (W-1165C) • 29,520,000		

F-No. (W-No.) • Printage *(rarity)*	Grade	Comments
Series of 1950-A–1950-E *(continued)*		
❑ F-1964C★ (W-1165C★) • 1,800,000		
❑ F-1964D (W-1165D) • 33,840,000		
❑ F-1964D★ (W-1165D★) • 1,800,000		
❑ F-1964E (W-1165E) • 33,480,000		
❑ F-1964E★ (W-1165E★) • 2,160,000		
❑ F-1964F (W-1165F) • 54,360,000		
❑ F-1964F★ (W-1165F★) • 3,240,000		
❑ F-1964G (W-1165G) • 56,880,000		
❑ F-1964G★ (W-1165G★) • 3,240,000		
❑ F-1964H (W-1165H) • 22,680,000		
❑ F-1964H★ (W-1165H★) • 720,000		
❑ F-1964I (W-1165I) • 12,960,000		
❑ F-1964I★ (W-1165I★) • 720,000		
❑ F-1964J (W-1165J) • 24,760,000		
❑ F-1964J★ (W-1165J★) • 1,800,000		
❑ F-1964K (W-1165K) • 3,960,000		
❑ F-1964K★ (W-1165K★) • 360,000		
❑ F-1964L (W-1165L) • 25,920,000		
❑ F-1964L★ (W-1165L★) • 1,440,000		
❑ F-1965A (W-1166A) • 25,200,000		
❑ F-1965A★ (W-1166A★) • 1,080,000		
❑ F-1965B (W-1166B) • 102,160,000		
❑ F-1965B★ (W-1166B★) • 5,040,000		
❑ F-1965C (W-1166C) • 21,520,000		
❑ F-1965C★ (W-1166C★) • 1,080,000		
❑ F-1965D (W-1166D) • 23,400,000		
❑ F-1965D★ (W-1166D★) • 1,080,000		
❑ F-1965E (W-1166E) • 42,490,000		
❑ F-1965E★ (W-1166E★) • 1,080,000		
❑ F-1965F (W-1166F) • 35,200,000		
❑ F-1965F★ (W-1166F★) • 1,800,000		
❑ F-1965G (W-1166G) • 67,240,000		
❑ F-1965G★ (W-1166G★) • 3,600,000		

F-No. (W-No.) • Printage *(rarity)*	Grade	Comments
❑ F-1965H (W-1166H) • 20,160,000		
❑ F-1965H★ (W-1166H★) • 720,000		
❑ F-1965I (W-1166I) • 7,920,000		
❑ F-1965I★ (W-1166I★) • 360,000		
❑ F-1965J (W-1166J) • 11,160,000		
❑ F-1965J★ (W-1166J★) • 720,000		
❑ F-1965K (W-1166K) • 7,200,000		
❑ F-1965K★ (W-1166K★) • 360,000		
❑ F-1965L (W-1166L) • 53,280,000		
❑ F-1965L★ (W-1166L★) • 3,600,000		
❑ F-1966B (W-1168B) • 82,000,000		
❑ F-1966B★ (W-1168B★) • 6,678,000		
❑ F-1966G (W-1168G) • 14,760,000		
❑ F-1966G★ (W-1168G★) • 1,080,000		
❑ F-1966L (W-1168H) • 24,400,000		
❑ F-1966L★ (W-1168H★) • 1,800,000		
Series of 1963 and 1963-A		
❑ F-1967A (W-1170A) • 4,480,000		
❑ F-1967A★ (W-1170A★) • 640,000		
❑ F-1967B (W-1170B) • 12,160,000		
❑ F-1967B★ (W-1170B★) • 1,280,000		
❑ F-1967C (W-1170C) • 8,320,000		
❑ F-1967C★ (W-1170C★) • 1,920,000		
❑ F-1967D (W-1170D) • 10,240,000		
❑ F-1967D★ (W-1170D★) • 1,920,000		
❑ F-1967F (W-1170F) • 17,920,000		
❑ F-1967F★ (W-1170F★) • 2,560,000		
❑ F-1967G (W-1170G) • 22,400,000		
❑ F-1967G★ (W-1170G★) • 3,200,000		
❑ F-1967H (W-1170H) • 14,080,000		
❑ F-1967H★ (W-1170H★) • 1,920,000		
❑ F-1967J (W-1170J) • 1,920,000		
❑ F-1967J★ (W-1170J★) • 640,000		
❑ F-1967K (W-1170K) • 5,760,000		

F-No. (W-No.) • Printage *(rarity)*	Grade	Comments
Series of 1963 and 1963-A *(continued)*		
❏ F-1967K★ (W-1170K★) • 1,920,000		
❏ F-1967L (W-1170L) • 18,560,000		
❏ F-1967L★ (W-1170L★) • 1,920,000		
❏ F-1968A (W-1171A) • 77,440,000		
❏ F-1968A★ (W-1171A★) • 5,760,000		
❏ F-1968B (W-1171B) • 98,080,000		
❏ F-1968B★ (W-1171B★) • 7,680,000		
❏ F-1968C (W-1171C) • 106,400,000		
❏ F-1968C★ (W-1171C★) • 10,240,000		
❏ F-1968D (W-1171D) • 83,840,000		
❏ F-1968D★ (W-1171D★) • 7,040,000		
❏ F-1968E (W-1171E) • 18,560,000		
❏ F-1968E★ (W-1171E★) • 10,880,000		
❏ F-1968F (W-1171F) • 117,920,000		
❏ F-1968F★ (W-1171F★) • 9,600,000		
❏ F-1968G (W-1171G) • 213,440,000		
❏ F-1968G★ (W-1171G★) • 16,640,000		
❏ F-1968H (W-1171H) • 56,960,000		
❏ F-1968H★ (W-1171H★) • 5,120,000		
❏ F-1968I (W-1171I) • 32,640,000		
❏ F-1968I★ (W-1171I★) • 3,200,000		
❏ F-1968J (W-1171J) • 55,040,000		
❏ F-1968J★ (W-1171J★) • 5,760,000		
❏ F-1968K (W-1171K) • 64,000,000		
❏ F-1968K★ (W-1171K★) • 3,840,000		
❏ F-1968L (W-1171L) • 128,900,000		
❏ F-1968L★ (W-1171L★) • 12,153,000		
Series of 1969–1969-C		
❏ F-1969A (W-1172A) • 51,200,000		
❏ F-1969A★ (W-1172A★) • 1,920,000		
❏ F-1969B (W-1172B) • 198,560,000		
❏ F-1969B★ (W-1172B★) • 8,960,000		
❏ F-1969C (W-1172C) • 69,120,000		

F-No. (W-No.) • Printage *(rarity)*	Grade	Comments
❑ F-1969C★ (W-1172C★) • 2,560,000		
❑ F-1969D (W-1172D) • 56,320,000		
❑ F-1969D★ (W-1172D★) • 2,560,000		
❑ F-1969E (W-1172E) • 84,480,000		
❑ F-1969E★ (W-1172E★) • 3,200,000		
❑ F-1969F (W-1172F) • 84,480,000		
❑ F-1969F★ (W-1172F★) • 3,840,000		
❑ F-1969G (W-1172G) • 125,600,000		
❑ F-1969G★ (W-1172G★) • 5,120,000		
❑ F-1969H (W-1172H) • 27,520,000		
❑ F-1969H★ (W-1172H★) • 1,280,000		
❑ F-1969I (W-1172I) • 16,640,000		
❑ F-1969I★ (W-1172I★) • 640,000		
❑ F-1969J (W-1172J) • 48,640,000		
❑ F-1969J★ (W-1172J★) • 3,192,000		
❑ F-1969K (W-1172K) • 39,680,000		
❑ F-1969K★ (W-1172K★) • 1,920,000		
❑ F-1969L (W-1172L) • 103,840,000		
❑ F-1969L★ (W-1172L★) • 4,480,000		
❑ F-1970A (W-1173A) • 23,040,000		
❑ F-1970A★ (W-1173A★) • 1,280,000		
❑ F-1970B (W-1173B) • 62,240,000		
❑ F-1970B★ (W-1173B★) • 1,760,000		
❑ F-1970C (W-1173C) • 41,160,000		
❑ F-1970C★ (W-1173C★) • 1,920,000		
❑ F-1970D (W-1173D) • 21,120,000		
❑ F-1970D★ (W-1173D★) • 640,000		
❑ F-1970E (W-1173E) • 37,920,000		
❑ F-1970E★ (W-1173E★) • 1,120,000		
❑ F-1970F (W-1173F) • 25,120,000		
❑ F-1970F★ (W-1173F★) • 480,000		
❑ F-1970G (W-1173G) • 60,800,000		
❑ F-1970G★ (W-1173G★) • 1,920,000		
❑ F-1970H (W-1173H) • 15,360,000		

F-No. (W-No.) • Printage *(rarity)*	Grade	Comments
Series of 1969–1969-C *(continued)*		
❑ F-1970H★ (W-1173H★) • 640,000		
❑ F-1970I (W-1173I) • 8,960,000		
❑ F-1970I★ (W-1173I★) • 640,000		
❑ F-1970J (W-1173J) • 17,920,000		
❑ F-1970J★ (W-1173J★) • 640,000		
❑ F-1970K (W-1173K) • 21,120,000		
❑ F-1970K★ (W-1173K★) • 640,000		
❑ F-1970L (W-1173L) • 44,800,000		
❑ F-1970L★ (W-1173L★) • 1,920,000		
❑ F-1971A (W-1174A) • 5,760,000		
❑ F-1971B (W-1174B) • 34,560,000		
❑ F-1971B★ (W-1174B★) • 634,000		
❑ F-1971C (W-1174C) • 5,120,000		
❑ F-1971D (W-1174D) • 12,160,000		
❑ F-1971E (W-1174E) • 15,360,000		
❑ F-1971E★ (W-1174E★) • 640,000		
❑ F-1971F (W-1174F) • 18,560,000		
❑ F-1971F★ (W-1174F★) • 640,000		
❑ F-1971G (W-1174G) • 27,040,000		
❑ F-1971G★ (W-1174G★) • 480,000		
❑ F-1971H (W-1174H) • 5,120,000		
❑ F-1971I (W-1174I) • 8,320,000		
❑ F-1971J (W-1174J) • 8,320,000		
❑ F-1971J★ (W-1174J★) • 640,000		
❑ F-1971K (W-1174K) • 12,160,000		
❑ F-1971L (W-1174L) • 23,160,000		
❑ F-1971L★ (W-1174L★) • 640,000		
❑ F-1972A (W-1175A) • 50,720,000		
❑ F-1972A★ (W-1175A★) • 1,920,000		
❑ F-1972B (W-1175B) • 120,000,000		
❑ F-1972B★ (W-1175B★) • 2,400,000		
❑ F-1972C (W-1175C) • 53,760,000		
❑ F-1972C★ (W-1175C★) • 1,280,000		

F-No. (W-No.) • Printage *(rarity)*	Grade	Comments
❑ F-1972D (W-1175D) • 43,680,000		
❑ F-1972D★ (W-1175D★) • 1,120,000		
❑ F-1972E (W-1175E) • 73,760,000		
❑ F-1972E★ (W-1175E★) • 640,000		
❑ F-1972F (W-1175F) • 81,440,000		
❑ F-1972F★ (W-1175F★) • 3,200,000		
❑ F-1972G (W-1175G) • 54,400,000		
❑ F-1972H (W-1175H) • 37,760,000		
❑ F-1972H★ (W-1175H★) • 1,280,000		
❑ F-1972I (W-1175I) • 14,080,000		
❑ F-1972J (W-1175J) • 41,120,000		
❑ F-1972J★ (W-1175J★) • 1,920,000		
❑ F-1972K (W-1175K) • 41,120,000		
❑ F-1972K★ (W-1175K★) • 1,920,000		
❑ F-1972L (W-1175L) • 80,800,000		
❑ F-1972L★ (W-1175L★) • 3,680,000		
Series of 1974		
❑ F-1973A (W-1177A) • 58,240,000		
❑ F-1973A★ (W-1177A★) • 1,408,000		
❑ F-1973B (W-1177B) • 153,120,000		
❑ F-1973B★ (W-1177B★) • 2,656,000		
❑ F-1973C (W-1177C) • 52,920,000		
❑ F-1973C★ (W-1177C★) • 3,040,000		
❑ F-1973D (W-1177D) • 78,080,000		
❑ F-1973D★ (W-1177D★) • 1,920,000		
❑ F-1973E (W-1177E) • 135,200,000		
❑ F-1973E★ (W-1177E★) • 1,760,000		
❑ F-1973F (W-1177F) • 127,520,000		
❑ F-1973F★ (W-1177F★) • 3,040,000		
❑ F-1973G (W-1177G) • 95,520,000		
❑ F-1973G★ (W-1177G★) • 1,760,000		
❑ F-1973H (W-1177H) • 64,800,000		
❑ F-1973H★ (W-1177H★) • 1,760,000		
❑ F-1973I (W-1177I) • 41,600,000		

$5

F-No. (W-No.) • Printage *(rarity)*	Grade	Comments
Series of 1974 *(continued)*		
❑ F-1973I★ (W-1177I★) • 2,560,000		
❑ F-1973J (W-1177J) • 42,240,000		
❑ F-1973J★ (W-1177J★) • 2,176,000		
❑ F-1973K (W-1177K) • 57,600,000		
❑ F-1973K★ (W-1177K★) • 1,408,000		
❑ F-1973L (W-1177L) • 139,680,000		
❑ F-1973L★ (W-1177L★) • 5,088,000		
Series of 1977 and 1977-A		
❑ F-1974A (W-1178A) • 60,800,000		
❑ F-1974A★ (W-1178A★) • 1,664,000		
❑ F-1974B (W-1178B) • 183,040,000		
❑ F-1974B★ (W-1178B★) • 3,072,000		
❑ F-1974C (W-1178C) • 78,720,000		
❑ F-1974C★ (W-1178C★) • 1,280,000		
❑ F-1974D (W-1178D) • 72,960,000		
❑ F-1974D★ (W-1178D★) • 1,152,000		
❑ F-1974E (W-1178E) • 110,720,000		
❑ F-1974E★ (W-1178E★) • 2,816,000		
❑ F-1974F (W-1178F) • 127,360,000		
❑ F-1974F★ (W-1178F★) • 1,920,000		
❑ F-1974G (W-1178G) • 177,920,000		
❑ F-1974G★ (W-1178G★) • 2,816,000		
❑ F-1974H (W-1178H) • 46,080,000		
❑ F-1974H★ (W-1178H★) • 128,000		
❑ F-1974I (W-1178I) • 21,760,000		
❑ F-1974J (W-1178J) • 78,080,000		
❑ F-1974J★ (W-1178J★) • 1,408,000		
❑ F-1974K (W-1178K) • 60,800,000		
❑ F-1974K★ (W-1178K★) • 2,408,000		
❑ F-1974L (W-1178L) • 135,040,000		
❑ F-1974L★ (W-1178L★) • 2,432,000		
❑ F-1975A (W-1179A) • 48,000,000		
❑ F-1975A★ (W-1179A★) • 512,000		

F-No. (W-No.) • Printage *(rarity)*	Grade	Comments
❑ F-1975B (W-1179B) • 113,920,000		
❑ F-1975B★ (W-1179B★) • 2,304,000		
❑ F-1975C (W-1179C) • 55,680,000		
❑ F-1975C★ (W-1179C★) • 640,000		
❑ F-1975D (W-1179D) • 85,880,000		
❑ F-1975D★ (W-1179D★) • 1,280,000		
❑ F-1975E (W-1179E) • 77,440,000		
❑ F-1975E★ (W-1179E★) • 768,000		
❑ F-1975F (W-1179F) • 76,160,000		
❑ F-1975F★ (W-1179F★) • 1,152,000		
❑ F-1975G (W-1179G) • 80,640,000		
❑ F-1975G★ (W-1179G★) • 1,408,000		
❑ F-1975H (W-1179H) • 42,240,000		
❑ F-1975H★ (W-1179H★) • 640,000		
❑ F-1975I (W-1179I) • 10,240,000		
❑ F-1975I★ (W-1179I★) • 256,000		
❑ F-1975J (W-1179J) • 52,480,000		
❑ F-1975J★ (W-1179J★) • 1,024,000		
❑ F-1975K (W-1179K) • 76,160,000		
❑ F-1975K★ (W-1179K★) • 1,408,000		
❑ F-1975L (W-1179L) • 106,880,000		
❑ F-1975L★ (W-1179L★) • 1,152,000		
Series of 1981 and 1981-A		
❑ F-1976A (W-1181A) • 109,000,000		
❑ F-1976B (W-1181B) • 250,880,000		
❑ F-1976B★ (W-1181B★) • 4,464,000		
❑ F-1976C (W-1181C) • 112,640,000		
❑ F-1976C★ (W-1181C★) • 640,000		
❑ F-1976D (W-1181D) • 122,240,000		
❑ F-1976D★ (W-1181D★) • 1,268,000		
❑ F-1976E (W-1181E) • 234,880,000		
❑ F-1976E★ (W-1181E★) • 640,000		
❑ F-1976F (W-1181F) • 234,880,000		
❑ F-1976F★ (W-1181F★) • 1,644,000		

F-No. (W-No.) • Printage *(rarity)*	Grade	Comments
Series of 1981 and 1981-A *(continued)*		
❏ F-1976G (W-1181G) • 241,280,000		
❏ F-1976G★ (W-1181G★) • 768,000		
❏ F-1976H (W-1181H) • 199,680,000		
❏ F-1976H★ (W-1181H★) • 628,000		
❏ F-1976I (W-1181I) • 109,440,000		
❏ F-1976I★ (W-1181I★) • 640,000		
❏ F-1976J (W-1181J) • 125,440,000		
❏ F-1976J★ (W-1181J★) • 960,000		
❏ F-1976K (W-1181K) • 138,240,000		
❏ F-1976K★ (W-1181K★) • 640,000		
❏ F-1976L (W-1181L) • 263,680,000		
❏ F-1976L★ (W-1181L★) • 1,792,000		
❏ F-1977A (W-1182A) • 192,000,000		
❏ F-1977B (W-1182B) • 448,000,000		
❏ F-1977B★ (W-1182B★) • 3,200,000		
❏ F-1977C (W-1182C) • 169,600,000		
❏ F-1977D (W-1182D) • 214,400,000		
❏ F-1977E (W-1182E) • 332,800,000		
❏ F-1977F (W-1182F) • 352,000,000		
❏ F-1977G (W-1182G) • 345,600,000		
❏ F-1977H (W-1182H) • 128,000,000		
❏ F-1977I (W-1182I) • 73,800,000		
❏ F-1977J (W-1182J) • 134,400,000		
❏ F-1977K (W-1182K) • 176,000,000		
❏ F-1977L (W-1182L) • 150,400,000		
❏ F-1977L★ (W-1182L★) • 3,200,000		
Series of 1985		
❏ F-1978A (W-1183A) • 192,000,000		
❏ F-1978B (W-1183B) • 451,200,000		
❏ F-1978B★ (W-1183B★) • 3,200,000		
❏ F-1978C (W-1183C) • 170,400,000		
❏ F-1978C★ (W-1183C★) • 6,400,000		
❏ F-1978D (W-1183D) • 216,000,000		

F-No. (W-No.) • Printage *(rarity)*	Grade	Comments
❑ F-1978E (W-1183E) • 335,200,000		
❑ F-1978E★ (W-1183E★) • 3,200,000		
❑ F-1978F (W-1183F) • 354,400,000		
❑ F-1978F★ (W-1183F★) • 6,400,000		
❑ F-1978G (W-1183G) • 348,000,000		
❑ F-1978G★ (W-1183G★) • 6,400,000		
❑ F-1978H (W-1183H) • 128,000,000		
❑ F-1978I (W-1183I) • 173,600,000		
❑ F-1978J (W-1183J) • 135,200,000		
❑ F-1978K (W-1183K) • 176,800,000		
❑ F-1978K★ (W-1183K★) • 3,200,000		
❑ F-1978L (W-1183L) • 460,800,000		
❑ F-1978L★ (W-1183L★) • 3,200,000		
Series of 1988 and 1988-A		
❑ F-1979A (W-1184A) • 86,400,000		
❑ F-1979A★ (W-1184A★) • 768,000		
❑ F-1979B (W-1184B) • 185,600,000		
❑ F-1979B★ (W-1184B★) • 3,200,000		
❑ F-1979C (W-1184C) • 54,400,000		
❑ F-1979D (W-1184D) • 111,200,000		
❑ F-1979E (W-1184E) • 131,200,000		
❑ F-1979F (W-1184F) • 137,200,000		
❑ F-1979F★ (W-1184F★) • 6,400,000		
❑ F-1979G (W-1184G) • 134,400,000		
❑ F-1979H (W-1184H) • 51,200,000		
❑ F-1979I (W-1184I) • 9,600,000		
❑ F-1979J (W-1184J) • 44,800,000		
❑ F-1979K (W-1184K) • 54,500,000		
❑ F-1979L (W-1184L) • 70,400,000		
❑ F-1980A (W-1185A) • 140,800,000		
❑ F-1980A★ (W-1185A★) • 3,200,000		
❑ F-1980B (W-1185B) • 640,000,000		
❑ F-1980B★ (W-1185B★) • 4,608,000		
❑ F-1980C (W-1185C) • 70,400,000		

F-No. (W-No.) • Printage *(rarity)*	Grade	Comments
Series of 1988 and 1988-A *(continued)*		
❑ F-1980D (W-1185D) • 166,000,000		
❑ F-1980D★ (W-1185D★) • 4,864,000		
❑ F-1980E (W-1185E) • 486,400,000		
❑ F-1980E★ (W-1185E★) • 3,020,000		
❑ F-1980F (W-1185F) • 192,000,000		
❑ F-1980F★ (W-1185F★) • 2,640,000		
❑ F-1980G (W-1185G) • 633,600,000		
❑ F-1980G★ (W-1185G★)		
❑ F-1980H (W-1185H) • 185,600,000		
❑ F-1980H★ (W-1185H★) • 1,280,000		
❑ F-1980I (W-1185I) • 73,600,000		
❑ F-1980I★ (W-1185I★) • 3,200,000		
❑ F-1980J (W-1185J) • 115,200,000		
❑ F-1980K (W-1185K) • 128,000,000		
❑ F-1980L (W-1185L) • 492,800,000		
❑ F-1981C (W-1186C) • 25,600,000		
❑ F-1981F (W-1186F) • 282,400,000		
❑ F-1981F★ (W-1186F★) • 640,000		
❑ F-1981G (W-1186G) • 76,800,000		
❑ F-1981G★ (W-1186G★) • 1,280,000		
❑ F-1981J (W-1186J) • 25,600,000		
❑ F-1981K (W-1186K) • 44,800,000		
❑ F-1981L (W-1186L) • 179,200,000		
❑ F-1981L★ (W-1186L★) • 3,200,000		
Series of 1993		
❑ F-1982A (W-1187A) • 38,400,000		
❑ F-1982B (W-1187B) • 102,400,000		
❑ F-1982B★ (W-1187B★) • 2,816,000		
❑ F-1982C (W-1187C) • 38,400,000		
❑ F-1982E (W-1187E) • 76,800,000		
❑ F-1982E★ (W-1187E★) • 1,920,000		
❑ F-1982F (W-1187F) • 70,400,000		
❑ F-1983G (W-1188G) • 64,000,000		

F-No. (W-No.) • Printage *(rarity)*	Grade	Comments
❏ F-1983G★ (W-1188G★) • 1,280,000		
❏ F-1983H (W-1188H) • 64,000,000		
❏ F-1983H★ (W-1188H★) • 2,560,000		
❏ F-1983I (W-1188I) • 6,400,000		
❏ F-1983J (W-1188J) • 32,000,000		
❏ F-1983K (W-1188K) • 57,600,000		
❏ F-1983L (W-1188L) • 185,600,000		
❏ F-1983L★ (W-1188L★) • 2,560,000		
Series of 1995		
❏ F-1984A (W-1189A) • 160,000,000		
❏ F-1984A★ (W-1189A★) • 640,000		
❏ F-1984B (W-1189B) • 390,040,444		
❏ F-1984B★ (W-1189B★) • 3,840,000		
❏ F-1984C (W-1189C) • 128,000,000		
❏ F-1984D (W-1189D) • 89,600,000		
❏ F-1984E (W-1189E) • 300,800,000		
❏ F-1984F (W-1189F) • 179,200,000		
❏ F-1985A (W-1190A) • 57,600,000		
❏ F-1985B (W-1190B) • 76,800,000		
❏ F-1985C (W-1190C) • 38,000,000		
❏ F-1985D (W-1190D) • 64,000,000		
❏ F-1985D★ (W-1190D★) • 3,200,000		
❏ F-1985E (W-1190E) • 108,000,000		
❏ F-1985F (W-1190F) • 448,000,000		
❏ F-1985F★ (W-1190F★) • 70,400,000		
❏ F-1985G (W-1190G) • 524,800,000		
❏ F-1985G★ (W-1190G★) • 9,600,000		
❏ F-1985H (W-1190H) • 204,800,000		
❏ F-1985I (W-1190I) • 64,000,000		
❏ F-1985J (W-1190J) • 160,000,000		
❏ F-1985K (W-1190K) • 204,800,000		
❏ F-1985L (W-1190L) • 706,800,000		
Series of 1999		
❏ F-1986A (W-1191A) • 19,200,000		
❏ F-1986B (W-1191B) • 76,800,000		

F-No. (W-No.) • Printage (rarity)	Grade	Comments
Series of 1999 (continued)		
❑ F-1986C (W-1191C) • 57,600,000		
❑ F-1986D (W-1191D) • 25,600,000		
❑ F-1986E (W-1191E) • 96,000,000		
❑ F-1986E★ (W-1191E★) • 739,200		
❑ F-1987A (W-1192A) • 70,400,000		
❑ F-1987A★ (W-1192A★) • 3,200,000		
❑ F-1987B (W-1192B) • 256,000,000		
❑ F-1987B★ (W-1192B★) • 3,840,000		
❑ F-1987C (W-1192C) • 89,600,000		
❑ F-1987D (W-1192D) • 12,800,000		
❑ F-1987E (W-1192E) • 185,600,000		
❑ F-1987E★ (W-1192E★) • 3,200,000		
❑ F-1987F (W-1192F) • 211,200,000		
❑ F-1987F★ (W-1192F★) • 10,915,200		
❑ F-1987G (W-1192G) • 140,800,000		
❑ F-1987G★ (W-1192G★) • 3,200,000		
❑ F-1987H (W-1192H) • 44,800,000		
❑ F-1987I (W-1192I) • 12,800,000		
❑ F-1987J (W-1192J) • 32,000,000		
❑ F-1987J★ (W-1192J★) • 3,200,000		
❑ F-1987K (W-1192K) • 121,600,000		
❑ F-1987L (W-1192L) • 243,200,000		
Series of 2001		
❑ F-1988A (W-1193A) • 128,000,000		
❑ F-1988B (W-1193B) • 121,600,000		
❑ F-1988C (W-1193C) • 64,000,000		
❑ F-1988D (W-1193D) • 83,200,000		
❑ F-1988E (W-1193E) • 51,200,000		
❑ F-1988F (W-1193F) • 224,000,000		
❑ F-1988G (W-1193G) • 185,600,000		
❑ F-1988H (W-1193H) • 102,400,000		
❑ F-1988I (W-1193I) • 32,000,000		
❑ F-1988J (W-1193J) • 76,800,000		

F-No. (W-No.) • Printage *(rarity)*	Grade	Comments
❑ F-1988K (W-1193K) • 211,200,000		
❑ F-1988K★ (W-1193K★)		
❑ F-1988L (W-1193L) • 281,600,000		
❑ F-1988L★ (W-1193L★) • 5,120,000		
Series of 2003 and 2003-A		
❑ F-1989A (W-1194A) • 32,000,000		
❑ F-1989C (W-1194C) • 32,000,000		
❑ F-1989D (W-1194D) • 32,000,000		
❑ F-1989F (W-1194F) • 89,600,000		
❑ F-1989G (W-1194G) • 32,000,000		
❑ F-1989G★ (W-1194G★) • 3,200,000		
❑ F-1990A (W-1195A) • 25,600,000		
❑ F-1990B (W-1195B) • 147,200,000		
❑ F-1990C (W-1195C) • 38,400,000		
❑ F-1990C★ (W-1195C★)		
❑ F-1990D (W-1195D) • 32,000,000		
❑ F-1990E (W-1195E) • 108,800,000		
❑ F-1990F (W-1195F) • 96,000,000		
❑ F-1990G (W-1195G) • 89,600,000		
❑ F-1990H (W-1195H) • 51,200,000		
❑ F-1990I (W-1195I) • 32,000,000		
❑ F-1990J (W-1195J) • 51,200,000		
❑ F-1990K (W-1195K) • 96,000,000		
❑ F-1990L (W-1195L) • 243,200,000		
❑ F-1990L★ (W-1195L★) • 3,520,000		
❑ F-1991A (W-1197A) • 38,400,000		
❑ F-1991B (W-1197B) • 96,000,000		
❑ F-1991B★ (W-1197B★)		
❑ F-1991C (W-1197C) • 44,800,000		
❑ F-1991D (W-1197D) • 38,400,000		
❑ F-1991E (W-1197E) • 70,400,000		
❑ F-1991F (W-1197F) • 134,400,000		
❑ F-1991F★ (W-1197F★) • 52,000		
❑ F-1991G (W-1197G) • 83,200,000		

F-No. (W-No.) • Printage *(rarity)*	Grade	Comments
Series of 2003 and 2003-A *(continued)*		
❏ F-1991G★ (W-1197G★) • 40,000		
❏ F-1991H (W-1197H) • 6,400,000		
❏ F-1991I (W-1197I) • 19,200,000		
❏ F-1991J (W-1197J) • 102,400,000		
❏ F-1991K (W-1197K) • 172,800,000		
❏ F-1991L (W-1197L) • 57,600,000		
Series of 2006		
❏ F-1992F (W-1198F) • 275,200,000		
❏ F-1992G (W-1198G) • 108,800,000		
❏ F-1992I (W-1198I) • 25,600,000		
❏ F-1993A (W-1199A) • 121,600,000		
❏ F-1993A★ (W-1199A★) • 3,840,000		
❏ F-1993B (W-1199B) • 256,600,000		
❏ F-1993B★ (W-1199B★)		
❏ F-1993C (W-1199C) • 140,800,000		
❏ F-1993D (W-1199D) • 153,600,000		
❏ F-1993E (W-1199E) • 217,600,000		
❏ F-1993E★ (W-1199E★) • 640,000		
❏ F-1993F (W-1199F) • 339,200,000		
❏ F-1993F★ (W-1199F★) • 4,224,000		
❏ F-1993G (W-1199G) • 224,000,000		
❏ F-1993G★ (W-1199G★) • 3,840,000		
❏ F-1993H (W-1199H) • 76,800,000		
❏ F-1993I (W-1199I) • 44,800,000		
❏ F-1993J (W-1199J) • 89,600,000		
❏ F-1993K (W-1199K) • 179,200,000		
❏ F-1993L (W-1199L) • 288,000,000		
❏ F-1993L★ (W-1199L★) • 640,000		
Series of 2009		
❏ F-1994A • 32,000,000		
❏ F-1994B • 76,800,000		
❏ F-1994C • 38,400,000		
❏ F-1994D • 51,200,000		
❏ F-1994E • 64,000,000		

F-No. (W-No.) • Printage *(rarity)*	Grade	Comments
❏ F-1994F • 140,800,000		
❏ F-1994G • 96,000,000		
❏ F-1994H • 32,000,000		
❏ F-1994I • 19,200,000		
❏ F-1994J • 32,000,000		
❏ F-1994K • 83,200,000		
❏ F-1994L • 326,400,000		
❏ F-1995A • 19,200,000		
❏ F-1995A★ • 3,520,000		
❏ F-1995B • 44,800,000		
❏ F-1995C • 25,600,000		
❏ F-1995D • 32,000,000		
❏ F-1995E • 38,400,000		
❏ F-1995F • 51,200,000		
❏ F-1995F★ • 960,000		
Series of 2013		
❏ F-1996A		
❏ F-1996A★		
❏ F-1996B		
❏ F-1996C		
❏ F-1996D		
❏ F-1996E		
❏ F-1996F		
❏ F-1996G		
❏ F-1996H		
❏ F-1996I		
❏ F-1996J		
❏ F-1996K		
❏ F-1996K★		
❏ F-1996L		
❏ F-1996L★		
Series of 2017		
❏		
❏		
❏		

LARGE-SIZE

$10 Demand Notes

F-No. (W-No.) • Printage (rarity)	Grade	Comments
Series of 1861		
❑ F-6 (W-1217) • est. 72,000 (4 known)		
❑ F-6 (W-1218) • 540,000 (45–50)		
❑ F-6a (W-1216) • est. 28,000 (5 known)		
❑ F-7 (W-1220) • est. 93,000 (4 known)		
❑ F-7 (W-1221) • 480,000 (50–55)		
❑ F-7a (W-1219) • est. 7,000 (3 known)		
❑ F-8 (W-1212) • est. 71,000 (1 known)		
❑ F-8 (W-1213) • 560,000 (42–45)		
❑ F-8a (W-1211) • est. 29,000 (2 known)		
❑ F-9 (W-1215) • est. 64,000 (6 known)		
❑ F-9a (W-1214) • est. 11,000 (1 known)		
❑ F-10 (W-1222) • est. 47,000 (4 known)		

$10 Interesting-Bearing Notes of 1863

F-No. (W-No.) • Printage (rarity)	Grade	Comments
❑ F-196 (W-1226) • 620,000 (9–10)		
❑ F-196a (W-1228) • incl. above (35–40)		

$10 Compound Interest Treasury Notes of 1864

F-No. (W-No.) • Printage (rarity)	Grade	Comments
❑ F-190 (W-1230) • 2,328,520 (16–18)		

F-No. (W-No.) • Printage *(rarity)*	Grade	Comments
❑ F-190a (W-1232) • incl. above *(21–24)*		
❑ F-190a (W-1234) • incl. above *(4 known)*		
❑ F-190b (W-1236) • incl. above *(110–120)*		

$10 Legal Tender Notes

F-No. (W-No.) • Printage *(rarity)*	Grade	Comments
Series of 1862, First Obligation		
❑ F-93 (W-1254) • est. 2,302,000 *(80–100)*		
❑ F-93 (W-1256) • est. 220,000 *(15–25)*		
❑ F-93 (W-1257) • est. 3,580,000 *(130–150)*		
❑ F-93a (W-1251) • est. 78,000 *(5 known)*		
❑ F-93b (W-1252) • est. 120,000 *(9 known)*		
❑ F-93b (W-1253) • incl. above *(4 known)*		
Series of 1862 and 1863, Second Obligation		
❑ F-94 (W-1260) • 1,400,000 *(50–60)*		
❑ F-95 (W-1261) • 2,530,504 *(55–60)*		
❑ F-95 (W-1262) • 370,000 *(11–15)*		
❑ F-95a (W-1263) • 400,000 *(35–40)*		
❑ F-95b (W-1264) • 800,496 *(165–180)*		
Series of 1869		
❑ F-96 (W-1275) • 8,376,000 *(500–600)*		
Series of 1875		
❑ F-97 (W-1277) • 866,000 *(12–14)*		
❑ F-98 (W-1276) • 1,500,000 *(35–40)*		
Series of 1878		
❑ F-99 (W-1278) • est. 2,600,000 *(85–95)*		
Series of 1880		
❑ F-100 (W-1279) • est. 1,800,000 *(100–140)*		
❑ F-101 (W-1281) • est. 1,700,000 *(50–55)*		
❑ F-102 (W-1282, Back Style 1) • est. 2,664,000 *(110–120)*		
❑ F-102 (W-1282, Back Style 2) • incl. above *(incl. above)*		
❑ F-103 (W-1283) • 972,000 *(115–125)*		
❑ F-104 (W-1284) • est. 1,288,000 *(48–54)*		
❑ F-105 (W-1285) • est. 1,440,000 *(65–70)*		
❑ F-106 (W-1286) • est. 2,540,000 *(110–120)*		
❑ F-107 (W-1287) • est. 2,652,000 *(135–150)*		

F-No. (W-No.) • Printage *(rarity)*	Grade	Comments
Series of 1880 *(continued)*		
❏ F-108 (W-1288) • est. 1,708,000 *(115–125)*		
❏ F-109 (W-1289) • est. 100,000 *(2 known)*		
❏ F-110 (W-1290) • est. 3,500,000 *(110–120)*		
❏ F-111 (W-1291) • est. 9,200,000 *(220–235)*		
❏ F-112 (W-1292) • est. 1,900,000 *(45–50)*		
❏ F-113 (W-1293) • est. 11,876,000 *(325–375)*		
Series of 1901		
❏ F-114 (W-1294) • est. 47,140,000 *(400–500)*		
❏ F-115 (W-1295) • est. 11,060,000 *(130–150)*		
❏ F-116 (W-1296) • est. 15,330,000 *(165–180)*		
❏ F-117 (W-1297) • 5,760,000 *(95–115)*		
❏ F-117★ (W-1297★) • *(3 known)*		
❏ F-118 (W-1298) • 8,476,000 *(120–130)*		
❏ F-118★ (W-1298★) • *(3 known)*		
❏ F-119 (W-1299) • 11,592,000 *(275–325)*		
❏ F-119★ (W-1299★) • *(2 known)*		
❏ F-120 (W-1300) • est. 4,776,000 *(225–250)*		
❏ F-120★ (W-1300★) • *(10–12)*		
❏ F-121 (W-1301) • est. 500,000 *(30–36)*		
❏ F-121 (W-1301 Mule) • est. 7,636,000 *(550–650)*		
❏ F-121★ (W-1301 Mule★) • *(35–40)*		
❏ F-122 (W-1302) • est. 34,688,000 *(1,500–1,700)*		
❏ F-122★ (W-1302★) • *(55–58)*		
❏ F-122 (W-1302 Mule) • est. 2,000,000 *(90–110)*		
❏ F-122★ (W-1302 Mule★) • *(11–13)*		
Series of 1923		
❏ F-123 (W-1303) • 696,000 *(450–550)*		
❏ F-123★ (W-1303★) • *(2 known)*		

$10 National Bank Notes

F-No. (W-No.) • Printage *(rarity)*	Grade	Comments
Original Series ("First Charter Period")		
❏ F-409 (W-1310) • *(65–70)*		
❏ F-412 (W-1312) • *(115–125)*		
❏ F-413 (W-1314) • *(1 known)*		

F-No. (W-No.) • Printage *(rarity)*	Grade	Comments
❏ F-414 (W-1316) • *(24–28)*		
Series of 1875 ("First Charter Period")		
❏ F-416 (W-1330) • *(300–325)*		
❏ F-417 (W-1332) • *(75–85)*		
❏ F-418 (W-1334) • *(46–50)*		
❏ F-419 (W-1336) • *(225–250)*		
❏ F-420 (W-1338) • *(180–200)*		
❏ F-421 (W-1340) • *(5 known)*		
❏ F-422 (W-1342) • *(18–20)*		
❏ F-423 (W-1344) • *(11–13)*		
❏ F-423a (W-1346) • *(1 known)*		
Series of 1882, Brown Back ("Second Charter Period")		
❏ F-479 (W-1360) • *(400–500)*		
❏ F-480 (W-1361) • *(900–1,100)*		
❏ F-481 (W-1362) • *(225–275)*		
❏ F-482 (W-1363) • *(450–550)*		
❏ F-483 (W-1364) • *(200–240)*		
❏ F-484 (W-1365) • *(800–1,000)*		
❏ F-485 (W-1366) • *(600–750)*		
❏ F-486 (W-1367) • *(11–13)*		
❏ F-487 (W-1368) • *(575–700)*		
❏ F-488 (W-1369) • *(65–75)*		
❏ F-489 (W-1370) • *(55–65)*		
❏ F-490 (W-1371) • *(1,200–1,400)*		
❏ F-491 (W-1372) • *(11–13)*		
❏ F-492 (W-1373) • *(15–17)*		
Series of 1882, Date Back ("Second Charter Period")		
❏ F-539 (W-1380) • *(90–100)*		
❏ F-540 (W-1381) • *(220–240)*		
❏ F-541 (W-1382) • *(2 known)*		
❏ F-542 (W-1383) • *(360–400)*		
❏ F-543 (W-1384) • *(48–54)*		
❏ F-544 (W-1385) • *(40–45)*		
❏ F-545 (W-1386) • *(1,400–1,500)*		

F-No. (W-No.) • Printage (rarity)	Grade	Comments
Series of 1882, Date Back ("Second Charter Period") (continued)		
❏ F-546 (W-1387) • (75–85)		
❏ F-547 (W-1388) • (2 known)		
❏ F-548 (W-1389) • (7 known)		
❏ F-548a (W-1390) • (1 known)		
Series of 1882, Value Back ("Second Charter Period")		
❏ F-576 (W-1394) • (7 known)		
❏ F-576a (W-1395) • (6 known)		
❏ F-576b (W-1396) • (5 known)		
❏ F-577 (W-1397) • (1,100–1,300)		
❏ F-578 (W-1399) • (40–45)		
❏ F-579 (W-1400) • (30–35)		
❏ F-579b (W-1402) • (13–15)		
Series of 1902, Red Seal ("Third Charter Period")		
❏ F-613 (W-1404) • (1,750–1,900)		
❏ F-614 (W-1405) • (250–300)		
❏ F-615 (W-1406) • (275–325)		
Series of 1902, Blue Seal, Date Back ("Third Charter Period")		
❏ F-616 (W-1408) • (2,600–3,000)		
❏ F-617 (W-1409) • (400–450)		
❏ F-618 (W-1410) • (1,300–1,450)		
❏ F-619 (W-1411) • (700–800)		
❏ F-620 (W-1412) • (400–500)		
❏ F-621 (W-1413) • (64–68)		
❏ F-622 (W-1414) • (48–52)		
❏ F-623 (W-1415) • (100–110)		
❏ F-623a (W-1416) • (18–20)		
Series of 1902, Blue Seal, Plain Back ("Third Charter Period")		
❏ F-624 (W-1420) • (10,000–12,000)		
❏ F-625 (W-1421) • (2,000–2,300)		
❏ F-626 (W-1422) • (5,500–6,000)		
❏ F-627 (W-1423) • (3,400–3,800)		
❏ F-628 (W-1424) • (2,700–3,100)		
❏ F-629 (W-1425) • (475–525)		
❏ F-630 (W-1426) • (400–450)		
❏ F-631 (W-1427) • (1,500–1,700)		

F-No. (W-No.) • Printage *(rarity)*	Grade	Comments
❑ F-632 (W-1428) • *(3,500–4,000)*		
❑ F-633 (W-1429) • *(2,750–3,000)*		
❑ F-634 (W-1430) • *(1,200–1,600)*		
❑ F-635 (W-1431) • *(1,450–1,600)*		
❑ F-636 (W-1432) • *(60–70)*		
❑ F-637 (W-1433) • *(55–60)*		
❑ F-638 (W-1434) • *(12–14)*		

$10 National Gold Bank Notes

F-No. (W-No.) • Printage *(rarity)*	Grade	Comments
❑ F-1142 (W-1320) • 18,004 *(35–40)*		
❑ F-1143 (W-1322) • 12,669 *(13–15)*		
❑ F-1144 (W-1321) • 3,823 *(5 known)*		
❑ F-1145 (W-1323) • 2,400 *(3 known)*		
❑ F-1146 (W-1324) • 15,000 *(18–20)*		
❑ F-1147 (W-1353) • 879 *(8 known)*		
❑ F-1148 (W-1326) • 8,547 *(12–14)*		
❑ F-1149 (W-1325) • 6,000 *(7 known)*		
❑ F-1150 (W-1352) • 4,800 *(6 known)*		
❑ F-1151 (W-1327) • 1,500 *(7 known)*		
❑ F-1151a (W-1328) • 1,500 *(3 known)*		

$10 Silver Certificates

F-No. (W-No.) • Printage *(rarity)*	Grade	Comments
Series of 1878		
❑ F-283 (W-1460) • est. 500 *(1 known)*		
❑ F-284 (W-1463) • est. 19,500 *(4 known)*		
❑ F-284b (W-1469) • est. 40,000 *(2 known)*		
❑ F-285 (W-1475) • est. 4,000 *(2 known)*		
❑ F-285a (W-1478) • est. 196,000 *(8 known)*		
Series of 1880, Countersigned		
❑ F-286 (W-1480) • 400,000 *(20–23)*		
Series of 1880, Not Countersigned		
❑ F-287 (W-1490) • est. 3,000,000 *(95–115)*		
❑ F-288 (W-1491) • est. 1,300,000 *(90–100)*		
❑ F-289 (W-1492) • est. 3,596,000 *(190–210)*		

F-No. (W-No.) • Printage *(rarity)*	Grade	Comments
Series of 1880, Not Countersigned *(continued)*		
❏ F-290 (W-1493) • 304,000 *(50–55)*		
Series of 1886		
❏ F-291 (W-1494) • 400,000 *(25–30)*		
❏ F-292 (W-1495) • est. 2,500,000 *(75–85)*		
❏ F-293 (W-1496) • est. 5,700,000 *(148–155)*		
❏ F-294 (W-1497) • est. 2,200,000 *(75–85)*		
❏ F-295 (W-1498) • est. 1,500,000 *(55–60)*		
❏ F-296 (W-1499) • est. 1,500,000 *(63–68)*		
❏ F-297 (W-1500) • est. 404,000 *(15–17)*		
Series of 1891		
❏ F-298 (W-1501) • est. 3,400,000 *(72–76)*		
❏ F-299 (W-1502) • est. 19,460,000 *(280–320)*		
❏ F-300 (W-1503) • est. 4,940,000 *(100–110)*		
❏ F-301 (W-1504) • est. 6,620,000 *(155–165)*		
Series of 1908		
❏ F-302 (W-1505) • est. 4,828,000 *(150–160)*		
❏ F-303 (W-1506) • 1,756,000 *(120–130)*		
❏ F-303★ (W-1506★) • *(1 known)*		
❏ F-304 (W-1507) • 3,624,000 *(275–325)*		
❏ F-304★ (W-1507★) • *(1 known)*		

$10 Refunding Certificates of 1879

F-No. (W-No.) • Printage *(rarity)*	Grade	Comments
❏ F-213 (W-1510) • 25,000 *(2 known)*		
❏ F-214 (W-1511) • 4,000,000 *(165–180)*		

$10 Treasury or Coin Notes

F-No. (W-No.) • Printage *(rarity)*	Grade	Comments
Series of 1890		
❏ F-366 (W-1520) • est. 2,900,000 *(120–130)*		
❏ F-367 (W-1521) • est. 240,000 *(35–40)*		
❏ F-368 (W-1522) • est. 1,460,000 *(145–153)*		
Series of 1891		
❏ F-369 (W-1523) • est. 1,100,000 *(135–145)*		
❏ F-370 (W-1524) • est. 4,000,000 *(120–130)*		

F-No. (W-No.) • Printage *(rarity)*	Grade	Comments
❏ F-371 (W-1525) • est. 928,000 *(55–60)*		

$10 Gold Certificates

F-No. (W-No.) • Printage *(rarity)*	Grade	Comments
Series of 1907		
❏ F-1167 (W-1530) • 21,366,800 *(155–165)*		
❏ F-1168 (W-1531) • 17,476,000 *(100–115)*		
❏ F-1168★ (W-1531★) • *(4 known)*		
❏ F-1169 (W-1532) • est. 23,348,000 *(180–200)*		
❏ F-1169★ (W-1532★) • *(3 known)*		
❏ F-1169a (W-1533) • est. 10,086,000 *(120–140)*		
❏ F-1170 (W-1534) • est. 720,000 *(25–35)*		
❏ F-1170a (W-1535) • est. 1,556,000 *(55–65)*		
❏ F-1171 (W-1536) • est. 20,200,000 *(250–350)*		
❏ F-1171★ (W-1536★) • *(6 known)*		
❏ F-1172 (W-1537) • est. 40,340,000 *(600–800)*		
❏ F-1172★ (W-1537★) • *(15–17)*		
Series of 1922		
❏ F-1173 (W-1541) • 144,100,000 *(3,800–4,300)*		
❏ F-1173★ (W-1541★) • *(240–280)*		
❏ F-1173 (W-1541 Mule) • est. 3,000,000 *(80–95)*		
❏ F-1173★ (W-1541 Mule★) • *(6 known)*		
❏ F-1173a (W-1540) • est. 9,480,000 *(110–130)*		
❏ F-1173a★ (W-1540★) • *(2 known)*		
❏ F-1173a (W-1540 Mule) • est. 4,024,000 *(25–30)*		
❏ F-1173a★ (W-1540 Mule★) • *(7 known)*		

$10 Federal Reserve Notes

F-No. (W-No.) • Printage *(rarity)*	Grade	Comments
Series of 1914, Red Seal		
❏ F-892A (W-1550A-a) • 1,000,000 *(33–36)*		
❏ F-892B (W-1550A-b) • 360,000 *(8 known)*		
❏ F-893A (W-1550B-a) • 4,000,000 *(75–85)*		
❏ F-893B (W-1550B-b) • 8,900,000 *(180–200)*		
❏ F-894A (W-1550C-a) • 600,000 *(28–32)*		

F-No. (W-No.) • Printage (rarity)	Grade	Comments
Series of 1914, Red Seal (continued)		
❏ F-894B (W-1550C-b) • 900,000 (55–65)		
❏ F-895A (W-1550D-a) • 400,000 (13–15)		
❏ F-895B (W-1550D-b) • 1,112,000 (45–55)		
❏ F-896A (W-1550E-a) • 400,000 (18–20)		
❏ F-896B (W-1550E-b) • 352,000 (20–23)		
❏ F-897A (W-1550F-a) • 400,000 (20–24)		
❏ F-897B (W-1550F-b) • 140,000 (7 known)		
❏ F-898A (W-1550G-a) • 1,000,000 (75–85)		
❏ F-898B (W-1550G-b) • 804,000 (60–70)		
❏ F-899A (W-1550H-a) • 600,000 (55–65)		
❏ F-899B (W-1550H-b) • 296,000 (19–22)		
❏ F-900A (W-1550I-a) • 400,000 (55–65)		
❏ F-900B (W-1550I-b) • 212,000 (20–23)		
❏ F-901A (W-1550J-a) • 400,000 (35–40)		
❏ F-901B (W-1550J-b) • 216,000 (16–18)		
❏ F-902A (W-1550K-a) • 400,000 (20–24)		
❏ F-902B (W-1550K-b) • 180,000 (10–12)		
❏ F-903A (W-1550L-a) • 400,000 (23–25)		
❏ F-903B (W-1550L-b) • 660,000 (20–24)		
Series of 1914, Blue Seal		
❏ F-904 (W-1560A-b) • est. 10,552,000 (105–115)		
❏ F-904★ (W-1560A-b★) • (1 known)		
❏ F-905 (W-1561A-b) • est. 9,088,000 (65–70)		
❏ F-905★ (W-1561A-b★) • (1 known)		
❏ F-906 (W-1562A-b) • est. 16,284,000 (120–130)		
❏ F-906★ (W-1562A-b★) • (15–17)		
❏ F-907A (W-1563A-b) • est. 28,008,000 (310–340)		
❏ F-907A★ (W-1563A-b★) • (13–15)		
❏ F-907B (W-1563A-c) • est. 4,464,000 (90–100)		
❏ F-907B★ (W-1563A-c★) • (1 known)		
❏ F-908 (W-1564B-b) • est. 35,368,000 (130–140)		
❏ F-908★ (W-1564B-b★) • (3 known)		
❏ F-909 (W-1565B-b) • est. 24,332,000 (115–125)		

F-No. (W-No.) • Printage *(rarity)*	Grade	Comments
❑ F-909★ (W-1565B-b★) • *(9–10)*		
❑ F-910 (W-1566B-b) • est. 29,904,000 *(300–350)*		
❑ F-910★ (W-1566B-b★) • *(25–28)*		
❑ F-911A (W-1567B-b) • est. 42,696,000 *(600–800)*		
❑ F-911A★ (W-1567B-b★) • *(22–24)*		
❑ F-911B (W-1567B-c) • est. 13,184,000 *(170–190)*		
❑ F-911B★ (W-1567B-c★) • *(6 known)*		
❑ F-911C (W-1567B-d) • est. 18,344,000 *(250–300)*		
❑ F-911C★ (W-1567B-d★) • *(13–15)*		
❑ F-912 (W-1568C-b) • est. 11,112,000 *(110–125)*		
❑ F-912★ (W-1568C-b★) • *(2 known)*		
❑ F-913 (W-1569C-b) • est. 5,088,000 *(60–70)*		
❑ F-913★ (W-1569C-b★) • *(3 known)*		
❑ F-914 (W-1570C-b) • est. 9,300,000 *(90–100)*		
❑ F-914★ (W-1570C-b★) • *(10–11)*		
❑ F-915A (W-1571C-b) • est. 27,140,000 *(320–340)*		
❑ F-915A★ (W-1571C-b★) • *(18–20)*		
❑ F-915C (W-1571C-d) • est. 2,476,000 *(100–110)*		
❑ F-915C★ (W-1571C-d★) • *(2 known)*		
❑ F-916 (W-1572D-b) • est. 6,720,000 *(75–85)*		
❑ F-916★ (W-1572D-b★) • *(3 known)*		
❑ F-917 (W-1573D-b) • est. 4,628,000 *(65–75)*		
❑ F-917★ (W-1573D-b★) • *(5 known)*		
❑ F-918 (W-1574D-b) • est. 7,940,000 *(95–115)*		
❑ F-918★ (W-1574D-b★) • *(10–12)*		
❑ F-919A (W-1575D-b) • est. 18,692,000 *(320–340)*		
❑ F-919A★ (W-1575D-b★) • *(16–18)*		
❑ F-919B (W-1575D-c) • est. 2,676,000 *(60–70)*		
❑ F-919C (W-1575D-d) • est. 1,688,000 *(70–80)*		
❑ F-919C★ (W-1575D-d★) • *(1 known)*		
❑ F-920 (W-1576E-b) • est. 5,600,000 *(80–90)*		
❑ F-920★ (W-1576E-b★) • *(1 known)*		
❑ F-921 (W-1577E-b) • est. 4,148,000 *(44–48)*		

F-No. (W-No.) • Printage *(rarity)*	Grade	Comments
Series of 1914, Blue Seal *(continued)*		
❑ F-921★ (W-1577E-b★) • *(2 known)*		
❑ F-922 (W-1578E-b) • est. 6,560,000 *(110–120)*		
❑ F-922★ (W-1578E-b★) • *(13–14)*		
❑ F-923 (W-1579E-b) • est. 10,468,000 *(200–220)*		
❑ F-923★ (W-1579E-b★) • *(3 known)*		
❑ F-924 (W-1580F-b) • est. 7,560,000 *(70–80)*		
❑ F-924★ (W-1580F-b★) • *(2 known)*		
❑ F-925 (W-1581F-b) • est. 4,500,000 *(48–54)*		
❑ F-925★ (W-1581F-b★) • *(5 known)*		
❑ F-926 (W-1582F-b) • est. 5,140,000 *(95–115)*		
❑ F-926★ (W-1582F-b★) • *(2 known)*		
❑ F-927A (W-1583F-b) • est. 9,392,000 *(130–150)*		
❑ F-927A★ (W-1583F-b★) • *(4 known)*		
❑ F-927B (W-1583F-c) • est. 4,268,000 *(75–85)*		
❑ F-928 (W-1584G-b) • est. 20,896,000 *(220–240)*		
❑ F-928★ (W-1584G-b★) • *(2 known)*		
❑ F-929 (W-1585G-b) • est. 9,300,000 *(130–145)*		
❑ F-929★ (W-1585G-b★) • *(7 known)*		
❑ F-930 (W-1586G-b) • est. 19,512,000 *(210–230)*		
❑ F-930★ (W-1586G-b★) • *(35–37)*		
❑ F-931A (W-1587G-b) • est. 19,692,000 *(320–360)*		
❑ F-931A★ (W-1587G-b★) • *(28–32)*		
❑ F-931B (W-1587G-c) • est. 11,116,000 *(225–250)*		
❑ F-931B★ (W-1587G-c★) • *(4 known)*		
❑ F-931C (W-1587G-d) • est. 2,484,000 *(70–80)*		
❑ F-931C★ (W-1587G-d★) • *(2 known)*		
❑ F-932 (W-1588H-b) • est. 6,404,000 *(75–85)*		
❑ F-933 (W-1589H-b) • est. 4,312,000 *(75–85)*		
❑ F-933★ (W-1589H-b★) • *(3 known)*		
❑ F-934 (W-1590H-b) • est. 7,336,000 *(170–190)*		
❑ F-934★ (W-1590H-b★) • *(15–16)*		
❑ F-935 (W-1591H-b) • est. 2,560,000 *(70–80)*		

F-No. (W-No.) • Printage (rarity)	Grade	Comments
❑ F-936 (W-1592I-b) • est. 4,940,000 (90–105)		
❑ F-936★ (W-1592I-b★) • (2 known)		
❑ F-937 (W-1593I-b) • est. 1,348,000 (40–45)		
❑ F-937★ (W-1593I-b★) • (7 known)		
❑ F-938 (W-1594I-b) • est. 2,660,000 (7 known)		
❑ F-938★ (W-1594I-b★) • (10–12)		
❑ F-939 (W-1595I-b) • est. 4,816,000 (235–255)		
❑ F-939★ (W-1595I-b★) • (6 known)		
❑ F-940 (W-1596J-b) • est. 6,684,000 (120–130)		
❑ F-940★ (W-1596J-b★) • (4 known)		
❑ F-941 (W-1597J-b) • est. 1,000,000 (20–23)		
❑ F-942 (W-1598J-b) • est. 4,276,000 (115–125)		
❑ F-942★ (W-1598J-b★) • (14–16)		
❑ F-943A (W-1599J-b) • est. 3,868,000 (145–160)		
❑ F-944 (W-1600K-b) • est. 5,956,000 (95–115)		
❑ F-944★ (W-1600K-b★) • (3 known)		
❑ F-945 (W-1601K-b) • est. 1,324,000 (20–24)		
❑ F-946 (W-1602K-b) • est. 2,204,000 (70–80)		
❑ F-946★ (W-1602K-b★) • (6 known)		
❑ F-947 (W-1603K-b) • est. 3,336,000 (75–85)		
❑ F-948 (W-1604L-b) • est. 5,440,000 (35–42)		
❑ F-949 (W-1605L-b) • est. 4,200,000 (35–42)		
❑ F-949★ (W-1605L-b★) • (2 known)		
❑ F-950 (W-1606L-b) • est. 9,540,000 (60–70)		
❑ F-951A (W-1607L-b) • est. 16,020,000 (200–225)		
❑ F-951A★ (W-1607L-b★) • (8 known)		
❑ F-951B (W-1607L-c) • est. 3,272,000 (45–50)		
❑ F-951C (W-1607L-d) • est. 1,900,000 (75–85)		
❑ F-951C★ (W-1607L-d★) • (1 known)		

$10 Federal Reserve Bank Notes

F-No. (W-No.) • Printage (rarity)	Grade	Comments
Series of 1915		
❑ F-811 (W-1620F) • 48,000 (6 known)		

F-No. (W-No.) • Printage *(rarity)*	Grade	Comments
Series of 1915 *(continued)*		
❑ F-813 (W-1621G) • 180,000 *(58–62)*		
❑ F-816 (W-1625J) • est. 208,000 *(38–47)*		
❑ F-817 (W-1624J) • est. 276,000 *(100–110)*		
❑ F-817b (W-1622J) • est. 500 *(2 known)*		
❑ F-818 (W-1626J) • 16,000 *(7 known)*		
❑ F-819 (W-1627K) • est. 204,000 *(55–60)*		
❑ F-820 (W-1629K) • est. 8,000 *(6 known)*		
❑ F-821 (W-1628K) • est. 28,000 *(9–10)*		
Series of 1918		
❑ F-810 (W-1630B) • 200,000 *(30–35)*		
❑ F-812 (W-1631F) • 184,000 *(36–42)*		
❑ F-814 (W-1632G) • 200,000 *(24–48)*		
❑ F-815 (W-1633H) • 100,000 *(35–40)*		
❑ F-815★ (W-1633H★) • *(1 known)*		

SMALL-SIZE

$10 National Bank Notes

F-No. (W-No.) • Printage *(rarity)*	Grade	Comments
Series of 1929, Type 1		
❑ F-1801-1 (W-1720) • *(58,715 known)*		
Series of 1929, Type 2		
❑ F-1801-2 (W-1721) • *(19,270 known)*		

$10 Silver Certificates

F-No. (W-No.) • Printage *(rarity)*	Grade	Comments
Series of 1933		
❑ F-1700 (W-1745) • 216,000		
❑ F-1700★ (W-1745★) • *(1 known)*		
Series of 1934, Blue Seal		
❑ F-1701 (W-1750) • 88,692,864		
❑ F-1701★ (W-1750★)		
❑ F-1701 (W-1750 Mule)		
❑ F-1701★ (W-1750 Mule★)		
Series of 1934, Yellow Seal for North Africa		
❑ F-2308 (W-1752)		
❑ F-2308★ (W-1752★) • *(1 known)*		
Series of 1934-A, Blue Seal		
❑ F-1702 (W-1753) • 42,346,428		
❑ F-1702★ (W-1753★) • est. 310,000		
❑ F-unlisted (W-1753 Mule)		
Series of 1934-A, Yellow Seal for North Africa		
❑ F-2309 (W-1754) • 21,860,000		
❑ F-2309★ (W-1754★)		
Series of 1934-B and 1934-C		
❑ F-1703 (W-1755) • 337,740		
❑ F-1703★ (W-1755★) • est. 9,000		
❑ F-1704 (W-1756) • 20,032,632		
❑ F-1704★ (W-1756★) • est. 350,000		
Series of 1934-D, Wide Back		
❑ F-1705 (W-1757) • 11,801,112		
❑ F-1705★ (W-1757★) • est. 160,000		
Series of 1934-D, Narrow Back		
❑ F-1705 (W-1758)		
❑ F-1705★ (W-1758★)		
Series of 1953–1953-B		
❑ F-1706 (W-1759) • 10,440,000		
❑ F-1706★ (W-1759★) • 576,000		
❑ F-1707 (W-1760) • 1,080,000		
❑ F-1707★ (W-1760★) • 144,000		
❑ F-1708 (W-1761) • 720,000		

$10 Gold Certificates

F-No. (W-No.) • Printage *(rarity)*	Grade	Comments
Series of 1928 and 1928-A		
❑ F-2400 (W-1710) • 130,812,000		
❑ F-2400★ (W-1710★)		

$10 Federal Reserve Bank Notes

F-No. (W-No.) • Printage *(rarity)*	Grade	Comments
Series of 1929		
❑ F-1860A (W-1730A) • 1,680,000		
❑ F-1860A★ (W-1730A★)		
❑ F-1860B (W-1731B) • 5,556,000		
❑ F-1860B★ (W-1731B★)		
❑ F-1860C (W-1732C) • 1,416,000		
❑ F-1860C★ (W-1732C★)		
❑ F-1860D (W-1733D) • 2,412,000		
❑ F-1860D★ (W-1733D★)		
❑ F-1860E (W-1734E) • 1,356,000		
❑ F-1860E★ (W-1734E★)		
❑ F-1860F (W-1735F) • 1,056,000		
❑ F-1860F★ (W-1735F★)		
❑ F-1860G (W-1736G) • 3,156,000		
❑ F-1860G★ (W-1736G★)		
❑ F-1860H (W-1737H) • 1,584,000		
❑ F-1860H★ (W-1737H★)		
❑ F-1860I (W-1738I) • 58,000		
❑ F-1860I★ (W-1738I★)		
❑ F-1860J (W-1739J) • 1,284,000		
❑ F-1860J★ (W-1739J★)		
❑ F-1860K (W-1740K) • 504,000		
❑ F-1860K★ (W-1740K★)		
❑ F-1860L (W-1741L) • 1,080,000		
❑ F-1860L★ (W-1741L★)		

$10 Federal Reserve Notes

F-No. (W-No.) • Printage *(rarity)*	Grade	Comments
Series of 1928 and 1928-A		
❑ F-2000A (W-1800A) • 9,804,552		
❑ F-2000A★ (W-1800A★)		
❑ F-2000B (W-1800B) • 11,295,796		
❑ F-2000B★ (W-1800B★)		
❑ F-2000C (W-1800C) • 8,114,412		
❑ F-2000C★ (W-1800C★)		
❑ F-2000D (W-1800D) • 7,570,812		
❑ F-2000D★ (W-1800D★)		
❑ F-2000E (W-1800E) • 4,534,800		
❑ F-2000E★ (W-1800E★)		
❑ F-2000F (W-1800F) • 6,807,720		
❑ F-2000F★ (W-1800F★)		
❑ F-2000G (W-1800G) • 8,130,000		
❑ F-2000G★ (W-1800G★)		
❑ F-2000H (W-1800H) • 4,124,100		
❑ F-2000H★ (W-1800H★)		
❑ F-2000I (W-1800I) • 3,874,440		
❑ F-2000I★ (W-1800I★)		
❑ F-2000J (W-1800J) • 3,620,400		
❑ F-2000J★ (W-1800J★)		
❑ F-2000K (W-1800K) • 4,855,500		
❑ F-2000K★ (W-1800K★)		
❑ F-2000L (W-1800L) • 7,086,900		
❑ F-2000L★ (W-1800L★)		
❑ F-2001A (W-1801A) • 2,893,440		
❑ F-2001A★ (W-1801A★)		
❑ F-2001B (W-1801B) • 18,631,056		
❑ F-2001B★ (W-1801B★)		
❑ F-2001C (W-1801C) • 2,710,680		
❑ F-2001C★ (W-1801C★)		
❑ F-2001D (W-1801D) • 5,610,000		
❑ F-2001D★ (W-1801D★)		

F-No. (W-No.) • Printage *(rarity)*	Grade	Comments
Series of 1928 and 1928-A *(continued)*		
❏ F-2001E (W-1801E) • 552,300		
❏ F-2001E★ (W-1801E★)		
❏ F-2001F (W-1801F) • 3,033,480		
❏ F-2001F★ (W-1801F★)		
❏ F-2001G (W-1801G) • 8,715,000		
❏ F-2001G★ (W-1801G★)		
❏ F-2001H (W-1801H) • 531,600		
❏ F-2001H★ (W-1801H★)		
❏ F-2001I (W-1801I) • 102,600		
❏ F-2001J (W-1801J) • 410,400		
❏ F-2001K (W-1801K) • 961,800		
❏ F-2001L (W-1801L) • 2,547,900		
❏ F-2001L★ (W-1801L★)		
Series of 1928-B, Dark Green Seal		
❏ F-2002A (W-1802A) • 33,218,088		
❏ F-2002A★ (W-1802A★)		
❏ F-2002B (W-1802B) • 44,808,308		
❏ F-2002B★ (W-1802B★)		
❏ F-2002C (W-1802C) • 22,689,216		
❏ F-2002C★ (W-1802C★)		
❏ F-2002D (W-1802D) • 17,418,024		
❏ F-2002D★ (W-1802D★)		
❏ F-2002E (W-1802E) • 12,714,504		
❏ F-2002E★ (W-1802E★)		
❏ F-2002F (W-1802F) • 5,246,700		
❏ F-2002F★ (W-1802F★)		
❏ F-2002G (W-1802G) • 38,035,000		
❏ F-2002G★ (W-1802G★)		
❏ F-2002H (W-1802H) • 10,814,664		
❏ F-2002H★ (W-1802H★)		
❏ F-2002I (W-1802I) • 5,294,460		
❏ F-2002I★ (W-1802I★)		
❏ F-2002J (W-1802J) • 7,748,040		

F-No. (W-No.) • Printage *(rarity)*	Grade	Comments
❏ F-2002J★ (W-1802J★)		
❏ F-2002K (W-1802K) • 3,396,096		
❏ F-2002L (W-1802L) • 22,695,300		
❏ F-2002L★ (W-1802L★)		
Series of 1928-B, Light Yellow-Green Seal		
❏ F-2002A (W-1803A) • incl. in F-2002A/W-1802A		
❏ F-2002A★ (W-1803A★)		
❏ F-2002B (W-1803B) • incl. in F-2002B/W-1802B		
❏ F-2002B★ (W-1803B★)		
❏ F-2002C (W-1803C) • incl. in F-2002C/W-1802C		
❏ F-2002C★ (W-1803C★)		
❏ F-2002D (W-1803D) • incl. in F-2002D/W-1802D		
❏ F-2002D★ (W-1803D★)		
❏ F-2002E (W-1803E) • incl. in F-2002E/W-1802E		
❏ F-2002E★ (W-1803E★)		
❏ F-2002F (W-1803F) • incl. in F-2002F/W-1802F		
❏ F-2002F★ (W-1803F★)		
❏ F-2002G (W-1803G) • incl. in F-2002G/W-1802G		
❏ F-2002G★ (W-1803G★)		
❏ F-2002H (W-1803H) • incl. in F-2002H/W-1802H		
❏ F-2002H★ (W-1803H★)		
❏ F-2002I (W-1803I) • incl. in F-2002I/W-1802I		
❏ F-2002I★ (W-1803I★)		
❏ F-2002J (W-1803J) • incl. in F-2002J/W-1802J		
❏ F-2002J★ (W-1803J★)		
❏ F-2002L (W-1803L) • incl. in F-2002L/W-1802L		
❏ F-2002L★ (W-1803L★)		
Series of 1928-C		
❏ F-2003B (W-1804B) • 2,902,678		
❏ F-2003D (W-1804D) • 4,230,428		
❏ F-2003D★ (W-1804D★)		
❏ F-2003E (W-1804E) • 304,800		
❏ F-2003G (W-1804G) • 2,423,400		

F-No. (W-No.) • Printage *(rarity)*	Grade	Comments
Series of 1934, Light Yellow-Green Seal		
❏ F-2004A (W-1805A) • 46,276,152		
❏ F-2004A★ (W-1805A★)		
❏ F-2004B (W-1805B) • 117,298,008		
❏ F-2004B★ (W-1805B★)		
❏ F-2004C (W-1805C) • 34,770,768		
❏ F-2004C★ (W-1805C★)		
❏ F-2004D (W-1805D) • 28,764,108		
❏ F-2004D★ (W-1805D★)		
❏ F-2004E (W-1805E) • 16,437,252		
❏ F-2004E★ (W-1805E★)		
❏ F-2004F (W-1805F) • 20,656,872		
❏ F-2004F★ (W-1805F★)		
❏ F-2004G (W-1805G) • 69,962,064		
❏ F-2004G★ (W-1805G★)		
❏ F-2004H (W-1805H) • 22,593,204		
❏ F-2004H★ (W-1805H★)		
❏ F-2004I (W-1805I) • 16,840,980		
❏ F-2004I★ (W-1805I★)		
❏ F-2004J (W-1805J) • 22,627,824		
❏ F-2004J★ (W-1805J★)		
❏ F-2004K (W-1805K) • 21,403,488		
❏ F-2004K★ (W-1805K★)		
❏ F-2004L (W-1805L) • 37,402,308		
❏ F-2004L★ (W-1805L★)		
Series of 1934, Green Seal		
❏ F-2005A (W-1806A) • incl. in F-2004A/W-1805A		
❏ F-2005A★ (W-1806A★)		
❏ F-2005A (W-1806A Mule)		
❏ F-2005A★ (W-1806A Mule★)		
❏ F-2005B (W-1806B) • incl. in F-2004B/W-1805B		
❏ F-2005B★ (W-1806B★)		
❏ F-2005B (W-1806B Mule)		
❏ F-2005B★ (W-1806B Mule★)		

F-No. (W-No.) • Printage *(rarity)*	Grade	Comments
❏ F-2005C (W-1806C) • incl. in F-2004C/W-1805C		
❏ F-2005C★ (W-1806C★)		
❏ F-2005C (W-1806C Mule)		
❏ F-2005C★ (W-1806C Mule★)		
❏ F-2005D (W-1806D) • incl. in F-2004D/W-1805D		
❏ F-2005D★ (W-1806D★)		
❏ F-2005D (W-1806D Mule)		
❏ F-2005D★ (W-1806D Mule★)		
❏ F-2005E (W-1806E) • incl. in F-2004E/W-1805E		
❏ F-2005E★ (W-1806E★)		
❏ F-2005E (W-1806E Mule)		
❏ F-2005E★ (W-1806E Mule★)		
❏ F-2005F (W-1806F) • incl. in F-2004F/W-1805F		
❏ F-2005F★ (W-1806F★)		
❏ F-2005F (W-1806F Mule)		
❏ F-2005F★ (W-1806F Mule★)		
❏ F-2005G (W-1806G) • incl. in F-2004G/W-1805G		
❏ F-2005G★ (W-1806G★)		
❏ F-2005G (W-1806G Mule)		
❏ F-2005G★ (W-1806G Mule★)		
❏ F-2005H (W-1806H) • incl. in F-2004H/W-1805H		
❏ F-2005H★ (W-1806H★)		
❏ F-2005H (W-1806H Mule)		
❏ F-2005H★ (W-1806H Mule★)		
❏ F-2005I (W-1806I) • incl. in F-2004I/W-1805I		
❏ F-2005I★ (W-1806I★)		
❏ F-2005I (W-1806I Mule)		
❏ F-2005I★ (W-1806I Mule★)		
❏ F-2005J (W-1806J) • incl. in F-2004J/W-1805J		
❏ F-2005J★ (W-1806J★)		
❏ F-2005J (W-1806J Mule)		
❏ F-2005J★ (W-1806J Mule★)		
❏ F-2005K (W-1806K) • incl. in F-2004K/W-1805K		
❏ F-2005K★ (W-1806K★)		

F-No. (W-No.) • Printage *(rarity)*	Grade	Comments
Series of 1934, Green Seal *(continued)*		
❏ F-2005K (W-1806K Mule)		
❏ F-2005K★ (W-1806K Mule★)		
❏ F-2005L (W-1806L) • incl. in F-2004L/W-1805L		
❏ F-2005L★ (W-1806L★)		
❏ F-2005L (W-1806L Mule)		
❏ F-2005L★ (W-1806L Mule★)		
Series of 1934-A, Green Seal		
❏ F-2006A (W-1807A) • 104,540,088		
❏ F-2006A★ (W-1807A★)		
❏ F-2006A (W-1807A Mule)		
❏ F-2006B (W-1807B) • 281,940,996		
❏ F-2006B★ (W-1807B★)		
❏ F-2006B (W-1807B Mule)		
❏ F-2006B★ (W-1807B Mule★)		
❏ F-2006C (W-1807C) • 95,338,032		
❏ F-2006C★ (W-1807C★)		
❏ F-2006C (W-1807C Mule)		
❏ F-2006C★ (W-1807C Mule★)		
❏ F-2006D (W-1807D) • 93,332,004		
❏ F-2006D★ (W-1807D★)		
❏ F-2006D (W-1807D Mule)		
❏ F-2006D★ (W-1807D Mule★)		
❏ F-2006E (W-1807E) • 101,037,912		
❏ F-2006E★ (W-1807E★)		
❏ F-2006E (W-1807E Mule)		
❏ F-2006E★ (W-1807E Mule★)		
❏ F-2006F (W-1807F) • 85,478,160		
❏ F-2006F★ (W-1807F★)		
❏ F-2006F (W-1807F Mule)		
❏ F-2006F★ (W-1807F Mule★)		
❏ F-2006G (W-1807G) • 177,285,960		
❏ F-2006G★ (W-1807G★)		
❏ F-2006G (W-1807G Mule)		

F-No. (W-No.) • Printage *(rarity)*	Grade	Comments
❑ F-2006G★ (W-1807G Mule★)		
❑ F-2006H (W-1807H) • 50,694,312		
❑ F-2006H★ (W-1807H★)		
❑ F-2006I (W-1807I) • 16,340,016		
❑ F-2006I★ (W-1807I★)		
❑ F-2006I (W-1807I Mule)		
❑ F-2006J (W-1807J) • 31,069,978		
❑ F-2006J★ (W-1807J★)		
❑ F-2006K (W-1807K) • 28,263,156		
❑ F-2006K★ (W-1807K★)		
❑ F-2006L (W-1807L) • 125,537,592		
❑ F-2006L★ (W-1807L★)		
❑ F-2006L (W-1807L Mule)		
Series of 1934-A, Brown Seal, HAWAII Overprint		
❑ F-2303 (W-1808L) • 10,424,000		
❑ F-2303★ (W-1808L★)		
Series of 1934-B		
❑ F-2007A (W-1809A) • 3,999,600		
❑ F-2007A★ (W-1809A★)		
❑ F-2007B (W-1809B) • 34,815,948		
❑ F-2007B★ (W-1809B★)		
❑ F-2007C (W-1809C) • 10,339,020		
❑ F-2007C★ (W-1809C★)		
❑ F-2007D (W-1809D) • 1,394,700		
❑ F-2007D★ (W-1809D★)		
❑ F-2007E (W-1809E) • 4,018,272		
❑ F-2007E★ (W-1809E★)		
❑ F-2007F (W-1809F) • 6,746,076		
❑ F-2007F★ (W-1809F★)		
❑ F-2007G (W-1809G) • 18,130,836		
❑ F-2007G★ (W-1809G★)		
❑ F-2007H (W-1809H) • 6,849,348		
❑ F-2007H★ (W-1809H★)		
❑ F-2007I (W-1809I) • 2,254,800		

F-No. (W-No.) • Printage *(rarity)*	Grade	Comments
Series of 1934-B *(continued)*		
❑ F-2007I★ (W-1809I★)		
❑ F-2007J (W-1809J) • 3,835,764		
❑ F-2007J★ (W-1809J★)		
❑ F-2007K (W-1809K) • 3,085,200		
❑ F-2007K★ (W-1809K★)		
❑ F-2007L (W-1809L) • 9,076,800		
❑ F-2007L★ (W-1809L★)		
Series of 1934-C, Wide Face		
❑ F-2008A (W-1810A) • 42,431,404		
❑ F-2008A★ (W-1810A★)		
❑ F-2008B (W-1810B) • 115,675,644		
❑ F-2008B★ (W-1810B★)		
❑ F-2008C (W-1810C) • 46,874,760		
❑ F-2008C★ (W-1810C★)		
❑ F-2008D (W-1810D) • 33,240,000		
❑ F-2008D★ (W-1810D★)		
❑ F-2008E (W-1810E) • 37,422,600		
❑ F-2008E★ (W-1810E★)		
❑ F-2008F (W-1810F) • 44,838,264		
❑ F-2008F★ (W-1810F★)		
❑ F-2008G (W-1810G) • 105,875,412		
❑ F-2008G★ (W-1810G★)		
❑ F-2008H (W-1810H) • 36,541,404		
❑ F-2008H★ (W-1810H★)		
❑ F-2008I (W-1810I) • 11,944,848		
❑ F-2008I★ (W-1810I★)		
❑ F-2008J (W-1810J) • 20,874,072		
❑ F-2008J★ (W-1810J★)		
❑ F-2008K (W-1810K) • 25,642,620		
❑ F-2008K★ (W-1810K★)		
❑ F-2008L (W-1810L) • 49,164,480		
❑ F-2008L★ (W-1810L★)		
Series of 1934-C, Narrow Face		
❑ F-2008J (W-1811J) • incl. in F-2008J (W-1810J)		

F-No. (W-No.) • Printage *(rarity)*	Grade	Comments
Series of 1934-D		
❑ F-2009A (W-1812A) • 19,917,900		
❑ F-2009A★ (W-1812A★)		
❑ F-2009B (W-1812B) • 64,067,904		
❑ F-2009B★ (W-1812B★)		
❑ F-2009C (W-1812C) • 18,432,000		
❑ F-2009C★ (W-1812C★)		
❑ F-2009D (W-1812D) • 20,291,316		
❑ F-2009D★ (W-1812D★)		
❑ F-2009E (W-1812E) • 18,090,312		
❑ F-2009E★ (W-1812E★)		
❑ F-2009F (W-1812F) • 17,064,816		
❑ F-2009F★ (W-1812F★)		
❑ F-2009G (W-1812G) • 55,943,844		
❑ F-2009G★ (W-1812G★)		
❑ F-2009H (W-1812H) • 15,828,048		
❑ F-2009H★ (W-1812H★)		
❑ F-2009I (W-1812I) • 5,237,220		
❑ F-2009I★ (W-1812I★)		
❑ F-2009J (W-1812J) • 7,992,000		
❑ F-2009J★ (W-1812J★)		
❑ F-2009K (W-1812K) • 7,178,196		
❑ F-2009K★ (W-1812K★)		
❑ F-2009L (W-1812L) • 23,956,584		
❑ F-2009L★ (W-1812L★)		
Series of 1950, Wide Back		
❑ F-2010A (W-1813A) • 70,992,000		
❑ F-2010A★ (W-1813A★) • 1,008,000		
❑ F-2010B (W-1813B) • 218,576,000		
❑ F-2010B★ (W-1813B★) • 2,586,000		
❑ F-2010C (W-1813C) • 76,320,000		
❑ F-2010C★ (W-1813C★) • 1,008,000		
❑ F-2010D (W-1813D) • 76,032,000		
❑ F-2010D★ (W-1813D★) • 1,008,000		

F-No. (W-No.) • Printage *(rarity)*	Grade	Comments
Series of 1950, Wide Back *(continued)*		
❑ F-2010E (W-1813E) • 61,776,000		
❑ F-2010E★ (W-1813E★) • 876,000		
❑ F-2010F (W-1813F) • 63,792,000		
❑ F-2010F★ (W-1813F★) • 864,000		
❑ F-2010G (W-1813G) • 161,056,000		
❑ F-2010G★ (W-1813G★) • 2,088,000		
❑ F-2010H (W-1813H) • 47,808,000		
❑ F-2010H★ (W-1813H★) • 648,000		
❑ F-2010I (W-1813I) • 18,864,000		
❑ F-2010I★ (W-1813I★) • 552,000		
❑ F-2010J (W-1813J) • 36,332,000		
❑ F-2010J★ (W-1813J★) • 456,000		
❑ F-2010K (W-1813K) • 33,264,000		
❑ F-2010K★ (W-1813K★) • 480,000		
❑ F-2010L (W-1813L) • 76,896,000		
❑ F-2010L★ (W-1813L★) • 1,152,000		
Series of 1950, Narrow Back		
❑ F-2010A (W-1814A) • incl. in F-2010A/W-1813A		
❑ F-2010A★ (W-1814A★) • incl. in F-2010A★/W-1813A★		
❑ F-2010B (W-1814B) • incl. in F-2010B/W-1813B		
❑ F-2010B★ (W-1814B★) • incl. in F-2010B★/W-1813B★		
❑ F-2010C (W-1814C) • incl. in F-2010C/W-1813C		
❑ F-2010C★ (W-1814C★) • incl. in F-2010C★/W-1813C★		
❑ F-2010D (W-1814D) • incl. in F-2010D/W-1813D		
❑ F-2010D★ (W-1814D★) • incl. in F-2010D★/W-1813D★		
❑ F-2010E (W-1814E) • incl. in F-2010E/W-1813E		
❑ F-2010E★ (W-1814E★) • incl. in F-2010E★/W-1813E★		
❑ F-2010F (W-1814F) • incl. in F-2010F/W-1813F		
❑ F-2010G (W-1814G) • incl. in F-2010G/W-1813G		
❑ F-2010G★ (W-1814G★) • incl. in F-2010G★/W-1813G★		
❑ F-2010H (W-1814H) • incl. in F-2010H/W-1813H		
❑ F-2010H★ (W-1814H★) • incl. in F-2010H★/W-1813H★		
❑ F-2010I (W-1814I) • incl. in F-2010I/W-1813I		

F-No. (W-No.) • Printage *(rarity)*	Grade	Comments
☐ F-2010I★ (W-1814I★) • incl. in F-2010I★/W-1813I★		
☐ F-2010J (W-1814J) • incl. in F-2010J/W-1813J		
☐ F-2010J★ (W-1814J★) • incl. in F-2010J★/W-1813J★		
☐ F-2010K (W-1814K) • incl. in F-2010K/W-1813K		
☐ F-2010K★ (W-1814K★) • incl. in F-2010K★/W-1813K★		
☐ F-2010L (W-1814L) • incl. in F-2010L/W-1813L		
☐ F-2010L★ (W-1814L★) • incl. in F-2010L★/W-1813L★		
Series of 1950-A–1950-E		
☐ F-2011A (W-1815A) • 104,248,000		
☐ F-2011A★ (W-1815A★) • 5,112,000		
☐ F-2011B (W-1815B) • 356,664,000		
☐ F-2011B★ (W-1815B★) • 16,992,000		
☐ F-2011C (W-1815C) • 71,920,000		
☐ F-2011C★ (W-1815C★) • 3,672,000		
☐ F-2011D (W-1815D) • 75,088,000		
☐ F-2011D★ (W-1815D★) • 3,672,000		
☐ F-2011E (W-1815E) • 82,144,000		
☐ F-2011E★ (W-1815E★) • 4,392,000		
☐ F-2011F (W-1815F) • 73,288,000		
☐ F-2011F★ (W-1815F★) • 3,816,000		
☐ F-2011G (W-1815G) • 235,064,000		
☐ F-2011G★ (W-1815G★) • 11,160,000		
☐ F-2011H (W-1815H) • 46,512,000		
☐ F-2011H★ (W-1815H★) • 2,880,000		
☐ F-2011I (W-1815I) • 8,136,000		
☐ F-2011I★ (W-1815I★) • 432,000		
☐ F-2011J (W-1815J) • 25,488,000		
☐ F-2011J★ (W-1815J★) • 2,304,000		
☐ F-2011K (W-1815K) • 21,816,000		
☐ F-2011K★ (W-1815K★) • 1,584,000		
☐ F-2011L (W-1815L) • 101,584,000		
☐ F-2011L★ (W-1815L★) • 6,408,000		
☐ F-2012A (W-1816A) • 49,240,000		
☐ F-2012A★ (W-1816A★) • 2,880,000		

F-No. (W-No.) • Printage *(rarity)*	Grade	Comments
Series of 1950-A–1950-E *(continued)*		
❏ F-2012B (W-1816B) • 170,840,000		
❏ F-2012B★ (W-1816B★) • 8,280,000		
❏ F-2012C (W-1816C) • 66,880,000		
❏ F-2012C★ (W-1816C★) • 3,240,000		
❏ F-2012D (W-1816D) • 55,360,000		
❏ F-2012D★ (W-1816D★) • 2,880,000		
❏ F-2012E (W-1816E) • 51,120,000		
❏ F-2012E★ (W-1816E★) • 2,880,000		
❏ F-2012F (W-1816F) • 66,520,000		
❏ F-2012F★ (W-1816F★) • 2,880,000		
❏ F-2012G (W-1816G) • 165,080,000		
❏ F-2012G★ (W-1816G★) • 6,480,000		
❏ F-2012H (W-1816H) • 33,040,000		
❏ F-2012H★ (W-1816H★) • 1,800,000		
❏ F-2012I (W-1816I) • 13,320,000		
❏ F-2012I★ (W-1816I★) • 720,000		
❏ F-2012J (W-1816J) • 33,480,000		
❏ F-2012J★ (W-1816J★) • 2,520,000		
❏ F-2012K (W-1816K) • 26,280,000		
❏ F-2012K★ (W-1816K★) • 1,440,000		
❏ F-2012L (W-1816L) • 55,000,000		
❏ F-2012L★ (W-1816L★) • 2,880,000		
❏ F-2013A (W-1817A) • 51,120,000		
❏ F-2013A★ (W-1817A★) • 2,160,000		
❏ F-2013B (W-1817B) • 126,520,000		
❏ F-2013B★ (W-1817B★) • 6,840,000		
❏ F-2013C (W-1817C) • 25,200,000		
❏ F-2013C★ (W-1817C★) • 720,000		
❏ F-2013D (W-1817D) • 33,120,000		
❏ F-2013D★ (W-1817D★) • 1,800,000		
❏ F-2013E (W-1817E) • 45,640,000		
❏ F-2013E★ (W-1817E★) • 1,800,000		
❏ F-2013F (W-1817F) • 38,880,000		

F-No. (W-No.) • Printage *(rarity)*	Grade	Comments
❑ F-2013F★ (W-1817F★) • 2,880,000		
❑ F-2013G (W-1817G) • 69,400,000		
❑ F-2013G★ (W-1817G★) • 3,600,000		
❑ F-2013H (W-1817H) • 23,040,000		
❑ F-2013H★ (W-1817H★) • 1,080,000		
❑ F-2013I (W-1817I) • 9,000,000		
❑ F-2013I★ (W-1817I★) • 720,000		
❑ F-2013J (W-1817J) • 23,320,000		
❑ F-2013J★ (W-1817J★) • 800,000		
❑ F-2013K (W-1817K) • 17,640,000		
❑ F-2013K★ (W-1817K★) • 720,000		
❑ F-2013L (W-1817L) • 35,640,000		
❑ F-2013L★ (W-1817L★) • 1,800,000		
❑ F-2014A (W-1818A) • 38,800,000		
❑ F-2014A★ (W-1818A★) • 1,800,000		
❑ F-2014B (W-1818B) • 150,320,000		
❑ F-2014B★ (W-1818B★) • 6,840,000		
❑ F-2014C (W-1818C) • 19,080,000		
❑ F-2014C★ (W-1818C★) • 1,080,000		
❑ F-2014D (W-1818D) • 24,120,000		
❑ F-2014D★ (W-1818D★) • 360,000		
❑ F-2014E (W-1818E) • 33,840,000		
❑ F-2014E★ (W-1818E★) • 720,000		
❑ F-2014F (W-1818F) • 36,000,000		
❑ F-2014F★ (W-1818F★) • 1,440,000		
❑ F-2014G (W-1818G) • 115,480,000		
❑ F-2014G★ (W-1818G★) • 5,040,000		
❑ F-2014H (W-1818H) • 10,440,000		
❑ F-2014H★ (W-1818H★) • 720,000		
❑ F-2014J (W-1818J) • 15,480,000		
❑ F-2014J★ (W-1818J★) • 1,080,000		
❑ F-2014K (W-1818K) • 18,280,000		
❑ F-2014K★ (W-1818K★) • 800,000		
❑ F-2014L (W-1818L) • 62,560,000		

F-No. (W-No.) • Printage *(rarity)*	Grade	Comments
Series of 1950-A–1950-E *(continued)*		
❑ F-2014L★ (W-1818L★) • 3,600,000		
❑ F-2015B (W-1819B) • 12,600,000		
❑ F-2015B★ (W-1819B★) • 2,621,000		
❑ F-2015G (W-1819G) • 65,080,000		
❑ F-2015G★ (W-1819G★) • 4,320,000		
❑ F-2015L (W-1819L) • 17,280,000		
❑ F-2015L★ (W-1819L★) • 720,000		
Series of 1963 and 1963-A		
❑ F-2016A (W-1820A) • 5,760,000		
❑ F-2016A★ (W-1820A★) • 640,000		
❑ F-2016B (W-1820B) • 24,960,000		
❑ F-2016B★ (W-1820B★) • 1,920,000		
❑ F-2016C (W-1820C) • 6,400,000		
❑ F-2016C★ (W-1820C★) • 1,280,000		
❑ F-2016D (W-1820D) • 7,040,000		
❑ F-2016D★ (W-1820D★) • 640,000		
❑ F-2016E (W-1820E) • 4,480,000		
❑ F-2016E★ (W-1820E★) • 640,000		
❑ F-2016F (W-1820F) • 10,880,000		
❑ F-2016F★ (W-1820F★) • 1,280,000		
❑ F-2016G (W-1820G) • 35,200,000		
❑ F-2016G★ (W-1820G★) • 2,560,000		
❑ F-2016H (W-1820H) • 13,440,000		
❑ F-2016H★ (W-1820H★) • 1,280,000		
❑ F-2016J (W-1820J) • 3,840,000		
❑ F-2016J★ (W-1820J★) • 640,000		
❑ F-2016K (W-1820K) • 5,120,000		
❑ F-2016K★ (W-1820K★) • 640,000		
❑ F-2016L (W-1820L) • 14,080,000		
❑ F-2016L★ (W-1820L★) • 1,280,000		
❑ F-2017A (W-1821A) • 131,360,000		
❑ F-2017A★ (W-1821A★) • 6,400,000		
❑ F-2017B (W-1821B) • 199,360,000		

F-No. (W-No.) • Printage *(rarity)*	Grade	Comments
❏ F-2017B★ (W-1821B★) • 9,600,000		
❏ F-2017C (W-1821C) • 100,000,000		
❏ F-2017C★ (W-1821C★) • 4,480,000		
❏ F-2017D (W-1821D) • 72,960,000		
❏ F-2017D★ (W-1821D★) • 3,840,000		
❏ F-2017E (W-1821E) • 114,720,000		
❏ F-2017E★ (W-1821E★) • 5,120,000		
❏ F-2017F (W-1821F) • 80,000,000		
❏ F-2017F★ (W-1821F★) • 3,840,000		
❏ F-2017G (W-1821G) • 195,520,000		
❏ F-2017G★ (W-1821G★) • 9,600,000		
❏ F-2017H (W-1821H) • 43,520,000		
❏ F-2017H★ (W-1821H★) • 1,920,000		
❏ F-2017I (W-1821I) • 16,640,000		
❏ F-2017I★ (W-1821I★) • 640,000		
❏ F-2017J (W-1821J) • 31,360,000		
❏ F-2017J★ (W-1821J★) • 1,920,000		
❏ F-2017K (W-1821K) • 51,200,000		
❏ F-2017K★ (W-1821K★) • 1,920,000		
❏ F-2017L (W-1821L) • 87,200,000		
❏ F-2017L★ (W-1821L★) • 5,120,000		
Series of 1969–1969-C		
❏ F-2018A (W-1822A) • 71,880,000		
❏ F-2018A★ (W-1822A★) • 2,560,000		
❏ F-2018B (W-1822B) • 247,360,000		
❏ F-2018B★ (W-1822B★) • 10,240,000		
❏ F-2018C (W-1822C) • 56,960,000		
❏ F-2018C★ (W-1822C★) • 2,560,000		
❏ F-2018D (W-1822D) • 57,600,000		
❏ F-2018D★ (W-1822D★) • 2,560,000		
❏ F-2018E (W-1822E) • 56,960,000		
❏ F-2018E★ (W-1822E★) • 2,560,000		
❏ F-2018F (W-1822F) • 53,760,000		
❏ F-2018F★ (W-1822F★) • 2,560,000		

F-No. (W-No.) • Printage *(rarity)*	Grade	Comments
Series of 1969–1969-C *(continued)*		
❑ F-2018G (W-1822G) • 142,240,000		
❑ F-2018G★ (W-1822G★) • 6,400,000		
❑ F-2018H (W-1822H) • 22,400,000		
❑ F-2018H★ (W-1822H★) • 640,000		
❑ F-2018I (W-1822I) • 12,800,000		
❑ F-2018I★ (W-1822I★) • 1,280,000		
❑ F-2018J (W-1822J) • 31,360,000		
❑ F-2018J★ (W-1822J★) • 1,280,000		
❑ F-2018K (W-1822K) • 30,080,000		
❑ F-2018K★ (W-1822K★) • 1,280,000		
❑ F-2018L (W-1822L) • 56,320,000		
❑ F-2018L★ (W-1822L★) • 3,185,000		
❑ F-2019A (W-1823A) • 41,120,000		
❑ F-2019A★ (W-1823A★) • 1,920,000		
❑ F-2019B (W-1823B) • 111,840,000		
❑ F-2019B★ (W-1823B★) • 3,840,000		
❑ F-2019C (W-1823C) • 24,320,000		
❑ F-2019C★ (W-1823C★) • 1,920,000		
❑ F-2019D (W-1823D) • 23,680,000		
❑ F-2019D★ (W-1823D★) • 1,276,000		
❑ F-2019E (W-1823E) • 25,600,000		
❑ F-2019E★ (W-1823E★) • 640,000		
❑ F-2019F (W-1823F) • 13,440,000		
❑ F-2019F★ (W-1823F★) • 640,000		
❑ F-2019G (W-1823G) • 80,160,000		
❑ F-2019G★ (W-1823G★) • 3,560,000		
❑ F-2019H (W-1823H) • 15,360,000		
❑ F-2019H★ (W-1823H★) • 640,000		
❑ F-2019I (W-1823I) • 8,320,000		
❑ F-2019J (W-1823J) • 10,880,000		
❑ F-2019K (W-1823K) • 20,480,000		
❑ F-2019K★ (W-1823K★) • 640,000		
❑ F-2019L (W-1823L) • 23,840,000		

F-No. (W-No.) • Printage *(rarity)*	Grade	Comments
❑ F-2019L★ (W-1823L★) • 640,000		
❑ F-2020A (W-1824A) • 16,640,000		
❑ F-2020B (W-1824B) • 60,320,000		
❑ F-2020B★ (W-1824B★) • 1,920,000		
❑ F-2020C (W-1824C) • 16,000,000		
❑ F-2020D (W-1824D) • 12,800,000		
❑ F-2020E (W-1824E) • 12,160,000		
❑ F-2020E★ (W-1824E★) • 640,000		
❑ F-2020F (W-1824F) • 13,440,000		
❑ F-2020F★ (W-1824F★) • 640,000		
❑ F-2020G (W-1824G) • 32,640,000		
❑ F-2020G★ (W-1824G★) • 1,268,000		
❑ F-2020H (W-1824H) • 8,960,000		
❑ F-2020H★ (W-1824H★) • 1,280,000		
❑ F-2020I (W-1824I) • 3,200,000		
❑ F-2020J (W-1824J) • 5,120,000		
❑ F-2020J★ (W-1824J★) • 640,000		
❑ F-2020K (W-1824K) • 5,760,000		
❑ F-2020L (W-1824L) • 23,840,000		
❑ F-2020L★ (W-1824L★) • 640,000		
❑ F-2021A (W-1825A) • 44,800,000		
❑ F-2021A★ (W-1825A★) • 640,000		
❑ F-2021B (W-1825B) • 203,200,000		
❑ F-2021B★ (W-1825B★) • 7,040,000		
❑ F-2021C (W-1825C) • 69,920,000		
❑ F-2021C★ (W-1825C★) • 1,280,000		
❑ F-2021D (W-1825D) • 46,880,000		
❑ F-2021D★ (W-1825D★) • 2,400,000		
❑ F-2021E (W-1825E) • 45,600,000		
❑ F-2021E★ (W-1825E★) • 1,120,000		
❑ F-2021F (W-1825F) • 46,240,000		
❑ F-2021F★ (W-1825F★) • 1,920,000		
❑ F-2021G (W-1825G) • 55,200,000		
❑ F-2021G★ (W-1825G★) • 880,000		

F-No. (W-No.) • Printage *(rarity)*	Grade	Comments
Series of 1969–1969-C *(continued)*		
❑ F-2021H (W-1825H) • 29,800,000		
❑ F-2021H★ (W-1825H★) • 1,280,000		
❑ F-2021I (W-1825I) • 11,520,000		
❑ F-2021I★ (W-1825I★) • 640,000		
❑ F-2021J (W-1825J) • 23,040,000		
❑ F-2021J★ (W-1825J★) • 640,000		
❑ F-2021K (W-1825K) • 24,960,000		
❑ F-2021K★ (W-1825K★) • 640,000		
❑ F-2021L (W-1825L) • 56,960,000		
❑ F-2021L★ (W-1825L★) • 640,000		
Series of 1974		
❑ F-2022A (W-1826A) • 104,480,000		
❑ F-2022A★ (W-1826A★) • 2,560,000		
❑ F-2022B (W-1826B) • 239,040,000		
❑ F-2022B★ (W-1826B★) • 4,460,000		
❑ F-2022C (W-1826C) • 69,280,000		
❑ F-2022C★ (W-1826C★) • 2,560,000		
❑ F-2022D (W-1826D) • 82,080,000		
❑ F-2022D★ (W-1826D★) • 1,920,000		
❑ F-2022E (W-1826E) • 105,760,000		
❑ F-2022E★ (W-1826E★) • 1,920,000		
❑ F-2022F (W-1826F) • 75,520,000		
❑ F-2022F★ (W-1826F★) • 3,200,000		
❑ F-2022G (W-1826G) • 104,320,000		
❑ F-2022G★ (W-1826G★) • 4,480,000		
❑ F-2022H (W-1826H) • 46,240,000		
❑ F-2022H★ (W-1826H★) • 1,280,000		
❑ F-2022I (W-1826I) • 27,520,000		
❑ F-2022I★ (W-1826I★) • 2,560,000		
❑ F-2022J (W-1826J) • 24,320,000		
❑ F-2022J★ (W-1826J★) • 640,000		
❑ F-2022K (W-1826K) • 39,840,000		
❑ F-2022K★ (W-1826K★) • 1,920,000		

F-No. (W-No.) • Printage *(rarity)*	Grade	Comments
❏ F-2022L (W-1826L) • 1,920,000		
❏ F-2022L★ (W-1826L★) • 1,760,000		
Series of 1977 and 1977-A		
❏ F-2023A (W-1827A) • 96,640,000		
❏ F-2023A★ (W-1827A★) • 2,688,000		
❏ F-2023B (W-1827B) • 277,120,000		
❏ F-2023B★ (W-1827B★) • 7,168,000		
❏ F-2023C (W-1827C) • 83,200,000		
❏ F-2023C★ (W-1827C★) • 896,000		
❏ F-2023D (W-1827D) • 83,200,000		
❏ F-2023D★ (W-1827D★) • 768,000		
❏ F-2023E (W-1827E) • 71,040,000		
❏ F-2023E★ (W-1827E★) • 1,920,000		
❏ F-2023F (W-1827F) • 88,960,000		
❏ F-2023F★ (W-1827F★) • 1,536,000		
❏ F-2023G (W-1827G) • 174,720,000		
❏ F-2023G★ (W-1827G★) • 3,968,000		
❏ F-2023H (W-1827H) • 46,720,000		
❏ F-2023H★ (W-1827H★) • 896,000		
❏ F-2023I (W-1827I) • 10,240,000		
❏ F-2023I★ (W-1827I★) • 256,000		
❏ F-2023J (W-1827J) • 50,560,000		
❏ F-2023J★ (W-1827J★) • 896,000		
❏ F-2023K (W-1827K) • 53,760,000		
❏ F-2023K★ (W-1827K★) • 640,000		
❏ F-2023L (W-1827L) • 73,600,000		
❏ F-2023L★ (W-1827L★) • 1,792,000		
❏ F-2024A (W-1828A) • 83,840,000		
❏ F-2024A★ (W-1828A★) • 1,664,000		
❏ F-2024B (W-1828B) • 259,280,000		
❏ F-2024B★ (W-1828B★) • 5,248,000		
❏ F-2024C (W-1828C) • 96,000,000		
❏ F-2024C★ (W-1828C★) • 2,048,000		
❏ F-2024D (W-1828D) • 44,800,000		

F-No. (W-No.) • Printage *(rarity)*	Grade	Comments
Series of 1977 and 1977-A *(continued)*		
❑ F-2024D★ (W-1828D★) • 2,048,000		
❑ F-2024E (W-1828E) • 104,320,000		
❑ F-2024E★ (W-1828E★) • 3,072,000		
❑ F-2024F (W-1828F) • 33,920,000		
❑ F-2024F★ (W-1828F★) • 640,000		
❑ F-2024G (W-1828G) • 108,160,000		
❑ F-2024G★ (W-1828G★) • 3,200,000		
❑ F-2024H (W-1828H) • 27,520,000		
❑ F-2024H★ (W-1828H★) • 640,000		
❑ F-2024I (W-1828I) • 7,680,000		
❑ F-2024I★ (W-1828I★) • 128,000		
❑ F-2024J (W-1828J) • 40,320,000		
❑ F-2024J★ (W-1828J★) • 2,136,000		
❑ F-2024K (W-1828K) • 60,160,000		
❑ F-2024K★ (W-1828K★) • 4,224,000		
❑ F-2024L (W-1828L) • 59,520,000		
❑ F-2024L★ (W-1828L★) • 2,048,000		
Series of 1981 and 1981-A		
❑ F-2025A (W-1829A) • 172,160,000		
❑ F-2025A★ (W-1829A★) • 1,280,000		
❑ F-2025B (W-1829B) • 434,560,000		
❑ F-2025B★ (W-1829B★) • 1,920,000		
❑ F-2025C (W-1829C) • 131,840,000		
❑ F-2025C★ (W-1829C★) • 632,000		
❑ F-2025D (W-1829D) • 122,240,000		
❑ F-2025D★ (W-1829D★) • 1,268,000		
❑ F-2025E (W-1829E) • 131,840,000		
❑ F-2025E★ (W-1829E★) • 2,576,000		
❑ F-2025F (W-1829F) • 131,840,000		
❑ F-2025F★ (W-1829F★) • 1,908,000		
❑ F-2025G (W-1829G) • 254,080,000		
❑ F-2025G★ (W-1829G★) • 1,280,000		
❑ F-2025H (W-1829H) • 55,280,000		

F-No. (W-No.) • Printage *(rarity)*	Grade	Comments
❑ F-2025I (W-1829I) • 23,680,000		
❑ F-2025I★ (W-1829I★) • 256,000		
❑ F-2025J (W-1829J) • 53,120,000		
❑ F-2025K (W-1829K) • 50,560,000		
❑ F-2025L (W-1829L) • 144,000,000		
❑ F-2025L★ (W-1829L★) • 1,280,000		
❑ F-2026A (W-1830A) • 112,000,000		
❑ F-2026B (W-1830B) • 259,000,000		
❑ F-2026B★ (W-1830B★) • 3,200,000		
❑ F-2026C (W-1830C) • 48,000,000		
❑ F-2026D (W-1830D) • 80,000,000		
❑ F-2026E (W-1830E) • 92,800,000		
❑ F-2026E★ (W-1830E★) • 3,200,000		
❑ F-2026F (W-1830F) • 83,200,000		
❑ F-2026F★ (W-1830F★) • 4,736,000		
❑ F-2026G (W-1830G) • 183,600,000		
❑ F-2026H (W-1830H) • 25,600,000		
❑ F-2026I (W-1830I) • 19,200,000		
❑ F-2026J (W-1830J) • 48,000,000		
❑ F-2026K (W-1830K) • 48,000,000		
❑ F-2026L (W-1830L) • 115,200,000		
Series of 1985		
❑ F-2027A (W-1831A) • 380,800,000		
❑ F-2027A★ (W-1831A★) • 7,296,000		
❑ F-2027B (W-1831B) • 1,027,200,000		
❑ F-2027B★ (W-1831B★) • 3,200,000		
❑ F-2027C (W-1831C) • 163,200,000		
❑ F-2027D (W-1831D) • 304,000,000		
❑ F-2027D★ (W-1831D★) • 3,200,000		
❑ F-2027E (W-1831E) • 211,200,000		
❑ F-2027F (W-1831F) • 297,600,000		
❑ F-2027F★ (W-1831F★) • 3,200,000		
❑ F-2027G (W-1831G) • 358,400,000		
❑ F-2027H (W-1831H) • 131,200,000		

F-No. (W-No.) • Printage *(rarity)*	Grade	Comments
Series of 1985 *(continued)*		
❑ F-2027H★ (W-1831H★) • 3,200,000		
❑ F-2027I (W-1831I) • 64,000,000		
❑ F-2027J (W-1831J) • 86,400,000		
❑ F-2027K (W-1831K) • 115,200,000		
❑ F-2027K★ (W-1831K★) • 3,136,000		
❑ F-2027L (W-1831L) • 300,800,000		
❑ F-2027L★ (W-1831L★) • 3,200,000		
Series of 1988-A		
❑ F-2028A (W-1832A) • 198,400,000		
❑ F-2028A★ (W-1832A★) • 6,400,000		
❑ F-2028B (W-1832B) • 339,200,000		
❑ F-2028B★ (W-1832B★) • 3,200,000		
❑ F-2028C (W-1832C) • 57,600,000		
❑ F-2028D (W-1832D) • 128,000,000		
❑ F-2028D★ (W-1832D★) • 3,200,000		
❑ F-2028E (W-1832E) • 105,600,000		
❑ F-2028F (W-1832F) • 236,800,000		
❑ F-2028G (W-1832G) • 236,800,000		
❑ F-2028H (W-1832H) • 70,400,000		
❑ F-2028I (W-1832I) • 19,200,000		
❑ F-2028J (W-1832J) • 51,200,000		
❑ F-2028K (W-1832K) • 115,200,000		
❑ F-2028L (W-1832L) • 217,600,000		
❑ F-2028L★ (W-1832L★) • 3,200,000		
Series of 1990		
❑ F-2029A (W-1833A) • 128,000,000		
❑ F-2029B (W-1833B) • 742,400,000		
❑ F-2029B★ (W-1833B★) • 16,874,000		
❑ F-2029C (W-1833C) • 19,200,000		
❑ F-2029C★ (W-1833C★) • 2,560,000		
❑ F-2029D (W-1833D) • 89,600,000		
❑ F-2029E (W-1833E) • 105,600,000		
❑ F-2029F (W-1833F) • 160,000,000		
❑ F-2029G (W-1833G) • 307,200,000		

F-No. (W-No.) • Printage *(rarity)*	Grade	Comments
❏ F-2029G★ (W-1833G★) • 2,560,000		
❏ F-2029H (W-1833H) • 70,400,000		
❏ F-2029H★ (W-1833H★) • 1,920,000		
❏ F-2029I (W-1833I) • 12,800,000		
❏ F-2029J (W-1833J) • 70,400,000		
❏ F-2029K (W-1833K) • 57,600,000		
❏ F-2029L (W-1833L) • 83,200,000		
Series of 1993		
❏ F-2030A (W-1834A) • 147,200,000		
❏ F-2030B (W-1834B) • 480,000,000		
❏ F-2030B★ (W-1834B★) • 5,120,000		
❏ F-2030C (W-1834C) • 83,200,000		
❏ F-2030C★ (W-1834C★) • 1,920,000		
❏ F-2030D (W-1834D) • 115,200,000		
❏ F-2030F (W-1834F) • 121,600,000		
❏ F-2030G (W-1834G) • 128,000,000		
❏ F-2030G★ (W-1834G★) • 2,176,000		
❏ F-2030H (W-1834H) • 89,600,000		
❏ F-2030J (W-1834J) • 19,200,000		
❏ F-2030L (W-1834L) • 192,000,000		
Series of 1995		
❏ F-2031A (W-1835A) • 192,000,000		
❏ F-2031B (W-1835B) • 358,400,000		
❏ F-2031C (W-1835C) • 57,600,000		
❏ F-2031D (W-1835D) • 108,000,000		
❏ F-2031E (W-1835E) • 153,600,000		
❏ F-2031E★ (W-1835E★) • 1,280,000		
❏ F-2031F (W-1835F) • 70,400,000		
❏ F-2031F★ (W-1835F★) • 640,000		
❏ F-2032B (W-1836B) • 76,800,000		
❏ F-2032C (W-1836C) • 89,600,000		
❏ F-2032D (W-1836D) • 70,400,000		
❏ F-2032D★ (W-1836D★) • 1,920,000		
❏ F-2032E (W-1836E) • 134,400,000		

F-No. (W-No.) • Printage *(rarity)*	Grade	Comments
Series of 1995 *(continued)*		
❑ F-2032F (W-1836F) • 377,600,000		
❑ F-2032F★ (W-1836F★) • 320,000		
❑ F-2032G (W-1836G) • 448,000,000		
❑ F-2032G★ (W-1836G★) • 3,200,000		
❑ F-2032H (W-1836H) • 153,600,000		
❑ F-2032H★ (W-1836H★) • 6,400,000		
❑ F-2032I (W-1836I) • 70,400,000		
❑ F-2032J (W-1836J) • 147,200,000		
❑ F-2032K (W-1836K) • 166,400,000		
❑ F-2032L (W-1836L) • 275,000,000		
❑ F-2032L★ (W-1836L★) • 3,200,000		
Series of 1999		
❑ F-2033A (W-1837A) • 83,200,000		
❑ F-2033A★ (W-1837A★) • 3,200,000		
❑ F-2033B (W-1837B) • 300,800,000		
❑ F-2033C (W-1837C) • 64,000,000		
❑ F-2033C★ (W-1837C★) • 3,520,000		
❑ F-2033D (W-1837D) • 51,520,000		
❑ F-2033D★ (W-1837D★) • 2,240,000		
❑ F-2033E (W-1837E) • 112,800,000		
❑ F-2033E★ (W-1837E★) • 675,200		
❑ F-2033F (W-1837F) • 96,000,000		
❑ F-2033G (W-1837G) • 83,200,000		
❑ F-2033H (W-1837H) • 38,400,000		
❑ F-2033I (W-1837I) • 6,400,000		
❑ F-2033J (W-1837J) • 12,800,000		
❑ F-2033K (W-1837K) • 44,800,000		
❑ F-2033L (W-1837L) • 32,000,000		
❑ F-2034A★ (W-1838A★) • 3,200,000		
❑ F-2034B★ (W-1838B★) • 3,200,000		
❑ F-2034F (W-1838F) • 83,200,000		
❑ F-2034F★ (W-1838F★) • 7,715,200		
❑ F-2034G (W-1838G) • 44,800,000		

F-No. (W-No.) • Printage (rarity)	Grade	Comments
❑ F-2034J (W-1838J) • 51,200,000		
❑ F-2034K (W-1838K) • 128,000,000		
❑ F-2034K★ (W-1838K★) • 12,800,000		
❑ F-2034L (W-1838L) • 76,800,000		
Series of 2001		
❑ F-2035A (W-1839A) • 19,200,000		
❑ F-2035B (W-1839B) • 121,600,000		
❑ F-2035B★ (W-1839B★) • 320,000		
❑ F-2035C (W-1839C) • 108,800,000		
❑ F-2035D (W-1839D) • 57,600,000		
❑ F-2035D★ (W-1839D★) • 1,280,000		
❑ F-2035E (W-1839E) • 117,760,000		
❑ F-2035F (W-1839F) • 38,400,000		
❑ F-2035G★ (W-1839G★) • 640,000		
❑ F-2035H (W-1839H) • 12,800,000		
❑ F-2035I (W-1839I) • 6,400,000		
❑ F-2036A (W-1840A) • 147,200,000		
❑ F-2036B (W-1840B) • 121,600,000		
❑ F-2036E (W-1840E) • 44,800,000		
❑ F-2036F (W-1840F) • 76,800,000		
❑ F-2036G (W-1840G) • 160,000,000		
❑ F-2036H (W-1840H) • 64,000,000		
❑ F-2036I (W-1840I) • 32,000,000		
❑ F-2036K (W-1840K) • 38,400,000		
❑ F-2036K★ (W-1840K★) • 3,200,000		
❑ F-2036L★ (W-1840L★) • 3,200,000		
Series of 2003		
❑ F-2037A (W-1841A) • 32,000,000		
❑ F-2037A★ (W-1841A★) • 416,000		
❑ F-2037B (W-1841B) • 57,600,000		
❑ F-2037C (W-1841C) • 32,000,000		
❑ F-2037D (W-1841D) • 38,400,000		
❑ F-2037D★ (W-1841D★) • 1,280,000		
❑ F-2037E (W-1841E) • 38,400,000		

F-No. (W-No.) • Printage *(rarity)*	Grade	Comments
Series of 2003 *(continued)*		
❏ F-2037F (W-1841F) • 57,600,000		
❏ F-2037G (W-1841G) • 140,800,000		
❏ F-2037H (W-1841H) • 38,400,000		
❏ F-2037H★ (W-1841H★) • 768,000		
❏ F-2037I (W-1841I) • 6,400,000		
❏ F-2037J (W-1841J) • 51,200,000		
❏ F-2037J★ (W-1841J★) • 2,920,000		
❏ F-2037K (W-1841K) • 76,800,000		
❏ F-2037K★ (W-1841K★) • 320,000		
❏ F-2037L (W-1841L) • 108,800,000		
❏ F-2038A (W-1842A) • 32,000,000		
❏ F-2038B (W-1842B) • 89,600,000		
❏ F-2038C (W-1842C) • 44,800,000		
❏ F-2038D (W-1842D) • 32,000,000		
❏ F-2038E (W-1842E) • 44,800,000		
❏ F-2038F (W-1842F) • 76,800,000		
❏ F-2038G (W-1842G) • 6,400,000		
❏ F-2038I (W-1842I) • 6,400,000		
Series of 2004-A		
❏ F-2039A (W-1843A) • 51,200,000		
❏ F-2039A★ (W-1843A★) • 3,200,000		
❏ F-2039B (W-1843B) • 153,600,000		
❏ F-2039B★ (W-1843B★) • 640,000		
❏ F-2039C (W-1843C) • 64,000,000		
❏ F-2039D (W-1843D) • 44,800,000		
❏ F-2039E (W-1843E) • 70,400,000		
❏ F-2039F (W-1843F) • 134,400,000		
❏ F-2039F★ (W-1843F★) • 96,000		
❏ F-2039G (W-1843G) • 96,000,000		
❏ F-2039G★ (W-1843G★) • 512,000		
❏ F-2039H (W-1843H) • 38,400,000		
❏ F-2039I (W-1843I) • 12,800,000		
❏ F-2039J (W-1843J) • 38,400,000		
❏ F-2039K (W-1843K) • 57,600,000		

F-No. (W-No.) • Printage *(rarity)*	Grade	Comments
❑ F-2039L (W-1843L) • 89,600,000		
❑ F-2039L★ (W-1843L★) • 5,760,000		
Series of 2006		
❑ F-2040A (W-1844A) • 76,800,000		
❑ F-2040B (W-1844B) • 281,600,000		
❑ F-2040B★ (W-1844B★) • 1,920,000		
❑ F-2040C (W-1844C) • 102,400,000		
❑ F-2040C★ (W-1844C★) • 640,000		
❑ F-2040D (W-1844D) • 102,400,000		
❑ F-2040E (W-1844E) • 115,200,000		
❑ F-2040F (W-1844F) • 268,800,000		
❑ F-2040G (W-1844G) • 172,800,000		
❑ F-2040G★ (W-1844G★) • 768,000		
❑ F-2040H (W-1844H) • 57,600,000		
❑ F-2040I (W-1844I) • 19,200,000		
❑ F-2040J (W-1844J) • 57,600,000		
❑ F-2040K (W-1844K) • 102,400,000		
❑ F-2040L (W-1844L) • 172,800,000		
Series of 2009		
❑ F-2041A • 76,800,000		
❑ F-2041B • 243,200,000		
❑ F-2041B★ • 3,200,000		
❑ F-2041C • 102,400,000		
❑ F-2041D • 115,200,000		
❑ F-2041D★ • 1,920,000		
❑ F-2041E • 121,600,000		
❑ F-2041F • 249,600,000		
❑ F-2041F★ • 640,000		
❑ F-2041G • 153,600,000		
❑ F-2041H • 57,600,000		
❑ F-2041I • 25,600,000		
❑ F-2041J • 51,200,000		
❑ F-2041K • 102,400,000		
❑ F-2041L • 166,400,000		

F-No. (W-No.) • Printage *(rarity)*	Grade	Comments
Series of 2013		
❑ F-2042A		
❑ F-2042B		
❑ F-2042B★		
❑ F-2042C		
❑ F-2042D		
❑ F-2042E		
❑ F-2042F		
❑ F-2042G		
❑ F-2042H		
❑ F-2042I		
❑ F-2042J		
❑ F-2042K		
❑ F-2042L		
❑		
❑		
❑		
Series of 2017		
❑		
❑		
❑		
❑		
❑		
❑		
❑		
❑		
❑		
❑		
❑		
❑		
❑		
❑		
❑		
❑		

LARGE-SIZE

$20 Interest-Bearing Notes of 1863

F-No. (W-No.) • Printage (rarity)	Grade	Comments
❑ F-197 (W-1920) • 822,000 (9–10)		
❑ F-197a (W-1930) • incl. above (25–28)		

$20 Demand Notes

F-No. (W-No.) • Printage (rarity)	Grade	Comments
Series of 1861		
❑ F-11 (W-1906) • est. 92,000 (8 known)		
❑ F-11 (W-1907) • 220,000 (8 known)		
❑ F-11a (W-1905) • est. 8,000 (1 known)		
❑ F-12 (W-1909) • est. 99,000 (6 known)		
❑ F-12 (W-1910) • 140,000 (6 known)		
❑ F-13 (W-1901) • est. 99,000		
❑ F-13 (W-1902) • 200,000 (4 known)		
❑ F-14 (W-1904) • est. 24,000 (1 known)		

$20 Legal Tender Notes

F-No. (W-No.) • Printage (rarity)	Grade	Comments
Series of 1862, First Obligation		
❑ F-124 (W-1962) • est. 1,050,000 (40–50)		
❑ F-124 (W-1963) • est. 1,250,000 (45–55)		
❑ F-124a (W-1961) • 100,000 (2 known)		

F-No. (W-No.) • Printage *(rarity)*	Grade	Comments
Series of 1862 and 1863, Second Obligation		
❑ F-125 (W-1964) • 800,000 *(40–45)*		
❑ F-126 (W-1965) • 920,984 *(32–38)*		
❑ F-126a (W-1966) • 225,000 *(11–13)*		
❑ F-126b (W-1968) • est. 734,000 *(155–165)*		
❑ F-126c (W-1967) • est. 66,016 *(6 known)*		
Series of 1869		
❑ F-127 (W-2000) • 3,648,000 *(185–205)*		
Series of 1875		
❑ F-128 (W-2001) • 1,250,000 *(65–70)*		
Series of 1878		
❑ F-129 (W-2002) • 1,740,000 *(210–230)*		
Series of 1880		
❑ F-130 (W-2003) • est. 360,000 *(12–14)*		
❑ F-131 (W-2004) • est. 360,000 *(24–27)*		
❑ F-132 (W-2005) • est. 776,000 *(53–57)*		
❑ F-133 (W-2006) • est. 380,000 *(27–32)*		
❑ F-134 (W-2007) • est. 668,000 *(54–58)*		
❑ F-135 (W-2008) • est. 832,000 *(62–66)*		
❑ F-136 (W-2009) • est. 1,760,000 *(135–150)*		
❑ F-137 (W-2010) • est. 1,840,000 *(90–95)*		
❑ F-138 (W-2011) • est. 956,000 *(60–65)*		
❑ F-139 (W-2012) • est. 184,000 *(20–23)*		
❑ F-140 (W-2013) • est. 1,580,000 *(95–105)*		
❑ F-141 (W-2014) • est. 2,300,000 *(135–145)*		
❑ F-142 (W-2015) • est. 1,440,000 *(120–130)*		
❑ F-143 (W-2016) • est. 1,564,000 *(90–100)*		
❑ F-144 (W-2017) • 404,000 *(48–52)*		
❑ F-145 (W-2018) • 408,000 *(70–80)*		
❑ F-146 (W-2019) • 400,000 *(55–60)*		
❑ F-146★ (W-2019★) • *(4 known)*		
❑ F-147 (W-2020) • est. 4,000,000 *(700–800)*		
❑ F-147★ (W-2020★) • *(38–47)*		
❑ F-147 (W-2020 Mule) • est. 580,000 *(50–60)*		
❑ F-147★ (W-2020 Mule★) • *(32–36)*		

$20 Compound Interest Treasury Notes of 1864

F-No. (W-No.) • Printage (rarity)	Grade	Comments
❑ F-191 (W-1950) • 822,000 (4 known)		
❑ F-191a (W-1953) • incl. above (62–66)		

$20 National Bank Notes

F-No. (W-No.) • Printage (rarity)	Grade	Comments
Original Series ("First Charter Period")		
❑ F-424 (W-2030) • (33–36)		
❑ F-427 (W-2031) • (70–80)		
❑ F-428 (W-2032) • (1 known)		
❑ F-429 (W-2033) • (20–24)		
Series of 1875 ("First Charter Period")		
❑ F-431 (W-2050) • (130–140)		
❑ F-432 (W-2051) • (45–50)		
❑ F-433 (W-2052) • (7 known)		
❑ F-434 (W-2053) • (125–135)		
❑ F-435 (W-2054) • (120–130)		
❑ F-436 (W-2055) • (3 known)		
❑ F-437 (W-2056) • (5 known)		
❑ F-438 (W-2057) • (7 known)		
❑ F-439 (W-2058) • (1 known)		
Series of 1882, Brown Back ("Second Charter Period")		
❑ F-493 (W-2070) • (145–153)		
❑ F-494 (W-2071) • (370–410)		
❑ F-495 (W-2072) • (60–65)		
❑ F-496 (W-2073) • (200–220)		
❑ F-497 (W-2074) • (90–100)		
❑ F-498 (W-2075) • (250–275)		
❑ F-499 (W-2076) • (300–350)		
❑ F-500 (W-2077) • (3 known)		
❑ F-501 (W-2078) • (230–260)		
❑ F-502 (W-2079) • (40–45)		
❑ F-503 (W-2080) • (25–28)		
❑ F-504 (W-2081) • (550–650)		
❑ F-505 (W-2082) • (5 known)		
❑ F-506 (W-2083) • (7 known)		

F-No. (W-No.) • Printage *(rarity)*	Grade	Comments
Series of 1882, Date Back ("Second Charter Period")		
❏ F-549 (W-2090) • *(23–25)*		
❏ F-550 (W-2091) • *(115–125)*		
❏ F-551 (W-2092) • *(2 known)*		
❏ F-552 (W-2093) • *(290–320)*		
❏ F-553 (W-2094) • *(31–34)*		
❏ F-554 (W-2095) • *(28–32)*		
❏ F-555 (W-2096) • *(800–900)*		
❏ F-556 (W-2097) • *(55–60)*		
❏ F-556a (W-2098) • *(1 known)*		
❏ F-557 (W-2099) • *(10–12)*		
Series of 1882, Value Back ("Second Charter Period")		
❏ F-580 (W-2100) • *(6 known)*		
❏ F-580a (W-2101) • *(4 known)*		
❏ F-580b (W-2102) • *(3 known)*		
❏ F-581 (W-2103) • *(530–550)*		
❏ F-582 (W-2104) • *(1 known)*		
❏ F-583 (W-2105) • *(42–46)*		
❏ F-584 (W-2106) • *(10–12)*		
❏ F-584a (W-2107) • *(2 known)*		
❏ F-585 (W-2108) • *(5 known)*		
Series of 1902, Red Seal ("Third Charter Period")		
❏ F-639 (W-2109) • *(800–1,000)*		
❏ F-640 (W-2110) • *(125–140)*		
❏ F-641 (W-2111) • *(100–110)*		
Series of 1902, Blue Seal, Date Back ("Third Charter Period")		
❏ F-642 (W-2112) • *(1,350–1,500)*		
❏ F-643 (W-2113) • *(250–280)*		
❏ F-644 (W-2114) • *(575–650)*		
❏ F-645 (W-2115) • *(325–350)*		
❏ F-646 (W-2116) • *(210–230)*		
❏ F-647 (W-2117) • *(35–40)*		
❏ F-648 (W-2118) • *(20–24)*		
❏ F-649 (W-2119) • *(48–52)*		
❏ F-649a (W-2120) • *(6 known)*		

F-No. (W-No.) • Printage (rarity)	Grade	Comments
Series of 1902, Blue Seal, Plain Back ("Third Charter Period")		
❏ F-650 (W-2121) • (5,500–6,000)		
❏ F-651 (W-2122) • (1,200–1,400)		
❏ F-652 (W-2123) • (2,750–3,500)		
❏ F-653 (W-2124) • (1,700–2,100)		
❏ F-654 (W-2125) • (1,400–1,600)		
❏ F-655 (W-2126) • (225–250)		
❏ F-656 (W-2127) • (220–245)		
❏ F-657 (W-2129) • (700–800)		
❏ F-658 (W-2130) • (1,700–1,900)		
❏ F-659 (W-2131) • (1,500–1,700)		
❏ F-660 (W-2132) • (450–550)		
❏ F-661 (W-2133) • (700–800)		
❏ F-662 (W-2134) • (15–17)		
❏ F-663 (W-2135) • (19–22)		
❏ F-663a (W-2136) • (2 known)		

$20 National Gold Bank Notes

F-No. (W-No.) • Printage (rarity)	Grade	Comments
Original Series		
❏ F-1152 (W-2040) • 11,248 (35–40)		
❏ F-1154 (W-2041) • 3,641 (3 known)		
❏ F-1155 (W-2044) • 5,000 (8 known)		
❏ F-1156 (W-2045) • 2,849 (8 known)		
❏ F-1158 (W-2047) • 1,600 (8 known)		
❏ F-1159 (W-2048) • 500 (2 known)		
❏ F-1159a (W-2043) • 800 (1 known)		
Series of 1875		
❏ F-1153 (W-2060) • 3,600 (7 known)		
❏ F-1155a (W-2061) • 293 (1 known)		
❏ F-1157 (W-2062) • 363 (2 known)		

$20 Silver Certificates

F-No. (W-No.) • Printage (rarity)	Grade	Comments
Series of 1878		
❏ F-305 (W-2143) • est. 19,500 (3 known)		

F-No. (W-No.) • Printage *(rarity)*	Grade	Comments
Series of 1878 *(continued)*		
❑ F-306 (W-2146) • est. 38,000 *(3 known)*		
❑ F-306b (W-2152) • est. 4,000 *(2 known)*		
❑ F-307 (W-2153) • est. 104,000 *(18–20)*		
Series of 1880, Countersigned		
❑ F-308 (W-2160) • 200,000 *(11–13)*		
Series of 1880, Not Countersigned		
❑ F-309 (W-2170) • est. 1,240,000 *(58–62)*		
❑ F-310 (W-2171) • est. 660,000 *(46–50)*		
❑ F-311 (W-2172) • est. 1,814,000 *(150–160)*		
❑ F-312 (W-2173) • 124,000 *(40–45)*		
Series of 1886		
❑ F-313 (W-2174) • 12,000 *(18–20)*		
❑ F-314 (W-2175) • 1,068,000 *(75–85)*		
❑ F-315 (W-2176) • est. 280,000 *(29–33)*		
❑ F-316 (W-2177) • est. 352,000 *(29–33)*		
Series of 1891		
❑ F-317 (W-2178) • est. 1,300,000 *(57–61)*		
❑ F-318 (W-2179) • est. 6,088,000 *(190–210)*		
❑ F-319 (W-2180) • est. 1,212,000 *(65–75)*		
❑ F-320 (W-2181) • est. 504,000 *(65–75)*		
❑ F-321 (W-2182) • est. 1,520,000 *(300–350)*		
❑ F-321★ (W-2182★) • *(5 known)*		
❑ F-322 (W-2183) • est. 220,000 *(140–180)*		
❑ F-322 (W-2184) • est. 184,000 *(incl. above)*		

$20 Treasury or Coin Notes

F-No. (W-No.) • Printage *(rarity)*	Grade	Comments
Series of 1890		
❑ F-372 (W-2190) • est. 500,000 *(70–80)*		
❑ F-373 (W-2191) • est. 84,000 *(11–13)*		
❑ F-374 (W-2192) • 708,000 *(110–120)*		
Series of 1891		
❑ F-375 (W-2193) • est. 492,000 *(200+)*		
❑ F-375a (W-2194) • est. 656,000 *(2 known)*		

$20 Gold Certificates

F-No. (W-No.) • Printage *(rarity)*	Grade	Comments
Act of March 3, 1863		
❑ F-1166b (W-2200) • est. 36,000 *(2 known)*		
❑ F-1166b (W-2202) • est. 168,000 *(4 known)*		
Series of 1882		
❑ F-1174 (W-2214) • 448,000 *(16–18)*		
❑ F-1175 (W-2110) • 14,000 *(2 known)*		
❑ F-1175a (W-2212) • 586,000 *(29–33)*		
❑ F-1176 (W-2216) • 232,000 *(21–23)*		
❑ F-1177 (W-2218) • 200,000 *(35–40)*		
❑ F-1178 (W-2220) • 16,344,000 *(525–550)*		
Series of 1905		
❑ F-1179 (W-2225) • 1,664,000 *(130–140)*		
❑ F-1180 (W-2226) • 3,012,000 *(200–220)*		
Series of 1906		
❑ F-1181 (W-2228) • 12,176,000 *(145–160)*		
❑ F-1182 (W-2229) • 6,924,000 *(115–125)*		
❑ F-1182★ (W-2229★) • *(1 known)*		
❑ F-1183 (W-2230) • 8,248,000 *(180–200)*		
❑ F-1183★ (W-2230★) • *(8 known)*		
❑ F-1184 (W-2231) • 1,480,000 *(95–115)*		
❑ F-1185 (W-2232) • 10,200,000 *(275–300)*		
❑ F-1185★ (W-2232★) • *(10–12)*		
❑ F-1186 (W-2233) • est. 8,180,000 *(310–340)*		
❑ F-1186★ (W-2233★) • *(8 known)*		
Series of 1922		
❑ F-1187 (W-2235) • est. 75,120,000 *(3,500–4,000)*		
❑ F-1187★ (W-2235★) • *(125–135)*		
❑ F-1187 (W-2235 Mule) • est. 12,000,000 *(500–650)*		
❑ F-1187★ (W-2235 Mule★) • *(16–18)*		

$20 Federal Reserve Notes

F-No. (W-No.) • Printage *(rarity)*	Grade	Comments
Series of 1914, Red Seal		
❑ F-952A (W-2240A-a) • 300,000 *(20–23)*		
❑ F-952B (W-2240A-b) • 40,000 *(3 known)*		
❑ F-953A (W-2240B-a) • 1,200,000 *(20–30)*		

F-No. (W-No.) • Printage *(rarity)*	Grade	Comments
Series of 1914, Red Seal *(continued)*		
❏ F-953B (W-2240B-b) • 1,352,000 *(95–105)*		
❏ F-954A (W-2240C-a) • 180,000 *(16–18)*		
❏ F-954B (W-2240C-b) • 180,000 *(18–20)*		
❏ F-955A (W-2240D-a) • 120,000 *(5 known)*		
❏ F-955B (W-2240D-b) • 380,000 *(33–36)*		
❏ F-956A (W-2240E-a) • 120,000 *(8 known)*		
❏ F-956B (W-2240E-b) • 64,000 *(6 known)*		
❏ F-957A (W-2240F-a) • 160,000 *(15–17)*		
❏ F-958A (W-2240G-a) • 300,000 *(54–58)*		
❏ F-958B (W-2240G-b) • 148,000 *(20–23)*		
❏ F-959A (W-2240H-a) • 180,000 *(40–45)*		
❏ F-959B (W-2240H-b) • 44,000 *(13–15)*		
❏ F-960A (W-2240I-a) • 120,000 *(21–23)*		
❏ F-960B (W-2240I-b) • 32,000 *(5 known)*		
❏ F-961A (W-2240J-a) • 120,000 *(24–27)*		
❏ F-961B (W-2240J-b) • 32,000 *(4 known)*		
❏ F-962A (W-2240K-a) • 160,000 *(30–35)*		
❏ F-963A (W-2240L-a) • 120,000 *(7 known)*		
❏ F-963B (W-2240L-b) • 140,000 *(7 known)*		
Series of 1914, Blue Seal		
❏ F-964 (W-2250A-b) • est. 4,660,000 *(65–75)*		
❏ F-964★ (W-2250A-b★) • *(3 known)*		
❏ F-965 (W-2251A-b) • est. 2,780,000 *(20–24)*		
❏ F-965★ (W-2251A-b★) • *(3 known)*		
❏ F-966 (W-2252A-b) • est. 8,476,000 *(130–145)*		
❏ F-966★ (W-2252A-b★) • *(9–10)*		
❏ F-967 (W-2253A-b) • est. 9,768,000 *(150–160)*		
❏ F-968 (W-2254B-b) • est. 16,172,000 *(120–130)*		
❏ F-968★ (W-2254B-b★) • *(3 known)*		
❏ F-969 (W-2255B-b) • est. 10,712,000 *(120–130)*		
❏ F-969★ (W-2255B-b★) • *(5 known)*		
❏ F-970 (W-2256B-b) • est. 10,908,000 *(140–150)*		
❏ F-970★ (W-2256B-b★) • *(12–14)*		

F-No. (W-No.) • Printage *(rarity)*	Grade	Comments
❑ F-971A (W-2257B-b) • est. 14,252,000 *(200–210)*		
❑ F-971A★ (W-2257B-b★) • *(19–22)*		
❑ F-971B (W-2257B-c) • est. 4,224,000 *(70–80)*		
❑ F-972 (W-2258C-b) • est. 7,740,000 *(100–110)*		
❑ F-972★ (W-2258C-b★) • *(9–10)*		
❑ F-973 (W-2259C-b) • est. 3,160,000 *(44–48)*		
❑ F-974 (W-2260C-b) • est. 7,824,000 *(100–110)*		
❑ F-974★ (W-2260C-b★) • *(16–18)*		
❑ F-975 (W-2261C-b) • est. 11,004,000 *(240–260)*		
❑ F-975★ (W-2261C-b★) • *(10–12)*		
❑ F-976 (W-2262D-b) • est. 7,560,000 *(150–160)*		
❑ F-976★ (W-2262D-b★) • *(2 known)*		
❑ F-977 (W-2263D-b) • est. 3,996,000 *(90–100)*		
❑ F-977★ (W-2263D-b★) • *(3 known)*		
❑ F-978 (W-2264D-b) • est. 6,308,000 *(120–130)*		
❑ F-978★ (W-2264D-b★) • *(14–16)*		
❑ F-979A (W-2265D-b) • est. 19,208,000 *(370–390)*		
❑ F-979A★ (W-2265D-b★) • *(10–12)*		
❑ F-979B (W-2265D-c) • est. 972,000 *(55–60)*		
❑ F-980 (W-2266E-b) • est. 4,216,000 *(55–60)*		
❑ F-980★ (W-2266E-b★) • *(2 known)*		
❑ F-981 (W-2267E-b) • est. 2,100,000 *(55–60)*		
❑ F-982 (W-2268E-b) • est. 3,040,000 *(75–85)*		
❑ F-982★ (W-2268E-b★) • *(10–12)*		
❑ F-983A (W-2269E-b) • est. 7,788,000 *(185–200)*		
❑ F-983A★ (W-2269E-b★) • *(5 known)*		
❑ F-984 (W-2270F-b) • est. 8,580,000 *(155–165)*		
❑ F-984★ (W-2270F-b★) • *(11–13)*		
❑ F-986 (W-2272F-b) • est. 3,552,000 *(115–125)*		
❑ F-986★ (W-2272F-b★) • *(5 known)*		
❑ F-987A (W-2273F-b) • est. 3,660,000 *(110–120)*		
❑ F-988 (W-2274G-b) • est. 12,812,000 *(190–210)*		
❑ F-989 (W-2275G-b) • est. 5,140,000 *(100–110)*		
❑ F-989★ (W-2275G-b★) • *(6 known)*		

F-No. (W-No.) • Printage *(rarity)*	Grade	Comments
Series of 1914, Blue Seal *(continued)*		
❑ F-990 (W-2276G-b) • est. 14,644,000 *(220–240)*		
❑ F-990★ (W-2276G-b★) • *(35–40)*		
❑ F-991A (W-2277G-b) • est. 9,928,000 *(275–300)*		
❑ F-991A★ (W-2277G-b★) • *(11–13)*		
❑ F-991B (W-2277G-c) • est. 3,488,000 *(148–155)*		
❑ F-991C (W-2277G-d) • 316,000 *(25–35)*		
❑ F-992 (W-2278H-b) • est. 5,272,000 *(130–140)*		
❑ F-992★ (W-2278H-b★) • *(8 known)*		
❑ F-993 (W-2279H-b) • est. 904,000 *(20–24)*		
❑ F-993★ (W-2279H-b★) • *(1 known)*		
❑ F-994 (W-2280H-b) • est. 3,000,000 *(95–115)*		
❑ F-994★ (W-2280H-b★) • *(18–20)*		
❑ F-995 (W-2281H-b) • est. 1,348,000 *(95–105)*		
❑ F-996 (W-2282I-b) • est. 2,828,000 *(95–115)*		
❑ F-996★ (W-2282I-b★) • *(6 known)*		
❑ F-997 (W-2283I-b) • est. 160,000 *(18–20)*		
❑ F-998 (W-2284I-b) • est. 1,764,000 *(145–160)*		
❑ F-998★ (W-2284I-b★) • *(4 known)*		
❑ F-999 (W-2285I-b) • est. 1,968,000 *(155–165)*		
❑ F-1000 (W-2286J-b) • est. 4,808,000 *(105–115)*		
❑ F-1002 (W-2288J-b) • est. 2,412,000 *(115–125)*		
❑ F-1002★ (W-2288J-b★) • *(11–13)*		
❑ F-1003 (W-2289J-b) • est. 1,800,000 *(115–125)*		
❑ F-1004 (W-2290K-b) • est. 3,212,000 *(75–85)*		
❑ F-1004★ (W-2290K-b★) • *(12–14)*		
❑ F-1005 (W-2291K-b) • est. 468,000 *(15–17)*		
❑ F-1006 (W-2292K-b) • est. 1,460,000 *(75–85)*		
❑ F-1007 (W-2293K-b) • est. 1,764,000 *(120–130)*		
❑ F-1008 (W-2294L-b) • est. 6,860,000 *(90–100)*		
❑ F-1008★ (W-2294L-b★) • *(3 known)*		
❑ F-1009 (W-2295L-b) • est. 3,220,000 *(45–50)*		
❑ F-1009★ (W-2295L-b★) • *(2 known)*		
❑ F-1010 (W-2296L-b) • est. 4,464,000 *(70–80)*		
❑ F-1010★ (W-2296L-b★) • *(8 known)*		

F-No. (W-No.) • Printage *(rarity)*	Grade	Comments
❏ F-1011A (W-2297L-b) • est. 14,668,000 *(240–260)*		
❏ F-1011A★ (W-2297L-b★) • *(16–18)*		
❏ F-1011B (W-2297L-c) • est. 4,400,000 *(110–120)*		
❏ F-1011B★ (W-2297L-c★) • *(1 known)*		
❏ F-1011C (W-2297L-d) • est. 1,884,000 *(35–40)*		

$20 Federal Reserve Bank Notes

F-No. (W-No.) • Printage *(rarity)*	Grade	Comments
Series of 1915		
❏ F-822 (W-2302F) • est. 4,000 *(5 known)*		
❏ F-822-1 (W-2304F) • est. 20,000 *(5 known)*		
❏ F-822a (W-2300F) • *(1 known)*		
❏ F-824 (W-2306G) • 80,000 *(38–47)*		
❏ F-826 (W-2312J) • 80,000 *(32–36)*		
❏ F-827 (W-2311J) • 100,000 *(36–42)*		
❏ F-828 (W-2315K) • 88,000 *(35–40)*		
❏ F-829 (W-2319K) • 4,000 *(6 known)*		
❏ F-830 (W-2317K) • 8,000 *(3 known)*		
Series of 1918		
❏ F-823 (W-2340F) • 96,000 *(50–60)*		
❏ F-825 (W-2342H) • 24,000 *(25–35)*		

SMALL-SIZE

$20 National Bank Notes

F-No. (W-No.) • Printage *(rarity)*	Grade	Comments
Series of 1929, Type 1		
❏ F-1802-1 (W-2410) • *(50,000–55,000)*		

F-No. (W-No.) • Printage *(rarity)*	Grade	Comments
Series of 1929, Type 2		
❑ F-1802-2 (W-2411) • *(13,000–14,000)*		

$20 Gold Certificates

F-No. (W-No.) • Printage *(rarity)*	Grade	Comments
Series of 1928 and 1928-A		
❑ F-2402 (W-2450) • 66,204,000		
❑ F-2402★ (W-2450★)		

$20 Federal Reserve Bank Notes

F-No. (W-No.) • Printage *(rarity)*	Grade	Comments
Series of 1929		
❑ F-1870A (W-2430A) • 972,000		
❑ F-1870A★ (W-2430A★)		
❑ F-1870B (W-2431B) • 2,568,000		
❑ F-1870B★ (W-2431B★)		
❑ F-1870C (W-2432C) • 1,008,000		
❑ F-1870C★ (W-2432C★)		
❑ F-1870D (W-2433D) • 1,020,000		
❑ F-1870D★ (W-2433D★)		
❑ F-1870E (W-2434E) • 1,632,000		
❑ F-1870E★ (W-2434E★)		
❑ F-1870F (W-2435F) • 960,000		
❑ F-1870F★ (W-2435F★)		
❑ F-1870G (W-2436G) • 2,028,000		
❑ F-1870G★ (W-2436G★)		
❑ F-1870H (W-2437H) • 444,000		
❑ F-1870H★ (W-2437H★)		
❑ F-1870I (W-2438I) • 864,000		
❑ F-1870I★ (W-2438I★)		
❑ F-1870J (W-2439J) • 612,000		
❑ F-1870J★ (W-2439J★)		
❑ F-1870K (W-2440K) • 468,000		
❑ F-1870K★ (W-2440K★)		
❑ F-1870L (W-2441L) • 888,000		
❑ F-1870L★ (W-2441L★)		

$20 Federal Reserve Notes

F-No. (W-No.) • Printage *(rarity)*	Grade	Comments
Series of 1928 and 1928-A		
❑ F-2050A (W-2500A) • 3,790,880		
❑ F-2050A★ (W-2500A★)		
❑ F-2050B (W-2500B) • 12,797,200		
❑ F-2050B★ (W-2500B★)		
❑ F-2050C (W-2500C) • 3,797,200		
❑ F-2050C★ (W-2500C★)		
❑ F-2050D (W-2500D) • 10,626,900		
❑ F-2050D★ (W-2500D★)		
❑ F-2050E (W-2500E) • 4,119,600		
❑ F-2050E★ (W-2500E★)		
❑ F-2050F (W-2500F) • 3,842,388		
❑ F-2050F★ (W-2500F★)		
❑ F-2050G (W-2500G) • 10,891,740		
❑ F-2050G★ (W-2500G★)		
❑ F-2050H (W-2500H) • 2,523,300		
❑ F-2050H★ (W-2500H★)		
❑ F-2050I (W-2500I) • 2,633,100		
❑ F-2050I★ (W-2500I★)		
❑ F-2050J (W-2500J) • 2,584,500		
❑ F-2050J★ (W-2500J★)		
❑ F-2050K (W-2500K) • 1,568,500		
❑ F-2050K★ (W-2500K★)		
❑ F-2050L (W-2500L) • 8,404,800		
❑ F-2050L★ (W-2500L★)		
❑ F-2051A (W-2501A) • 1,293,900		
❑ F-2051A★ (W-2501A★)		
❑ F-2051B (W-2501B) • 1,055,800		
❑ F-2051B★ (W-2501B★)		
❑ F-2051C (W-2501C) • 1,717,200		
❑ F-2051C★ (W-2501C★)		
❑ F-2051D (W-2501D) • 625,200		
❑ F-2051D★ (W-2501D★)		

F-No. (W-No.) • Printage *(rarity)*	Grade	Comments
Series of 1928 and 1928-A *(continued)*		
❑ F-2051E (W-2501E) • 1,534,500		
❑ F-2051E★ (W-2501E★)		
❑ F-2051F (W-2501F) • 1,442,400		
❑ F-2051F★ (W-2501F★)		
❑ F-2051G (W-2501G) • 822,000		
❑ F-2051G★ (W-2501G★)		
❑ F-2061H (W-2501H) • 573,300		
❑ F-2051H★ (W-2501H★)		
❑ F-2051J (W-2501J) • 113,900		
❑ F-2051J★ (W-2501J★)		
❑ F-2051K (W-2501K) • 1,032,000		
❑ F-2051K★ (W-2501K★)		
Series of 1928-B, Green Seal		
❑ F-2052A (W-2502A) • 7,749,636		
❑ F-2052A★ (W-2502A★)		
❑ F-2052B (W-2502B) • 19,448,436		
❑ F-2052B★ (W-2502B★)		
❑ F-2052C (W-2502C) • 8,095,548		
❑ F-2052C★ (W-2502C★)		
❑ F-2052D (W-2502D) • 11,684,196		
❑ F-2052D★ (W-2502D★)		
❑ F-2052E (W-2502E) • 4,413,900		
❑ F-2052E★ (W-2502E★)		
❑ F-2052F (W-2502F) • 2,390,240		
❑ F-2052F★ (W-2502F★)		
❑ F-2052G (W-2502G) • 17,220,276		
❑ F-2052G★ (W-2502G★)		
❑ F-2052H (W-2502H) • 3,834,600		
❑ F-2052H★ (W-2502H★)		
❑ F-2052I (W-2502I) • 3,298,920		
❑ F-2052I★ (W-2502I★)		
❑ F-2052J (W-2502J) • 4,941,252		
❑ F-2052J★ (W-2502J★)		

F-No. (W-No.) • Printage (rarity)	Grade	Comments
❏ F-2052K (W-2502K) • 2,406,060		
❏ F-2052K★ (W-2502K★)		
❏ F-2052L (W-2502L) • 9,689,124		
❏ F-2052L★ (W-2502L★)		
Series of 1928-B, Light Yellow-Green Seal		
❏ F-2052A (W-2503A) • incl. in F-2052A/W-2502A		
❏ F-2052A★ (W-2503A★)		
❏ F-2052B (W-2503B) • incl. in F-2052B/W-2502B		
❏ F-2052B★ (W-2503B★)		
❏ F-2052C (W-2503C) • incl. in F-2052C/W-2502C		
❏ F-2052C★ (W-2503C★)		
❏ F-2052D (W-2503D) • incl. in F-2052D/W-2502D		
❏ F-2052D★ (W-2503D★)		
❏ F-2052E (W-2503E) • incl. in F-2052E/W-2502E		
❏ F-2052E★ (W-2503E★)		
❏ F-2052G (W-2503G) • incl. in F-2052G/W-2502G		
❏ F-2052G★ (W-2503G★)		
❏ F-2052H (W-2503H) • incl. in F-2052H/W-2502H		
❏ F-2052H★ (W-2503H★)		
❏ F-2052I (W-2503I) • incl. in F-2052I/W-2502I		
❏ F-2052I★ (W-2503I★)		
❏ F-2052J (W-2503J) • incl. in F-2052J/W-2502J		
❏ F-2052J★ (W-2503J★)		
❏ F-2052L (W-2503L) • incl. in F-2052L/W-2502L		
❏ F-2052L★ (W-2503L★)		
Series of 1928-C		
❏ F-2053G (W-2504G) • 3,363,300		
❏ F-2053L (W-2504L) • 1,420,200		
Series of 1934, Light Yellow-Green Seal		
❏ F-2054A (W-2505A) • 37,673,068		
❏ F-2054A★ (W-2505A★)		
❏ F-2054B (W-2505B) • 37,573,264		
❏ F-2054B★ (W-2505B★)		
❏ F-2054C (W-2505C) • 53,209,968		
❏ F-2054C★ (W-2505C★)		

F-No. (W-No.) • Printage *(rarity)*	Grade	Comments
Series of 1934, Light Yellow-Green Seal *(continued)*		
❏ F-2054D (W-2505D) • 48,301,416		
❏ F-2054D★ (W-2505D★)		
❏ F-2054E (W-2505E) • 36,259,224		
❏ F-2054E★ (W-2505E★)		
❏ F-2054F (W-2505F) • 41,547,660		
❏ F-2054F★ (W-2505F★)		
❏ F-2054G (W-2505G) • 20,777,832		
❏ F-2054G★ (W-2505G★)		
❏ F-2054H (W-2505H) • 21,174,552		
❏ F-2054H★ (W-2505H★)		
❏ F-2054I (W-2505I) • 16,795,116		
❏ F-2054I★ (W-2505I★)		
❏ F-2054J (W-2505J) • 28,865,304		
❏ F-2054J★ (W-2505J★)		
❏ F-2054K (W-2505K) • 20,852,160		
❏ F-2054K★ (W-2505K★)		
❏ F-2054L (W-2505L) • 32,203,956		
❏ F-2054L★ (W-2505L★)		
Series of 1934, Green Seal		
❏ F-2054A (W-2506A) • incl. in F-2054A/W-2505A		
❏ F-2054A★ (W-2506A★)		
❏ F-2054A (W-2506A Mule)		
❏ F-2054A★ (W-2506A Mule★)		
❏ F-2054B (W-2606B) • incl. in F-2054B/W-2505B		
❏ F-2054B★ (W-2506B★)		
❏ F-2054B (W-2506B Mule)		
❏ F-2054C (W-2506C) • incl. in F-2054C/W-2505C		
❏ F-2054C★ (W-2506C★)		
❏ F-2054C (W-2506C Mule)		
❏ F-2054C★ (W-2506C Mule★)		
❏ F-2054D (W-2506D) • incl. in F-2054D/W-2505D		
❏ F-2054D★ (W-2506D★)		
❏ F-2054D (W-2506D Mule)		
❏ F-2054D★ (W-2506D Mule★)		

F-No. (W-No.) • Printage *(rarity)*	Grade	Comments
❏ F-2054E (W-2506E) • incl. in F-2054E/W-2505E		
❏ F-2054E★ (W-2506E★)		
❏ F-2054E (W-2506E Mule)		
❏ F-2054E★ (W-2506E Mule★)		
❏ F-2054F (W-2506F) • incl. in F-2054F/W-2505F		
❏ F-2054F★ (W-2506F★)		
❏ F-2054F (W-2506F Mule)		
❏ F-2054F★ (W-2506F Mule★)		
❏ F-2054G (W-2506G) • incl. in F-2054G/W-2505G		
❏ F-2054G★ (W-2506G★)		
❏ F-2054H (W-2506H) • incl. in F-2054H/W-2505H		
❏ F-2054H★ (W-2506H★)		
❏ F-2054H (W-2506H Mule)		
❏ F-2054H★ (W-2506H Mule★)		
❏ F-2054I (W-2506I) • incl. in F-2054I/W-2505I		
❏ F-2054I★ (W-2506I★)		
❏ F-2054I (W-2506I Mule)		
❏ F-2054I★ (W-2506I Mule★)		
❏ F-2054J (W-2506J) • incl. in F-2054J/W-2505J		
❏ F-2054J★ (W-2506J★)		
❏ F-2054J (W-2506J Mule)		
❏ F-2054J★ (W-2506J Mule★)		
❏ F-2054K (W-2506K) • incl. in F-2054K/W-2505K		
❏ F-2054K★ (W-2506K★)		
❏ F-2054K (W-2506K Mule)		
❏ F-2054K★ (W-2506K Mule★)		
❏ F-2054L (W-2506L) • incl. in F-2054L/W-2505L		
❏ F-2054L★ (W-2506L★)		
❏ F-2054L (W-2506L Mule)		
❏ F-2054L★ (W-2506L Mule★)		
Series of 1934 and 1934-A, Brown Seal, HAWAII Overprint		
❏ F-2304 (W-2510L) • 11,246,000		
❏ F-2304★ (W-2510L★) • 52,000		
❏ F-2304 (W-2510L Mule)		

F-No. (W-No.) • Printage *(rarity)*	Grade	Comments
Series of 1934 and 1934-A, Brown Seal, HAWAII Overprint *(continued)*		
❏ F-2304★ (W-2510L Mule★)		
❏ F-2305 (W-2520L) • incl. in F-2304/W-2510L		
❏ F-2305★ (W-2520L★) • 2,500		
❏ F-2305 (W-2520L Mule)		
❏ F-2305★ (W-2520L Mule★)		
Series of 1934-A, Green Seal		
❏ F-2055A (W-2522A) • 3,302,416		
❏ F-2055A★ (W-2522A★)		
❏ F-2055A (W-2522A Mule)		
❏ F-2055B (W-2522B) • 102,555,538		
❏ F-2055B★ (W-2522B★)		
❏ F-2055B (W-2522B Mule)		
❏ F-2055B★ (W-2522B Mule★)		
❏ F-2055C (W-2522C) • 3,371,316		
❏ F-2055C★ (W-2522C★)		
❏ F-2055D (W-2522D) • 23,475,108		
❏ F-2055D★ (W-2522D★)		
❏ F-2055D (W-2522D Mule)		
❏ F-2055D★ (W-2522D Mule★)		
❏ F-2055E (W-2522E) • 46,816,224		
❏ F-2055E★ (W-2522E★)		
❏ F-2055E (W-2522E Mule)		
❏ F-2055F (W-2522F) • 6,756,816		
❏ F-2055F★ (W-2522F★)		
❏ F-2055G (W-2522G) • 91,141,452		
❏ F-2055G★ (W-2522G★)		
❏ F-2055G (W-2522G Mule)		
❏ F-2055G★ (W-2522G Mule★)		
❏ F-2055H (W-2522H) • 3,701,568		
❏ F-2055H★ (W-2522H★)		
❏ F-2055H (W-2522H Mule)		
❏ F-2055I (W-2522I) • 1,162,500		
❏ F-2055I★ (W-2522I★)		

F-No. (W-No.) • Printage *(rarity)*	Grade	Comments
❑ F-2055I (W-2522I Mule)		
❑ F-2055J (W-2522J) • 3,221,184		
❑ F-2055J★ (W-2522J★)		
❑ F-2055J (W-2522J Mule)		
❑ F-2055K (W-2522K) • 2,531,700		
❑ F-2055K★ (W-2522K★)		
❑ F-2055K (W-2522K Mule)		
❑ F-2055L (W-2522L) • 94,454,112		
❑ F-2055L★ (W-2522L★)		
❑ F-2055L (W-2522L Mule)		
❑ F-2055L★ (W-2522L Mule★)		
Series of 1934-B		
❑ F-2056A (W-2524A) • 3,904,800		
❑ F-2056A★ (W-2524A★)		
❑ F-2056B (W-2524B) • 14,876,436		
❑ F-2056B★ (W-2524B★)		
❑ F-2056C (W-2524C) • 3,271,452		
❑ F-2056C★ (W-2524C★)		
❑ F-2056D (W-2524D) • 2,814,600		
❑ F-2056D★ (W-2524D★)		
❑ F-2056E (W-2524E) • 9,451,632		
❑ F-2056E★ (W-2524E★)		
❑ F-2056F (W-2524F) • 6,887,640		
❑ F-2056F★ (W-2524F★)		
❑ F-2056G (W-2524G) • 9,084,600		
❑ F-2056G★ (W-2524G★)		
❑ F-2056H (W-2524H) • 5,817,300		
❑ F-2056H★ (W-2524H★)		
❑ F-2056I (W-2524I) • 2,304,800		
❑ F-2056I★ (W-2524I★)		
❑ F-2056J (W-2524J) • 3,524,244		
❑ F-2056J★ (W-2524J★)		
❑ F-2056K (W-2524K) • 2,807,388		
❑ F-2056K★ (W-2524K★)		

F-No. (W-No.) • Printage *(rarity)*	Grade	Comments
Series of 1934-B *(continued)*		
❏ F-2056L (W-2524L) • 5,289,540		
❏ F-2056L★ (W-2524L★)		
Series of 1934-C, Old Back		
❏ F-2057A (W-2525A) • 7,397,352		
❏ F-2057A★ (W-2525A★)		
❏ F-2057B (W-2525B) • 18,668,148		
❏ F-2057B★ (W-2525B★)		
❏ F-2057C (W-2525C) • 11,590,752		
❏ F-2057C★ (W-2525C★)		
❏ F-2057D (W-2525D) • 17,912,424		
❏ F-2057D★ (W-2525D★)		
❏ F-2057E (W-2525E) • 22,526,568		
❏ F-2057E★ (W-2525E★)		
❏ F-2057F (W-2525F) • 18,858,876		
❏ F-2057F★ (W-2525F★)		
❏ F-2057G (W-2525G) • 26,031,660		
❏ F-2057G★ (W-2525G★)		
❏ F-2057H (W-2525H) • 13,276,984		
❏ F-2057H★ (W-2525H★)		
❏ F-2057I (W-2525I) • 3,490,200		
❏ F-2057I★ (W-2525I★)		
❏ F-2057J (W-2525J) • 9,675,468		
❏ F-2057J★ (W-2525J★)		
❏ F-2057K (W-2525K) • 10,205,364		
❏ F-2057K★ (W-2525K★)		
❏ F-2057L (W-2525L) • 20,580,000		
❏ F-2057L★ (W-2525L★)		
Series of 1934-C, New Back		
❏ F-2057A (W-2526A) • incl. in F-2057A/W-2525A		
❏ F-2057A★ (W-2526A★)		
❏ F-2057B (W-2526B) • incl. in F-2057B/W-2525B		
❏ F-2057B★ (W-2526B★)		
❏ F-2057C (W-2526C) • incl. in F-2057C/W-2525C		
❏ F-2057C★ (W-2526C★)		

F-No. (W-No.) • Printage *(rarity)*	Grade	Comments
❑ F-2057D (W-2526D) • incl. in F-2057D/W-2525D		
❑ F-2057D★ (W-2526D★)		
❑ F-2057E (W-2526E) • incl. in F-2057E/W-2525E		
❑ F-2057E★ (W-2526E★)		
❑ F-2057F (W-2526F) • incl. in F-2057F/W-2525F		
❑ F-2057F★ (W-2526F★)		
❑ F-2057G (W-2526G) • incl. in F-2057G/W-2525G		
❑ F-2057G★ (W-2526G★)		
❑ F-2057H (W-2526H) • incl. in F-2057H/W-2525H		
❑ F-2057H★ (W-2526H★)		
❑ F-2057I (W-2526I) • incl. in F-2057I/W-2525I		
❑ F-2057I★ (W-2526I★)		
❑ F-2057J (W-2526J) • incl. in F-2057J/W-2525J		
❑ F-2057J★ (W-2526J★)		
❑ F-2057K (W-2526K) • incl. in F-2057K/W-2525K		
❑ F-2057K★ (W-2526K★)		
❑ F-2057L (W-2526L) • incl. in F-2057L/W-2525L		
❑ F-2057L★ (W-2526L★)		

Series of 1934-D, Wide Back

	Grade	Comments
❑ F-2058A (W-2527A) • 4,520,000		
❑ F-2058A★ (W-2527A★)		
❑ F-2058B (W-2527B) • 27,894,260		
❑ F-2058B★ (W-2527B★)		
❑ F-2058C (W-2527C) • 6,022,428		
❑ F-2058C★ (W-2527C★)		
❑ F-2058D (W-2527D) • 8,981,688		
❑ F-2058D★ (W-2527D★)		
❑ F-2058E (W-2527E) • 17,055,984		
❑ F-2058E★ (W-2527E★)		
❑ F-2058F (W-2527F) • 7,495,440		
❑ F-2058F★ (W-2527F★)		
❑ F-2058G (W-2527G) • 15,187,596		
❑ F-2058G★ (W-2527G★)		
❑ F-2058H (W-2527H) • 5,923,248		

F-No. (W-No.) • Printage *(rarity)*	Grade	Comments
Series of 1934-D, Wide Back *(continued)*		
❏ F-2058H★ (W-2527H★)		
❏ F-2058I (W-2527I) • 2,422,416		
❏ F-2058J (W-2527J) • 4,211,904		
❏ F-2058J★ (W-2527J★)		
❏ F-2058K (W-2527K) • 3,707,364		
❏ F-2058L (W-2527L) • 12,015,228		
❏ F-2058L★ (W-2527L★)		
Series of 1934-D, Narrow Back		
❏ F-2058A★ (W-2529A★)		
❏ F-2058B (W-2529B) • incl. in F-2058B/W-2527B		
❏ F-2058C (W-2529C) • incl. in F-2058C/W-2527C		
❏ F-2058D (W-2529D) • incl. in F-2058D/W-2527D		
❏ F-2058E (W-2529E) • incl. in F-2058E/W-2527E		
❏ F-2058F (W-2529F) • incl. in F-2058F/W-2527F		
❏ F-2058G (W-2529G) • incl. in F-2058G/W-2527G		
❏ F-2058H (W-2529H) • incl. in F-2058H/W-2527H		
❏ F-2058I (W-2529I) • incl. in F-2058I/W-2527I		
❏ F-2058J (W-2529J) • incl. in F-2058J/W-2527J		
❏ F-2058K (W-2529K) • incl. in F-2058K/W-2527K		
❏ F-2058L (W-2529L) • incl. in F-2058L/W-2527L		
Series of 1950–1950-E		
❏ F-2059A (W-2530A) • 23,184,000		
❏ F-2059A★ (W-2530A★)		
❏ F-2059B (W-2530B) • 80,064,000		
❏ F-2059B★ (W-2530B★)		
❏ F-2059C (W-2530C) • 29,520,000		
❏ F-2059C★ (W-2530C★)		
❏ F-2059D (W-2530D) • 51,120,000		
❏ F-2059D★ (W-2530D★)		
❏ F-2059E (W-2530E) • 67,536,000		
❏ F-2059E★ (W-2530E★)		
❏ F-2059F (W-2530F) • 39,312,000		
❏ F-2059F★ (W-2530F★)		
❏ F-2059G (W-2530G) • 70,464,000		

F-No. (W-No.) • Printage *(rarity)*	Grade	Comments
❑ F-2059G★ (W-2530G★)		
❑ F-2059H (W-2530H) • 27,352,000		
❑ F-2059H★ (W-2530H★)		
❑ F-2059I (W-2530I) • 9,216,000		
❑ F-2059I★ (W-2530I★)		
❑ F-2059J (W-2530J) • 22,752,000		
❑ F-2059J★ (W-2530J★)		
❑ F-2059K (W-2530K) • 22,656,000		
❑ F-2059K★ (W-2530K★)		
❑ F-2059L (W-2530L) • 70,272,000		
❑ F-2059L★ (W-2530L★)		
❑ F-2060A (W-2531A) • 19,656,000		
❑ F-2060A★ (W-2531A★)		
❑ F-2060B (W-2531B) • 82,568,000		
❑ F-2060B★ (W-2531B★)		
❑ F-2060C (W-2531C) • 16,560,000		
❑ F-2060C★ (W-2531C★)		
❑ F-2060D (W-2531D) • 50,320,000		
❑ F-2060D★ (W-2531D★)		
❑ F-2060E (W-2531E) • 69,544,000		
❑ F-2060E★ (W-2531E★)		
❑ F-2060F (W-2531F) • 27,648,000		
❑ F-2060F★ (W-2531F★)		
❑ F-2060G (W-2531G) • 73,720,000		
❑ F-2060G★ (W-2531G★)		
❑ F-2060H (W-2531H) • 22,680,000		
❑ F-2060H★ (W-2531H★)		
❑ F-2060I (W-2531I) • 5,544,000		
❑ F-2060I★ (W-2531I★)		
❑ F-2060J (W-2531J) • 22,968,000		
❑ F-2060J★ (W-2531J★)		
❑ F-2060K (W-2531K) • 10,728,000		
❑ F-2060K★ (W-2531K★)		
❑ F-2060L (W-2531L) • 85,528,000		

F-No. (W-No.) • Printage *(rarity)*	Grade	Comments
Series of 1950–1950-E *(continued)*		
❑ F-2060L★ (W-2531L★)		
❑ F-2061A (W-2532A) • 5,040,000		
❑ F-2061A★ (W-2532A★)		
❑ F-2061B (W-2532B) • 49,960,000		
❑ F-2061B★ (W-2532B★)		
❑ F-2061C (W-2532C) • 7,920,000		
❑ F-2061C★ (W-2532C★)		
❑ F-2061D (W-2532D) • 38,160,000		
❑ F-2061D★ (W-2532D★)		
❑ F-2061E (W-2532E) • 42,120,000		
❑ F-2061E★ (W-2532E★)		
❑ F-2061F (W-2532F) • 40,240,000		
❑ F-2061F★ (W-2532F★)		
❑ F-2061G (W-2532G) • 80,560,000		
❑ F-2061G★ (W-2532G★)		
❑ F-2061H (W-2532H) • 19,440,000		
❑ F-2061H★ (W-2532H★)		
❑ F-2061I (W-2532I) • 12,240,000		
❑ F-2061I★ (W-2532I★)		
❑ F-2061J (W-2532J) • 28,440,000		
❑ F-2061J★ (W-2532J★)		
❑ F-2061K (W-2532K) • 11,880,000		
❑ F-2061K★ (W-2532K★)		
❑ F-2061L (W-2532L) • 51,040,000		
❑ F-2061L★ (W-2532L★)		
❑ F-2062A (W-2533A) • 7,200,000		
❑ F-2062A★ (W-2533A★)		
❑ F-2062B (W-2533B) • 43,200,000		
❑ F-2062B★ (W-2533B★)		
❑ F-2062C (W-2533C) • 7,560,000		
❑ F-2062C★ (W-2533C★)		
❑ F-2062D (W-2533D) • 28,440,000		
❑ F-2062D★ (W-2533D★)		

F-No. (W-No.) • Printage *(rarity)*	Grade	Comments
❑ F-2062E (W-2533E) • 37,000,000		
❑ F-2062E★ (W-2533E★)		
❑ F-2062F (W-2533F) • 19,080,000		
❑ F-2062F★ (W-2533F★)		
❑ F-2062G (W-2533G) • 29,160,000		
❑ F-2062G★ (W-2533G★)		
❑ F-2062H (W-2533H) • 12,960,000		
❑ F-2062H★ (W-2533H★)		
❑ F-2062I (W-2533I) • 6,480,000		
❑ F-2062I★ (W-2533I★)		
❑ F-2062J (W-2533J) • 18,360,000		
❑ F-2062K (W-2533K) • 9,000,000		
❑ F-2062K★ (W-2533K★)		
❑ F-2062L (W-2533L) • 45,360,000		
❑ F-2062L★ (W-2533L★)		
❑ F-2063A (W-2534A) • 9,320,000		
❑ F-2063A★ (W-2534A★)		
❑ F-2063B (W-2534B) • 64,280,000		
❑ F-2063B★ (W-2534B★)		
❑ F-2063C (W-2534C) • 5,400,000		
❑ F-2063C★ (W-2534C★)		
❑ F-2063D (W-2534D) • 23,760,000		
❑ F-2063D★ (W-2534D★)		
❑ F-2063E (W-2534E) • 30,240,000		
❑ F-2063E★ (W-2534E★)		
❑ F-2063F (W-2534F) • 22,680,000		
❑ F-2063F★ (W-2534F★)		
❑ F-2063G (W-2534G) • 67,960,000		
❑ F-2063G★ (W-2534G★)		
❑ F-2063H (W-2534H) • 6,120,000		
❑ F-2063H★ (W-2534H★)		
❑ F-2063I (W-2534I) • 3,240,000		
❑ F-2063I★ (W-2534I★)		
❑ F-2063J (W-2534J) • 8,200,000		

F-No. (W-No.) • Printage *(rarity)*	Grade	Comments
Series of 1950–1950-E *(continued)*		
❑ F-2063J★ (W-2534J★)		
❑ F-2063K (W-2534K) • 6,480,000		
❑ F-2063K★ (W-2534K★)		
❑ F-2063L (W-2534L) • 69,400,000		
❑ F-2063L★ (W-2534L★)		
❑ F-2064B (W-2535B) • 8,640,000		
❑ F-2064B★ (W-2535B★)		
❑ F-2064G (W-2535G) • 9,360,000		
❑ F-2064G★ (W-2535G★)		
❑ F-2064L (W-2535L) • 8,640,000		
❑ F-2064L★ (W-2535L★)		
Series of 1963 and 1963-A		
❑ F-2065A (W-2536A) • 2,560,000		
❑ F-2065A★ (W-2536A★)		
❑ F-2065B (W-2536B) • 16,640,000		
❑ F-2065B★ (W-2536B★)		
❑ F-2065D (W-2536D) • 7,680,000		
❑ F-2065D★ (W-2536D★)		
❑ F-2065E (W-2536E) • 4,480,000		
❑ F-2065E★ (W-2536E★)		
❑ F-2065F (W-2536F) • 10,240,000		
❑ F-2065F★ (W-2536F★)		
❑ F-2065G (W-2536G) • 2,560,000		
❑ F-2065G★ (W-2536G★)		
❑ F-2065H (W-2536H) • 3,200,000		
❑ F-2065H★ (W-2536H★)		
❑ F-2065J (W-2536J) • 3,840,000		
❑ F-2065J★ (W-2536J★)		
❑ F-2065K (W-2536K) • 2,560,000		
❑ F-2065K★ (W-2536K★)		
❑ F-2065L (W-2536L) • 7,040,000		
❑ F-2065L★ (W-2536L★)		
❑ F-2066A (W-2537A) • 32,680,000		

F-No. (W-No.) • Printage *(rarity)*	Grade	Comments
❏ F-2066A★ (W-2537A★) • 1,280,000		
❏ F-2066B (W-2537B) • 93,600,000		
❏ F-2066B★ (W-2537B★) • 3,840,000		
❏ F-2066C (W-2537C) • 17,920,000		
❏ F-2066C★ (W-2537C★) • 640,000		
❏ F-2066D (W-2537D) • 68,480,000		
❏ F-2066D★ (W-2537D★) • 2,560,000		
❏ F-2066E (W-2537E) • 128,800,000		
❏ F-2066E★ (W-2537E★) • 5,760,000		
❏ F-2066F (W-2537F) • 42,880,000		
❏ F-2066F★ (W-2537F★) • 1,920,000		
❏ F-2066G (W-2537G) • 156,320,000		
❏ F-2066G★ (W-2537G★) • 7,040,000		
❏ F-2066H (W-2537H) • 34,560,000		
❏ F-2066H★ (W-2537H★) • 1,920,000		
❏ F-2066I (W-2537I) • 10,240,000		
❏ F-2066I★ (W-2537I★) • 640,000		
❏ F-2066J (W-2537J) • 37,120,000		
❏ F-2066J★ (W-2537J★) • 1,920,000		
❏ F-2066K (W-2537K) • 38,400,000		
❏ F-2066K★ (W-2537K★) • 1,280,000		
❏ F-2066L (W-2537L) • 169,120,000		
❏ F-2066L★ (W-2537L★) • 8,320,000		

Series of 1969–1969-C

F-No. (W-No.) • Printage *(rarity)*	Grade	Comments
❏ F-2067A (W-2538A) • 19,200,000		
❏ F-2067A★ (W-2538A★) • 1,280,000		
❏ F-2067B (W-2538B) • 106,400,000		
❏ F-2067B★ (W-2538B★) • 5,106,000		
❏ F-2067C (W-2538C) • 10,880,000		
❏ F-2067C★ (W-2538C★) • 1,280,000		
❏ F-2067D (W-2538D) • 60,160,000		
❏ F-2067D★ (W-2538D★) • 2,560,000		
❏ F-2067E (W-2538E) • 66,560,000		
❏ F-2067E★ (W-2538E★) • 2,560,000		

F-No. (W-No.) • Printage *(rarity)*	Grade	Comments
Series of 1969–1969-C *(continued)*		
❏ F-2067F (W-2538F) • 36,480,000		
❏ F-2067F★ (W-2538F★) • 1,280,000		
❏ F-2067G (W-2538G) • 107,680,000		
❏ F-2067G★ (W-2538G★) • 3,200,000		
❏ F-2067H (W-2538H) • 19,200,000		
❏ F-2067H★ (W-2538H★) • 640,000		
❏ F-2067I (W-2538I) • 12,160,000		
❏ F-2067I★ (W-2538I★) • 640,000		
❏ F-2067J (W-2538J) • 39,040,000		
❏ F-2067J★ (W-2538J★) • 1,280,000		
❏ F-2067K (W-2538K) • 25,600,000		
❏ F-2067K★ (W-2538K★) • 640,000		
❏ F-2067L (W-2538L) • 103,840,000		
❏ F-2067L★ (W-2538L★) • 5,120,000		
❏ F-2068A (W-2539A) • 13,440,000		
❏ F-2068B (W-2539B) • 69,760,000		
❏ F-2068B★ (W-2539B★) • 2,460,000		
❏ F-2068C (W-2539C) • 13,440,000		
❏ F-2068D (W-2539D) • 29,440,000		
❏ F-2068D★ (W-2539D★) • 640,000		
❏ F-2068E (W-2539E) • 42,400,000		
❏ F-2068E★ (W-2539E★) • 1,920,000		
❏ F-2068F (W-2539F) • 13,440,000		
❏ F-2068G (W-2539G) • 81,640,000		
❏ F-2068G★ (W-2539G★) • 1,920,000		
❏ F-2068H (W-2539H) • 14,080,000		
❏ F-2068H★ (W-2539H★) • 640,000		
❏ F-2068I (W-2539I) • 7,040,000		
❏ F-2068J (W-2539J) • 16,040,000		
❏ F-2068K (W-2539K) • 14,720,000		
❏ F-2068K★ (W-2539K★) • 640,000		
❏ F-2068L (W-2539L) • 50,560,000		
❏ F-2068L★ (W-2539L★) • 1,280,000		

F-No. (W-No.) • Printage *(rarity)*	Grade	Comments
❑ F-2069B (W-2540B) • 39,200,000		
❑ F-2069B★ (W-2540B★) • 480,000		
❑ F-2069D (W-2540D) • 6,400,000		
❑ F-2069E (W-2540E) • 27,520,000		
❑ F-2069F (W-2540F) • 14,080,000		
❑ F-2069F★ (W-2540F★) • 640,000		
❑ F-2069G (W-2540G) • 14,240,000		
❑ F-2069G★ (W-2540G★) • 1,112,000		
❑ F-2069H (W-2540H) • 5,120,000		
❑ F-2069I (W-2540I) • 2,560,000		
❑ F-2069J (W-2540J) • 3,840,000		
❑ F-2069J★ (W-2540J★) • 640,000		
❑ F-2069K (W-2540K) • 12,160,000		
❑ F-2069L (W-2540L) • 26,000,000		
❑ F-2069L★ (W-2540L★) • 640,000		
❑ F-2070A (W-2541A) • 17,280,000		
❑ F-2070A★ (W-2541A★) • 640,000		
❑ F-2070B (W-2541B) • 135,200,000		
❑ F-2070B★ (W-2541B★) • 1,640,000		
❑ F-2070C (W-2541C) • 40,960,000		
❑ F-2070C★ (W-2541C★) • 640,000		
❑ F-2070D (W-2541D) • 57,760,000		
❑ F-2070D★ (W-2541D★) • 480,000		
❑ F-2070E (W-2541E) • 80,160,000		
❑ F-2070E★ (W-2541E★) • 1,920,000		
❑ F-2070F (W-2541F) • 35,840,000		
❑ F-2070F★ (W-2541F★) • 640,000		
❑ F-2070G (W-2541G) • 78,720,000		
❑ F-2070G★ (W-2541G★) • 640,000		
❑ F-2070H (W-2541H) • 33,920,000		
❑ F-2070H★ (W-2541H★) • 640,000		
❑ F-2070I (W-2541I) • 14,080,000		
❑ F-2070I★ (W-2541I★) • 640,000		
❑ F-2070J (W-2541J) • 32,000,000		

F-No. (W-No.) • Printage *(rarity)*	Grade	Comments
Series of 1969–1969-C *(continued)*		
❏ F-2070J★ (W-2541J★) • 640,000		
❏ F-2070K (W-2541K) • 31,360,000		
❏ F-2070K★ (W-2541K★) • 1,920,000		
❏ F-2070L (W-2541L) • 82,080,000		
❏ F-2070L★ (W-2541L★) • 1,120,000		
Series of 1974		
❏ F-2071A (W-2542A) • 56,960,000		
❏ F-2071A★ (W-2542A★) • 768,000		
❏ F-2071B (W-2542B) • 296,640,000		
❏ F-2071B★ (W-2542B★) • 7,616,000		
❏ F-2071C (W-2542C) • 59,680,000		
❏ F-2071C★ (W-2542C★) • 1,760,000		
❏ F-2071D (W-2542D) • 148,000,000		
❏ F-2071D★ (W-2542D★) • 3,296,000		
❏ F-2071E (W-2542E) • 149,920,000		
❏ F-2071E★ (W-2542E★) • 3,040,000		
❏ F-2071F (W-2542F) • 53,280,000		
❏ F-2071F★ (W-2542F★) • 480,000		
❏ F-2071G (W-2542G) • 249,920,000		
❏ F-2071G★ (W-2542G★) • 4,608,000		
❏ F-2071H (W-2542H) • 73,120,000		
❏ F-2071H★ (W-2542H★) • 1,120,000		
❏ F-2071I (W-2542I) • 39,040,000		
❏ F-2071I★ (W-2542I★) • 1,280,000		
❏ F-2071J (W-2542J) • 74,400,000		
❏ F-2071J★ (W-2542J★) • 736,000		
❏ F-2071K (W-2542K) • 68,640,000		
❏ F-2071K★ (W-2542K★) • 608,000		
❏ F-2071L (W-2542L) • 128,800,000		
❏ F-2071L★ (W-2542L★) • 4,320,000		
Series of 1977		
❏ F-2072A (W-2543A) • 94,720,000		
❏ F-2072A★ (W-2543A★) • 2,688,000		
❏ F-2072B (W-2543B) • 569,600,000		

F-No. (W-No.) • Printage *(rarity)*	Grade	Comments
❑ F-2072B★ (W-2543B★) • 12,416,000		
❑ F-2072C (W-2543C) • 117,760,000		
❑ F-2072C★ (W-2543C★) • 2,176,000		
❑ F-2072D (W-2543D) • 189,440,000		
❑ F-2072D★ (W-2543D★) • 5,632,000		
❑ F-2072E (W-2543E) • 257,280,000		
❑ F-2072E★ (W-2543E★) • 6,272,000		
❑ F-2072F (W-2543F) • 70,400,000		
❑ F-2072F★ (W-2543F★) • 2,698,000		
❑ F-2072G (W-2543G) • 358,400,000		
❑ F-2072G★ (W-2543G★) • 7,552,000		
❑ F-2072H (W-2543H) • 98,560,000		
❑ F-2072H★ (W-2543H★) • 1,792,000		
❑ F-2072I (W-2543I) • 15,360,000		
❑ F-2072I★ (W-2543I★) • 512,000		
❑ F-2072J (W-2543J) • 148,480,000		
❑ F-2072J★ (W-2543J★) • 4,864,000		
❑ F-2072K (W-2543K) • 163,840,000		
❑ F-2072K★ (W-2543K★) • 6,656,000		
❑ F-2072L (W-2543L) • 263,680,000		
❑ F-2072L★ (W-2543L★) • 6,528,000		

Series of 1981 and 1981-A

F-No. (W-No.) • Printage *(rarity)*	Grade	Comments
❑ F-2073A (W-2544A) • 191,360,000		
❑ F-2073A★ (W-2544A★) • 1,024,000		
❑ F-2073B (W-2544B) • 559,360,000		
❑ F-2073B★ (W-2544B★) • 5,312,000		
❑ F-2073C (W-2544C) • 146,560,000		
❑ F-2073C★ (W-2544C★) • 1,280,000		
❑ F-2073D (W-2544D) • 146,560,000		
❑ F-2073D★ (W-2544D★) • 1,280,000		
❑ F-2073E (W-2544E) • 296,320,000		
❑ F-2073E★ (W-2544E★) • 1,280,000		
❑ F-2073F (W-2544F) • 93,440,000		
❑ F-2073F★ (W-2544F★) • 3,200,000		

F-No. (W-No.) • Printage *(rarity)*	Grade	Comments
Series of 1981 and 1981-A *(continued)*		
❑ F-2073G (W-2544G) • 361,600,000		
❑ F-2073G★ (W-2544G★) • 2,688,000		
❑ F-2073H (W-2544H) • 76,160,000		
❑ F-2073H★ (W-2544H★) • 1,536,000		
❑ F-2073I (W-2544I) • 23,040,000		
❑ F-2073I★ (W-2544I★) • 256,000		
❑ F-2073J (W-2544J) • 147,840,000		
❑ F-2073J★ (W-2544J★) • 1,280,000		
❑ F-2073K (W-2544K) • 95,360,000		
❑ F-2073K★ (W-2544K★) • 896,000		
❑ F-2073L (W-2544L) • 404,480,000		
❑ F-2073L★ (W-2544L★) • 1,424,000		
❑ F-2074A (W-2545A) • 156,800,000		
❑ F-2074B (W-2545B) • 352,000,000		
❑ F-2074C (W-2545C) • 57,600,000		
❑ F-2074D (W-2545D) • 160,000,000		
❑ F-2074D★ (W-2545D★) • 3,840,000		
❑ F-2074E (W-2545E) • 214,400,000		
❑ F-2074F (W-2545F) • 140,800,000		
❑ F-2074F★ (W-2545F★) • 3,200,000		
❑ F-2074G (W-2545G) • 211,200,000		
❑ F-2074H (W-2545H) • 73,600,000		
❑ F-2074I (W-2545I) • 19,200,000		
❑ F-2074J (W-2545J) • 86,400,000		
❑ F-2074K (W-2545K) • 99,200,000		
❑ F-2074L (W-2545L) • 457,600,000		
❑ F-2074L★ (W-2545L★) • 6,400,000		
Series of 1985		
❑ F-2075A (W-2546A) • 416,000,000		
❑ F-2075A★ (W-2546A★) • 3,200,000		
❑ F-2075B (W-2546B) • 1,728,000,000		
❑ F-2075B★ (W-2546B★) • 5,760,000		
❑ F-2075C (W-2546C) • 224,000,000		

F-No. (W-No.) • Printage (rarity)	Grade	Comments
❑ F-2075C★ (W-2546C★) • 6,400,000		
❑ F-2075D (W-2546D) • 585,600,000		
❑ F-2075D★ (W-2546D★) • 6,400,000		
❑ F-2075E (W-2546E) • 864,000,000		
❑ F-2075E★ (W-2546E★) • 6,400,000		
❑ F-2075F (W-2546F) • 313,600,000		
❑ F-2075G (W-2546G) • 729,600,000		
❑ F-2075G★ (W-2546G★) • 5,760,000		
❑ F-2075H (W-2546H) • 203,400,000		
❑ F-2075I (W-2546I) • 112,000,000		
❑ F-2075J (W-2546J) • 204,800,000		
❑ F-2075J★ (W-2546J★) • 3,200,000		
❑ F-2075K (W-2546K) • 192,000,000		
❑ F-2075K★ (W-2546K★) • 3,200,000		
❑ F-2075L (W-2546L) • 1,129,600,000		
❑ F-2075L★ (W-2546L★) • 3,200,000		
Series of 1988-A		
❑ F-2076A (W-2547A) • 313,600,000		
❑ F-2076B (W-2547B) • 979,200,000		
❑ F-2076B★ (W-2547B★) • 6,560,000		
❑ F-2076C (W-2547C) • 96,000,000		
❑ F-2076C★ (W-2547C★) • 3,200,000		
❑ F-2076D (W-2547D) • 307,200,000		
❑ F-2076E (W-2547E) • 281,600,000		
❑ F-2076F (W-2547F) • 288,000,000		
❑ F-2076F★ (W-2547F★) • 3,200,000		
❑ F-2076G (W-2547G) • 563,200,000		
❑ F-2076G★ (W-2547G★) • 3,200,000		
❑ F-2076H (W-2547H) • 108,800,000		
❑ F-2076I (W-2547I) • 25,600,000		
❑ F-2076J (W-2547J) • 137,200,000		
❑ F-2076K (W-2547K) • 51,200,000		
❑ F-2076K★ (W-2547K★) • 3,200,000		
❑ F-2076L (W-2547L) • 729,600,000		

F-No. (W-No.) • Printage (rarity)	Grade	Comments
Series of 1990		
❑ F-2077A (W-2548A) • 345,600,000		
❑ F-2077A★ (W-2548A★) • 3,200,000		
❑ F-2077B (W-2548B) • 1,446,400,000		
❑ F-2077B★ (W-2548B★) • 16,640,000		
❑ F-2077C (W-2548C) • 96,000,000		
❑ F-2077D (W-2548D) • 281,600,000		
❑ F-2077D★ (W-2548D★) • 3,200,000		
❑ F-2077E (W-2548E) • 307,200,000		
❑ F-2077E★ (W-2548E★) • 3,200,000		
❑ F-2077F (W-2548F) • 460,800,000		
❑ F-2077G (W-2548G) • 652,800,000		
❑ F-2077H (W-2548H) • 172,800,000		
❑ F-2077H★ (W-2548H★) • 3,200,000		
❑ F-2077I (W-2548I) • 70,400,000		
❑ F-2077J (W-2548J) • 83,200,000		
❑ F-2077K (W-2548K) • 25,600,000		
❑ F-2077L (W-2548L) • 416,000,000		
❑ F-2078F★ (W-2549F★) • 1,280,000		
❑ F-2078G★ (W-2549G★) • 13,400,000		
❑ F-2078I★ (W-2549I★) • 5,120,000		
❑ F-2078L (W-2549L) • incl. in F-2077L/W-2548L		
Series of 1993		
❑ F-2079A (W-2550A) • 288,000,000		
❑ F-2079A★ (W-2550A★) • 2,560,000		
❑ F-2079B (W-2550B) • 640,000,000		
❑ F-2079B★ (W-2550B★) • 4,920,000		
❑ F-2079C (W-2550C) • 147,200,000		
❑ F-2079D (W-2550D) • 329,600,000		
❑ F-2079D★ (W-2550D★) • 1,920,000		
❑ F-2079E (W-2550E) • 656,000,000		
❑ F-2079E★ (W-2550E★) • 8,960,000		
❑ F-2079F (W-2550F) • 300,800,000		
❑ F-2079H (W-2550H) • 19,200,000		

F-No. (W-No.) • Printage *(rarity)*	Grade	Comments
❑ F-2080F (W-2551F) • 51,200,000		
❑ F-2080F★ (W-2551F★) • 3,200,000		
❑ F-2080G (W-2551G) • 390,400,000		
❑ F-2080H (W-2551H) • 166,400,000		
❑ F-2080J (W-2551J) • 102,400,000		
❑ F-2080L (W-2551L) • 806,400,000		
❑ F-2080L★ (W-2551L★) • 7,680,000		
Series of 1995		
❑ F-2081B (W-2552B) • 403,200,000		
❑ F-2081B★ (W-2552B★) • 5,760,000		
❑ F-2081C (W-2552C) • 70,400,000		
❑ F-2081D (W-2552D) • 140,800,000		
❑ F-2081D★ (W-2552D★) • 640,000		
❑ F-2081E (W-2552E) • 166,400,000		
❑ F-2082F (W-2553F) • 307,200,000		
❑ F-2082F★ (W-2553F★) • 3,200,000		
❑ F-2082G (W-2553G) • 492,800,000		
❑ F-2082H (W-2553H) • 140,800,000		
❑ F-2082I (W-2553I) • 44,800,000		
❑ F-2082J (W-2553J) • 230,400,000		
❑ F-2082K (W-2553K) • 249,600,000		
❑ F-2082L (W-2553L) • 614,400,000		
Series of 1996		
❑ F-2083A (W-2554A) • 883,200,000		
❑ F-2083A★ (W-2554A★) • 10,880,000		
❑ F-2083B (W-2554B) • 896,000,000		
❑ F-2083B★ (W-2554B★) • 3,200,000		
❑ F-2083C (W-2554C) • 506,400,000		
❑ F-2083C★ (W-2554C★) • 364,000,000		
❑ F-2083D (W-2554D) • 483,200,000		
❑ F-2083D★ (W-2554D★)		
❑ F-2083E (W-2554E) • 925,600,000		
❑ F-2083F (W-2554F)		
❑ F-2084E (W-2555E) • 243,200,000		

F-No. (W-No.) • Printage *(rarity)*	Grade	Comments
Series of 1996 *(continued)*		
❏ F-2084E★ (W-2555E★) • 3,200,000		
❏ F-2084F (W-2555F) • 925,600,000		
❏ F-2084F★ (W-2555F★) • 3,200,000		
❏ F-2084G (W-2555G) • 1,151,200,000		
❏ F-2084G★ (W-2555G★) • 12,800,000		
❏ F-2084H (W-2555H) • 257,600,000		
❏ F-2084H★ (W-2555H★) • 640,000		
❏ F-2084I (W-2555I) • 112,800,000		
❏ F-2084J (W-2555J) • 276,800,000		
❏ F-2084K (W-2555K) • 276,800,000		
❏ F-2084L (W-2555L) • 457,600,000		
❏ F-2084L★ (W-2555L★) • 7,040,000		
Series of 1999		
❏ F-2085A (W-2556A) • 57,600,000		
❏ F-2085A★ (W-2556A★) • 1,920,000		
❏ F-2085B (W-2556B) • 608,000,000		
❏ F-2085B★ (W-2556B★) • 1,920,000		
❏ F-2085C (W-2556C) • 192,000,000		
❏ F-2085D (W-2556D) • 268,800,000		
❏ F-2085D★ (W-2556D★) • 5,760,000		
❏ F-2085E (W-2556E) • 492,800,000		
❏ F-2086B★ (W-2557B★) • 3,200,000		
❏ F-2086D (W-2557D) • 12,800,000		
❏ F-2086F (W-2557F) • 409,600,000		
❏ F-2086G (W-2557G) • 704,000,000		
❏ F-2086G★ (W-2557G★) • 7,040,000		
❏ F-2086H (W-2557H) • 102,400,000		
❏ F-2086I (W-2557I) • 25,600,000		
❏ F-2086J (W-2557J) • 70,400,000		
❏ F-2086L (W-2557L) • 32,000,000		
❏ F-2086L★ (W-2557L★) • 3,200,000		
Series of 2001		
❏ F-2087B (W-2558B) • 403,200,000		
❏ F-2087B★ (W-2558B★) • 320,000		

F-No. (W-No.) • Printage *(rarity)*	Grade	Comments
❑ F-2087D (W-2558D) • 83,200,000		
❑ F-2087E (W-2558E) • 140,800,000		
❑ F-2088B (W-2559B) • 249,600,000		
❑ F-2088E (W-2559E) • 153,600,000		
❑ F-2088F (W-2559F) • 313,600,000		
❑ F-2088G (W-2559G) • 224,000,000		
❑ F-2088G★ (W-2559G★) • 3,200,000		
❑ F-2088H (W-2559H) • 44,800,000		
❑ F-2088I (W-2559I) • 57,600,000		
❑ F-2088J (W-2559J) • 112,000,000		
❑ F-2088J★ (W-2559J★) • 3,200,000		
❑ F-2088K (W-2559K) • 166,400,000		
❑ F-2088L (W-2559L) • 384,000,000		
❑ F-2088L★ (W-2559L★) • 3,200,000		
Series of 2004 and 2004-A		
❑ F-2089A (W-2560A)		
❑ F-2089A★ (W-2560A★)		
❑ F-2089B (W-2560B)		
❑ F-2089B★ (W-2560B★)		
❑ F-2089C (W-2560C)		
❑ F-2089C★ (W-2560C★)		
❑ F-2089D (W-2560D)		
❑ F-2089E (W-2560E)		
❑ F-2089E★ (W-2560E★)		
❑ F-2089F (W-2560F)		
❑ F-2090D (W-2561D)		
❑ F-2090E (W-2561E)		
❑ F-2090F (W-2561F)		
❑ F-2090F★ (W-2561F★)		
❑ F-2090G (W-2561G)		
❑ F-2090G★ (W-2561G★)		
❑ F-2090H (W-2561H)		
❑ F-2090I (W-2561I)		
❑ F-2090J (W-2561J)		

F-No. (W-No.) • Printage *(rarity)*	Grade	Comments
Series of 2004 and 2004-A *(continued)*		
❏ F-2090J★ (W-2561J★)		
❏ F-2090K (W-2561K)		
❏ F-2090K★ (W-2561K★)		
❏ F-2090L (W-2561L)		
❏ F-2090L★ (W-2561L★)		
❏ F-2091A (W-2562A) • 76,000,000		
❏ F-2091A★ (W-2562A★) • 384,000		
❏ F-2091B (W-2562B) • 192,000,000		
❏ F-2091B★ (W-2562B★) • 2,880,000		
❏ F-2091C (W-2562C) • 96,000,000		
❏ F-2091D (W-2562D) • 121,600,000		
❏ F-2091E (W-2562E) • 364,800,000		
❏ F-2091E★ (W-2562E★) • 3,200,000		
❏ F-2091F (W-2562F)		
❏ F-2091G (W-2562G)		
❏ F-2091I (W-2562I)		
❏ F-2091J (W-2562J)		
❏ F-2092F (W-2563F) • 288,000,000		
❏ F-2092H (W-2563H) • 76,800,000		
❏ F-2092I (W-2563I) • 64,000,000		
❏ F-2092J (W-2563J) • 134,400,000		
❏ F-2092K (W-2563K) • 275,200,000		
❏ F-2092K★ (W-2563K★) • 2,304,000		
❏ F-2092L (W-2563L) • 185,600,000		
Series of 2006 and 2006-A		
❏ F-2093A (W-2564A) • 268,000		
❏ F-2093B (W-2564B) • 486,400,000		
❏ F-2093C (W-2564C) • 243,200,000		
❏ F-2093D (W-2564D) • 307,200,000		
❏ F-2093E (W-2564E) • 390,400,000		
❏ F-2093E★ (W-2564E★) • 2,432,000		
❏ F-2093F (W-2564F) • 185,600,000		
❏ F-2093F★ (W-2564F★) • 6,720,000		
❏ F-2093G (W-2564G) • 189,200,000		

F-No. (W-No.) • Printage (rarity)	Grade	Comments
❏ F-2093G★ (W-2564G★) • 6,400,000		
❏ F-2093H (W-2564H) • 38,400,000		
❏ F-2093I (W-2564I) • 19,200,000		
❏ F-2093J (W-2564J) • 51,200,000		
❏ F-2093K (W-2564K) • 121,600,000		
❏ F-2093K★ (W-2564K★) • 3,200,000		
❏ F-2093L (W-2564L) • 198,400,000		
❏ F-2093L★ (W-2564L★) • 128,000		
❏ F-2094A★ (W-2565A★) • 1,024,000		
❏ F-2094D (W-2565D) • 83,200,000		
❏ F-2094F (W-2565F) • 588,800,000		
❏ F-2094G (W-2565G) • 252,400,000		
❏ F-2094G★ (W-2565G★) • 5,760,000		
❏ F-2094H (W-2565H) • 64,000,000		
❏ F-2094I (W-2565I) • 83,200,000		
❏ F-2094J (W-2565J) • 83,200,000		
❏ F-2094K (W-2565K) • 281,600,000		
❏ F-2094L (W-2565L) • 328,000,000		
❏ F-2094L★ (W-2565L★) • 6,400,000		
Series of 2009 and 2009-A		
❏ F-2095A • 185,600		
❏ F-2095B • 633,600,000		
❏ F-2095B★ • 3,200,000		
❏ F-2095C • 345,600,000		
❏ F-2095D • 185,600,000		
❏ F-2095D★ • 640,000		
❏ F-2095E • 620,800,000		
❏ F-2095E★ • 4,480,000		
❏ F-2095F • 460,800,000		
❏ F-2095F★ • 6,720,000		
❏ F-2095G • 282,000,000		
❏ F-2095G★ • 320,000		
❏ F-2095H • 153,600,000		
❏ F-2095I • 51,200,000		

F-No. (W-No.) • Printage (rarity)	Grade	Comments
Series of 2009 and 2009-A *(continued)*		
❏ F-2095J • 83,200,000		
❏ F-2095K • 147,200,000		
❏ F-2095L • 204,000,000		
❏ F-2095L★ • 6,880,000		
❏ F-2096D • 140,800,000		
❏ F-2096G • 134,000,000		
❏ F-2096G★ • 1,280,000		
❏ F-2096J • 96,000,000		
❏ F-2096J★ • 512,000		
❏ F-2096K • 108,800,000		
❏ F-2096K★ • 640,000		
❏ F-2096L • 384,000,000		
Series of 2013 and 2013-A		
❏ F-2097A		
❏ F-2097B		
❏ F-2097B★		
❏ F-2097C		
❏ F-2097D		
❏ F-2097E		
❏ F-2097E★		
❏ F-2097F		
❏ F-2097G		
❏ F-2097G★		
❏ F-2097H		
❏ F-2097I		
❏ F-2097J		
❏ F-2097K		
❏ F-2097L		
❏ F-2097L★		
❏ F-2098F		
❏ F-2098G		
❏ F-2098G★		
❏ F-2098I		
❏ F-2098J		

F-No. (W-No.) • Printage *(rarity)*	Grade	Comments
❏ F-2098K		
❏ F-2098L		
❏ F-2098L★		
❏		
❏		
❏		
❏		
❏		
❏		
❏		
❏		
Series of 2017		
❏		
❏		
❏		
❏		
❏		
❏		
❏		
❏		
❏		
❏		
❏		
❏		
❏		
❏		
❏		
❏		
❏		
❏		
❏		
❏		
❏		

LARGE-SIZE

$50 Interest-Bearing Notes

F-No. (W-No.) • Printage *(rarity)*	Grade	Comments
March 2, 1861, 6%, 2 Years		
❑ F-202a (W-2600) • 46,076 *(2 known)*		
❑ F-202a (W-2610) • incl. above		
July 17, 1861, 7.3%, 3 Years		
❑ F-207 (W-2620) • *(1 known)*		
March 3, 1863, 5%, 1 Year		
❑ F-198 (W-2650) • 164,800 *(3 known)*		
March 3, 1863, 5%, 2 Years		
❑ F-203 (W-2660) • 136,000 *(8 known)*		
❑ F-203 (W-2670) • 118,112 *(1 known)*		
June 30, 1864, 7.3%, 3 Years		
❑ F-212 (W-2680) • 363,952 *(7 known)*		
March 3, 1865, 7.3%, 3 Years		
❑ F-212d (W-2690) • 182,926 *(1 known)*		
❑ F-212d (W-2695) • 343,320 *(6 known)*		
❑ F-212d (W-2700) • incl. above *(incl. above)*		

$50 Legal Tender Notes

F-No. (W-No.) • Printage *(rarity)*	Grade	Comments
Series of 1862		
❑ F-148 (W-2771) • est. 280,000 *(10–15)*		
❑ F-148 (W-2772) • est. 153,600 *(15–20)*		
Series of 1863		
❑ F-150 (W-2773) • 32,000 *(9–10)*		

F-No. (W-No.) • Printage *(rarity)*	Grade	Comments
❑ F-150a (W-2775) • 70,504 *(1 known)*		
❑ F-150a (W-2776) • 65,000 *(10–12)*		
Series of 1869		
❑ F-151 (W-2800) • 604,000 *(70–80)*		
Series of 1874		
❑ F-152 (W-2801) • 489,200 *(60–70)*		
Series of 1875		
❑ F-unlisted (W-2802) • 40,000 *(4 known)*		
Series of 1878		
❑ F-154 (W-2803) • 210,000 *(21–25)*		
Series of 1880		
❑ F-155 (W-2804) • 80,000 *(9–10)*		
❑ F-156 (W-2805) • 160,000 *(19–22)*		
❑ F-157 (W-2806) • 80,000 *(12–14)*		
❑ F-158 (W-2807) • 20,000 *(8 known)*		
❑ F-159 (W-2808) • 220,000 *(20–23)*		
❑ F-160 (W-2809) • 80,000 *(18–20)*		
❑ F-161 (W-2810) • 100,000 *(70–80)*		
❑ F-162 (W-2811) • 212,000 *(26–30)*		
❑ F-163 (W-2812) • 28,000 *(5 known)*		
❑ F-164 (W-2813) • 300,000 *(220–230)*		

$50 Compound Interest Treasury Notes

F-No. (W-No.) • Printage *(rarity)*	Grade	Comments
Series of 1863		
❑ F-192 (W-2720) • 1,216,480 *(2 known)*		
Series of 1864		
❑ F-192b (W-2740) • incl. above *(14 known)*		

$50 National Bank Notes

F-No. (W-No.) • Printage *(rarity)*	Grade	Comments
Original Series ("First Charter Period")		
❑ F-440 (W-2820) • *(9–10)*		
❑ F-442 (W-2821) • *(12–14)*		
❑ F-443 (W-2822) • *(3 known)*		
Series of 1875 ("First Charter Period")		
❑ F-444 (W-2839) • *(24–28)*		
❑ F-444a (W-2840) • *(4 known)*		

F-No. (W-No.) • Printage *(rarity)*	Grade	Comments
Series of 1875 ("First Charter Period") *(continued)*		
❑ F-445 (W-2841) • *(5 known)*		
❑ F-446 (W-2842) • *(9–10)*		
❑ F-447 (W-2843) • *(12–14)*		
❑ F-448 (W-2844) • *(5 known)*		
❑ F-449 (W-2845) • *(1 known)*		
❑ F-450 (W-2846) • *(1 known)*		
❑ F-451 (W-2847) • *(2 known)*		
Series of 1882, Brown Back ("Second Charter Period")		
❑ F-507 (W-2855) • *(15–17)*		
❑ F-508 (W-2856) • *(70–80)*		
❑ F-509 (W-2857) • *(6 known)*		
❑ F-510 (W-2858) • *(26–30)*		
❑ F-511 (W-2859) • *(19–22)*		
❑ F-512 (W-2860) • *(36–42)*		
❑ F-513 (W-2861) • *(42–46)*		
❑ F-514 (W-2862) • *(11–13)*		
❑ F-515 (W-2863) • *(50–60)*		
❑ F-516 (W-2864) • *(4 known)*		
❑ F-517 (W-2865) • *(10–12)*		
❑ F-518 (W-2866) • *(30–35)*		
❑ F-518a (W-2867) • *(2 known)*		
Series of 1882, Date Back ("Second Charter Period")		
❑ F-558 (W-2870) • *(7 known)*		
❑ F-559 (W-2871) • *(3 known)*		
❑ F-560 (W-2872) • *(22–26)*		
❑ F-561 (W-2873) • *(18–20)*		
❑ F-562 (W-2874) • *(10–12)*		
❑ F-563 (W-2875) • *(130–140)*		
❑ F-564 (W-2876) • *(7 known)*		
❑ F-565 (W-2877) • *(5 known)*		
Series of 1882, Value Back ("Second Charter Period")		
❑ F-586 (W-2878) • 8,571 *(8 known)*		
Series of 1902, Red Seal ("Third Charter Period")		
❑ F-664 (W-2879) • *(75–85)*		

F-No. (W-No.) • Printage *(rarity)*	Grade	Comments
❏ F-665 (W-2880) • *(9–10)*		
❏ F-666 (W-2881) • *(6 known)*		
Series of 1902, Blue Seal, Date Back ("Third Charter Period")		
❏ F-667 (W-2882) • *(340–370)*		
❏ F-668 (W-2883) • *(120–130)*		
❏ F-669 (W-2884) • *(200–220)*		
❏ F-670 (W-2885) • *(145–160)*		
❏ F-671 (W-2886) • *(115–125)*		
❏ F-672 (W-2887) • *(24–28)*		
❏ F-673 (W-2888) • *(22–26)*		
❏ F-674 (W-2889) • *(45–50)*		
❏ F-674a (W-2890) • *(34–38)*		
Series of 1902, Blue Seal, Plain Back ("Third Charter Period")		
❏ F-675 (W-2891) • *(180–200)*		
❏ F-676 (W-2892) • *(55–60)*		
❏ F-677 (W-2893) • *(95–105)*		
❏ F-678 (W-2894) • *(165–180)*		
❏ F-679 (W-2895) • *(60–70)*		
❏ F-679a (W-2896) • *(35–40)*		
❏ F-680 (W-2897) • *(7 known)*		
❏ F-681 (W-2898) • *(38–47)*		
❏ F-682 (W-2899) • *(200–220)*		
❏ F-683 (W-2900) • *(115–125)*		
❏ F-684 (W-2901) • *(60–70)*		
❏ F-685 (W-2902) • *(95–105)*		
❏ F-685a (W-2903) • *(2 known)*		

$50 Gold Certificates

F-No. (W-No.) • Printage *(rarity)*	Grade	Comments
Series of 1882		
❏ F-1188 (W-2944) • 96,000 *(8 known)*		
❏ F-1189a (W-2942) • 231,000 *(12–14)*		
❏ F-1190 (W-2948) • 40,000 *(5 known)*		
❏ F-1191 (W-2950) • 40,000 *(4 known)*		

F-No. (W-No.) • Printage *(rarity)*	Grade	Comments
Series of 1882 *(continued)*		
❏ F-1192 (W-2952) • est. 99,996 *(20–24)*		
❏ F-1192a (W-2954) • est. 4 *(1 known)*		
❏ F-1193 (W-2956) • 1,724,000 *(115–125)*		
❏ F-1194 (W-2958) • 400,000 *(35–40)*		
❏ F-1195 (W-2960) • 400,000 *(55–60)*		
❏ F-1196 (W-2962) • 400,000 *(32–35)*		
❏ F-1197 (W-2964) • 1,204,000 *(175–185)*		

$50 National Gold Bank Notes

F-No. (W-No.) • Printage *(rarity)*	Grade	Comments
Original Series		
❏ F-1160 (W-2825) • 2,000 *(5 known)*		
❏ F-1161 (W-2831) • 400 *(1 known)*		
Series of 1875		
❏ F-1160a (W-2850) • 620 *(1 known)*		

$50 Silver Certificates

F-No. (W-No.) • Printage *(rarity)*	Grade	Comments
Series of 1878		
❏ F-324 (W-2912) • est. 12,000 *(2 known)*		
❏ F-324a (W-2916) • est. 4,000 *(1 known)*		
❏ F-324c (W-2922) • est. 60,000 *(3 known)*		
Series of 1880		
❏ F-325 (W-2925) • est. 16,000 *(1 known)*		
❏ F-326 (W-2926) • est. 80,000 *(5 known)*		
❏ F-327 (W-2927) • est. 100,000 *(11–13)*		
❏ F-328 (W-2928) • 100,000 *(32–35)*		
❏ F-329 (W-2929) • 120,000 *(32–35)*		
Series of 1891		
❏ F-330 (W-2930) • est. 120,000 *(6 known)*		
❏ F-331 (W-2931) • est. 380,000 *(30–35)*		
❏ F-332 (W-2932) • est. 300,000 *(24–28)*		
❏ F-333 (W-2933) • est. 304,000 *(40–44)*		
❏ F-334 (W-2934) • 200,000 *(50–60)*		
❏ F-335 (W-2935) • 812,000 *(170–185)*		

$50 Treasury or Coin Notes

F-No. (W-No.) • Printage *(rarity)*	Grade	Comments
Series of 1891		
❑ F-376 (W-2938) • 80,000 *(21 known)*		

$50 Gold Certificates

F-No. (W-No.) • Printage *(rarity)*	Grade	Comments
Series of 1913		
❑ F-1198 (W-2966) • 400,000 *(60–65)*		
❑ F-1199 (W-2967) • 1,224,000 *(210–230)*		
Series of 1922		
❑ F-1200 (W-2969) • est. 4,684,000 *(13–15)*		
❑ F-1200★ (W-2969★) • *(13–15)*		
❑ F-1200 (W-2969 Mule) • *(35–40)*		
❑ F-1200★ (W-2969 Mule★) • *(3 known)*		
❑ F-1200a (W-2968 Mule) • 800,000 *(145–160)*		

$50 Federal Reserve Notes

F-No. (W-No.) • Printage *(rarity)*	Grade	Comments
Series of 1914, Red Seal		
❑ F-1012A (W-2975A-a) • 20,000 *(4 known)*		
❑ F-1012B (W-2975A-b) • 24,000 *(5 known)*		
❑ F-1013A (W-2975B-a) • 80,000 *(10–12)*		
❑ F-1013B (W-2975B-b) • 40,000 *(13–15)*		
❑ F-1014A (W-2975C-a) • 12,000 *(16–18)*		
❑ F-1014B (W-2975C-b) • 40,000 *(9–10)*		
❑ F-1015A (W-2975D-a) • 8,000 *(5 known)*		
❑ F-1015B (W-2975D-b) • 40,000 *(9–10)*		
❑ F-1016A (W-2975E-a) • 28,000 *(8 known)*		
❑ F-1016B (W-2975E-b) • 40,000 *(18–20)*		
❑ F-1017A (W-2975F-a) • 28,000 *(11–13)*		
❑ F-1018A (W-2975G-a) • 20,000 *(6 known)*		
❑ F-1018B (W-2975G-b) • 40,000 *(12–14)*		
❑ F-1019A (W-2975H-a) • 12,000 *(11–13)*		
❑ F-1019B (W-2975H-b) • 16,000 *(16–18)*		
❑ F-1020A (W-2975I-a) • 8,000 *(6 known)*		
❑ F-1020B (W-2975I-b) • 8,000 *(18–20)*		

F-No. (W-No.) • Printage *(rarity)*	Grade	Comments
Series of 1914, Red Seal *(continued)*		
❑ F-1021A (W-2975J-a) • 8,000 *(5 known)*		
❑ F-1021B (W-2975J-b) • 8,000 *(4 known)*		
❑ F-1022A (W-2975K-a) • 28,000 *(22–26)*		
❑ F-1023A (W-2975L-a) • 8,000 *(3 known)*		
❑ F-1023B (W-2975L-b) • 24,000 *(18–20)*		
Series of 1914, Blue Seal		
❑ F-1024 (W-2980A-b) • est. 592,000 *(60–70)*		
❑ F-1025 (W-2981A-b) • est. 344,000 *(35–40)*		
❑ F-1026 (W-2982A-b) • est. 92,000 *(9–10)*		
❑ F-1028 (W-2984B-b) • est. 2,180,000 *(75–85)*		
❑ F-1029 (W-2985B-b) • est. 600,000 *(45–50)*		
❑ F-1030 (W-2986B-b) • est. 1,180,000 *(130–145)*		
❑ F-1030★ (W-2986B-b★) • *(3 known)*		
❑ F-1031A (W-2987B-b) • est. 528,000 *(38–47)*		
❑ F-1031B (W-2987B-c) • est. 656,000 *(18–20)*		
❑ F-1032 (W-2988C-b) • est. 652,000 *(35–40)*		
❑ F-1033 (W-2989C-b) • est. 244,000 *(15–17)*		
❑ F-1034 (W-2990C-b) • est. 732,000 *(60–65)*		
❑ F-1034★ (W-2990C-b★) • *(1 known)*		
❑ F-1035 (W-2991C-b) • est. 2,040,000 *(175–185)*		
❑ F-1035★ (W-2991C-b★) • *(2 known)*		
❑ F-1036 (W-2992D-b) • est. 1,488,000 *(95–115)*		
❑ F-1037 (W-2993D-b) • est. 404,000 *(35–45)*		
❑ F-1038 (W-2994D-b) • est. 1,260,000 *(90–100)*		
❑ F-1039A (W-2995D-b) • est. 2,368,000 *(170–185)*		
❑ F-1039A★ (W-2995D-b★) • *(11–13)*		
❑ F-1039B (W-2995D-c) • est. 568,000 *(70–80)*		
❑ F-1040 (W-2996E-b) • est. 512,000 *(40–45)*		
❑ F-1041 (W-2997E-b) • est. 160,000 *(15–17)*		
❑ F-1042 (W-2998E-b) • est. 732,000 *(70–80)*		
❑ F-1042★ (W-2998E-b★) • *(2 known)*		
❑ F-1043 (W-2999E-b) • est. 196,000 *(50–60)*		
❑ F-1044 (W-3000F-b) • est. 312,000 *(32–36)*		

F-No. (W-No.) • Printage *(rarity)*	Grade	Comments
❑ F-1045 (W-3001F-b) • est. 108,000 *(7 known)*		
❑ F-1046 (W-3002F-b) • est. 332,000 *(95–105)*		
❑ F-1047 (W-3003F-b) • est. 280,000 *(19–22)*		
❑ F-1048 (W-3004G-b) • est. 1,292,000 *(90–100)*		
❑ F-1049 (W-3005G-b) • est. 288,000 *(56–60)*		
❑ F-1049★ (W-3005G-b★) • *(1 known)*		
❑ F-1050 (W-3006G-b) • est. 1,336,000 *(90–95)*		
❑ F-1050★ (W-3006G-b★) • *(3 known)*		
❑ F-1051 (W-3007G-b) • est. 1,012,000 *(75–85)*		
❑ F-1052 (W-3008H-b) • est. 212,000 *(33–36)*		
❑ F-1053 (W-3009H-b) • est. 192,000 *(45–50)*		
❑ F-1053★ (W-3009H-b★) • *(1 known)*		
❑ F-1054 (W-3010H-b) • est. 152,000 *(45–50)*		
❑ F-1056 (W-3012I-b) • est. 96,000 *(45–50)*		
❑ F-1058 (W-3014I-b) • est. 32,000 *(8 known)*		
❑ F-1059 (W-3015I-b) • est. 20,000 *(3 known)*		
❑ F-1060 (W-3016J-b) • est. 308,000 *(44–48)*		
❑ F-1060★ (W-3017J-b★) • *(1 known)*		
❑ F-1063 (W-3019J-b) • est. 100,000 *(3 known)*		
❑ F-1064 (W-3020K-b) • est. 168,000 *(32–35)*		
❑ F-1066 (W-3022K-b) • est. 44,000 *(5 known)*		
❑ F-1068 (W-3024L-b) • est. 724,000 *(75–80)*		
❑ F-1068★ (W-3024L-b★) • *(1 known)*		
❑ F-1070 (W-3026L-b) • est. 292,000 *(38–42)*		
❑ F-1070★ (W-3026L-b★) • *(1 known)*		
❑ F-1071 (W-3027L-b) • est. 308,000 *(26–30)*		

$50 Federal Reserve Bank Notes

F-No. (W-No.) • Printage *(rarity)*	Grade	Comments
Series of 1918		
❑ F-831 (W-3030) • 4,000 *(54 known)*		

SMALL-SIZE

$50 National Bank Notes

F-No. (W-No.) • Printage *(rarity)*	Grade	Comments
Series of 1929, Type 1		
❑ F-1803-1 (W-3040) • *(4,300–4,600)*		
Series of 1929, Type 2		
❑ F-1803-2 (W-3041) • *(375–400)*		

$50 Gold Certificates

F-No. (W-No.) • Printage *(rarity)*	Grade	Comments
Series of 1928		
❑ F-2404 (W-3050) • 5,520,000		
❑ F-2404★ (W-3050★)		

$50 Federal Reserve Bank Notes

F-No. (W-No.) • Printage *(rarity)*	Grade	Comments
Series of 1929		
❑ F-1880B (W-3042B) • 636,000		
❑ F-1880B★ (W-3042B★)		
❑ F-1880D (W-3043D) • 684,000		
❑ F-1880D★ (W-3043D★)		
❑ F-1880G (W-3044G) • 300,000		
❑ F-1880G★ (W-3044G★)		
❑ F-1880I (W-3045I) • 276,000		
❑ F-1880I★ (W-3045I★)		
❑ F-1880J (W-3046J) • 276,000		
❑ F-1880J★ (W-3046J★)		

F-No. (W-No.) • Printage *(rarity)*	Grade	Comments
❏ F-1880K (W-3047K) • 168,000		
❏ F-1880L (W-3048L) • 576,000		
❏ F-1880L★ (W-3048L★)		

$50 Federal Reserve Notes

F-No. (W-No.) • Printage *(rarity)*	Grade	Comments
Series of 1928		
❏ F-2100A (W-3060A) • 265,200		
❏ F-2100A★ (W-3060A★)		
❏ F-2100B (W-3060B) • 1,351,800		
❏ F-2100B★ (W-3060B★)		
❏ F-2100C (W-3060C) • 997,056		
❏ F-2100C★ (W-3060C★)		
❏ F-2100D (W-3060D) • 1,161,900		
❏ F-2100D★ (W-3060D★)		
❏ F-2100E (W-3060E) • 539,400		
❏ F-2100E★ (W-3060E★)		
❏ F-2100F (W-3060F) • 538,800		
❏ F-2100F★ (W-3060F★)		
❏ F-2100G (W-3060G) • 1,348,620		
❏ F-2100G★ (W-3060G★)		
❏ F-2100H (W-3060H) • 627,300		
❏ F-2100H★ (W-3060H★)		
❏ F-2100I (W-3060I) • 106,200		
❏ F-2100I★ (W-3060I★)		
❏ F-2100J (W-3060J) • 252,600		
❏ F-2100J★ (W-3060J★)		
❏ F-2100K (W-3060K) • 109,920		
❏ F-2100K★ (W-3060K★)		
❏ F-2100L (W-3060L) • 447,600		
❏ F-2100L★ (W-3060L★)		
Series of 1928-A, Green Seal		
❏ F-2101A (W-3061A) • 1,834,989		
❏ F-2101B (W-3061B) • 3,392,328		
❏ F-2101C (W-3061C) • 3,078,944		

F-No. (W-No.) • Printage *(rarity)*	Grade	Comments
Series of 1928-A, Green Seal *(continued)*		
❑ F-2101D (W-3061D) • 2,453,364		
❑ F-2101E (W-3061E) • 1,516,500		
❑ F-2101F (W-3061F) • 338,400		
❑ F-2101G (W-3061G) • 5,263,956		
❑ F-2101G★ (W-3061G★)		
❑ F-2101H (W-3061H) • 880,500		
❑ F-2101I (W-3061I) • 780,240		
❑ F-2101J (W-3061J) • 791,604		
❑ F-2101K (W-3061K) • 701,496		
❑ F-2101L (W-3061L) • 1,522,620		
Series of 1928-A, Light Yellow-Green Seal		
❑ F-2101B (W-3062B) • incl. in F-2101B/W-3061B		
❑ F-2101G (W-3062G) • incl. in F-2101G/W-3061G		
❑ F-2101I (W-3062I) • incl. in F-2101I/W-3061I		
❑ F-2101J (W-3062J) • incl. in F-2101J/W-3061J		
❑ F-2101L (W-3062L) • incl. in F-2101L/W-3061L		
Series of 1934, Light Yellow-Green Seal		
❑ F-2102A (W-3063A) • 2,729,400		
❑ F-2102A★ (W-3063A★)		
❑ F-2102B (W-3063B) • 17,894,676		
❑ F-2102B★ (W-3063B★)		
❑ F-2102C (W-3063C) • 5,833,200		
❑ F-2102C★ (W-3063C★)		
❑ F-2102D (W-3063D) • 8,817,720		
❑ F-2102D★ (W-3063D★)		
❑ F-2102E (W-3063E) • 4,826,628		
❑ F-2102E★ (W-3063E★)		
❑ F-2102F (W-3063F) • 3,069,348		
❑ F-2102F★ (W-3063F★)		
❑ F-2102G (W-3063G) • 8,675,940		
❑ F-2102G★ (W-3063G★)		
❑ F-2102H (W-3063H) • 1,497,144		
❑ F-2102H★ (W-3063H★)		
❑ F-2102I (W-3063I) • 539,700		

F-No. (W-No.) • Printage *(rarity)*	Grade	Comments
❏ F-2102I★ (W-3063I★)		
❏ F-2102J (W-3063J) • 1,133,520		
❏ F-2102J★ (W-3063J★)		
❏ F-2102K (W-3063K) • 1,194,876		
❏ F-2102K★ (W-3063K★)		
❏ F-2102L (W-3063L) • 8,101,200		
❏ F-2102L★ (W-3063L★)		
Series of 1934, Green Seal		
❏ F-2102A (W-3064A) • incl. in F-2102A/W-3063A		
❏ F-2102A★ (W-3064A★)		
❏ F-2102B (W-3064B) • incl. in F-2102B/W-3063B		
❏ F-2102B★ (W-3064B★)		
❏ F-2102C (W-3064C) • incl. in F-2102C/W-3063C		
❏ F-2102C★ (W-3064C★)		
❏ F-2102D (W-3064D) • incl. in F-2102D/W-3063D		
❏ F-2102D★ (W-3064D★)		
❏ F-2102E (W-3064E) • incl. in F-2102E/W-3063E		
❏ F-2102E★ (W-3064E★)		
❏ F-2102F (W-3064F) • incl. in F-2102F/W-3063F		
❏ F-2102F★ (W-3064F★)		
❏ F-2102G (W-3064G) • incl. in F-2102G/W-3063G		
❏ F-2102G★ (W-3064G★)		
❏ F-2102H (W-3064H) • incl. in F-2102H/W-3063H		
❏ F-2102H★ (W-3064H★)		
❏ F-2102I (W-3064I) • incl. in F-2102I/W-3063I		
❏ F-2102I★ (W-3064I★)		
❏ F-2102J (W-3064J) • incl. in F-2102J/W-3063J		
❏ F-2102J★ (W-3064J★)		
❏ F-2102K (W-3064K) • incl. in F-2102K/W-3063K		
❏ F-2102K★ (W-3064K★)		
❏ F-2102L (W-3064L) • incl. in F-2102L/W-3063L		
❏ F-2102L★ (W-3064L★)		
Series of 1934-A–1934-D		
❏ F-2103A (W-3065A) • 406,200		
❏ F-2103A★ (W-3065A★)		

F-No. (W-No.) • Printage *(rarity)*	Grade	Comments
Series of 1934-A–1934-D *(continued)*		
❏ F-2103B (W-3065B) • 4,710,648		
❏ F-2103B★ (W-3065B★)		
❏ F-2103D (W-3065D) • 864,168		
❏ F-2103D★ (W-3065D★)		
❏ F-2103E (W-3065E) • 2,235,372		
❏ F-2103E★ (W-3065E★)		
❏ F-2103F (W-3065F) • 416,100		
❏ F-2103F★ (W-3065F★)		
❏ F-2103G (W-3065G) • 1,014,600		
❏ F-2103G★ (W-3065G★)		
❏ F-2103H (W-3065H) • 361,944		
❏ F-2103H★ (W-3065H★)		
❏ F-2103I (W-3065I) • 93,300		
❏ F-2103I★ (W-3065I★)		
❏ F-2103J (W-3065J) • 189,300		
❏ F-2103J★ (W-3065J★)		
❏ F-2103K (W-3065K) • 266,700		
❏ F-2103K★ (W-3065K★)		
❏ F-2103L (W-3065L) • 162,000		
❏ F-2103L★ (W-3065L★)		
❏ F-2104C (W-3066C) • 509,100		
❏ F-2104C★ (W-3066C★)		
❏ F-2104D (W-3066D) • 359,100		
❏ F-2104D★ (W-3066D★)		
❏ F-2104E (W-3066E) • 596,700		
❏ F-2104E★ (W-3066E★)		
❏ F-2104F (W-3066F) • 416,720		
❏ F-2104G (W-3066G) • 306,000		
❏ F-2104H (W-3066H) • 306,000		
❏ F-2104I (W-3066I) • 120,000		
❏ F-2104J (W-3066J) • 221,340		
❏ F-2104J★ (W-3066J★) • 2,500		
❏ F-2104K (W-3066K) • 120,108		

F-No. (W-No.) • Printage *(rarity)*	Grade	Comments
❏ F-2104L (W-3066L) • 441,000		
❏ F-2105A (W-3067A) • 117,600		
❏ F-2105B (W-3067B) • 1,556,400		
❏ F-2105B★ (W-3067B★)		
❏ F-2105C (W-3067C) • 107,283		
❏ F-2105C★ (W-3067C★)		
❏ F-2105D (W-3067D) • 374,400		
❏ F-2105D★ (W-3067D★)		
❏ F-2105E (W-3067E) • 1,821,960		
❏ F-2105E★ (W-3067E★)		
❏ F-2105F (W-3067F) • 104,640		
❏ F-2105G (W-3067G) • 294,432		
❏ F-2105G★ (W-3067G★)		
❏ F-2105H (W-3067H) • 535,200		
❏ F-2105I (W-3067I) • 118,800		
❏ F-2105I★ (W-3067I★)		
❏ F-2105J (W-3067J) • 303,600		
❏ F-2105K (W-3067K) • 429,900		
❏ F-2105K★ (W-3067K★)		
❏ F-2106A (W-3068A) • 279,600		
❏ F-2106A★ (W-3068A★)		
❏ F-2106B (W-3068B) • 898,776		
❏ F-2106B★ (W-3068B★)		
❏ F-2106C (W-3068C) • 699,000		
❏ F-2106C★ (W-3068C★)		
❏ F-2106E (W-3068E) • 156,000		
❏ F-2106F (W-3068F) • 216,000		
❏ F-2106F★ (W-3068F★)		
❏ F-2106G (W-3068G) • 494,016		
❏ F-2106G★ (W-3068G★)		
❏ F-2106I (W-3068I)		
❏ F-2106K (W-3068K) • 103,200		
Series of 1950–1950-E		
❏ F-2107A (W-3069A) • 1,248,000		
❏ F-2107A★ (W-3069A★)		

F-No. (W-No.) • Printage *(rarity)*	Grade	Comments
Series of 1950–1950-E *(continued)*		
❑ F-2107B (W-3069B) • 10,236,000		
❑ F-2107B★ (W-3069B★)		
❑ F-2107C (W-3069C) • 2,352,000		
❑ F-2107C★ (W-3069C★)		
❑ F-2107D (W-3069D) • 6,180,000		
❑ F-2107D★ (W-3069D★)		
❑ F-2107E (W-3069E) • 5,064,000		
❑ F-2107E★ (W-3069E★)		
❑ F-2107F (W-3069F) • 1,812,000		
❑ F-2107F★ (W-3069F★)		
❑ F-2107G (W-3069G) • 4,212,000		
❑ F-2107G★ (W-3069G★)		
❑ F-2107H (W-3069H) • 892,000		
❑ F-2107H★ (W-3069H★)		
❑ F-2107I (W-3069I) • 384,000		
❑ F-2107I★ (W-3069I★)		
❑ F-2107J (W-3069J) • 696,000		
❑ F-2107J★ (W-3069J★)		
❑ F-2107K (W-3069K) • 1,100,000		
❑ F-2107K★ (W-3069K★)		
❑ F-2107L (W-3069L) • 3,996,000		
❑ F-2107L★ (W-3069L★)		
❑ F-2108A (W-3070A) • 720,000		
❑ F-2108A★ (W-3070A★)		
❑ F-2108B (W-3070B) • 6,495,000		
❑ F-2108B★ (W-3070B★)		
❑ F-2108C (W-3070C) • 1,728,000		
❑ F-2108C★ (W-3070C★)		
❑ F-2108D (W-3070D) • 1,872,000		
❑ F-2108D★ (W-3070D★)		
❑ F-2108E (W-3070E) • 2,016,000		
❑ F-2108E★ (W-3070E★)		
❑ F-2108F (W-3070F) • 288,000		

F-No. (W-No.) • Printage *(rarity)*	Grade	Comments
❏ F-2108F★ (W-3070F★)		
❏ F-2108G (W-3070G) • 2,016,000		
❏ F-2108G★ (W-3070G★)		
❏ F-2108H (W-3070H) • 576,000		
❏ F-2108H★ (W-3070H★)		
❏ F-2108J (W-3070J) • 144,000		
❏ F-2108J★ (W-3070J★)		
❏ F-2108K (W-3070K) • 864,000		
❏ F-2108K★ (W-3070K★)		
❏ F-2108L (W-3070L) • 576,000		
❏ F-2108L★ (W-3070L★)		
❏ F-2109A (W-3071A) • 864,000		
❏ F-2109A★ (W-3071A★)		
❏ F-2109B (W-3071B) • 8,352,000		
❏ F-2109B★ (W-3071B★)		
❏ F-2109C (W-3071C) • 2,592,000		
❏ F-2109C★ (W-3071C★)		
❏ F-2109D (W-3071D) • 1,728,000		
❏ F-2109D★ (W-3071D★)		
❏ F-2109E (W-3071E) • 1,584,000		
❏ F-2109E★ (W-3071E★)		
❏ F-2109G (W-3071G) • 4,320,000		
❏ F-2109G★ (W-3071G★)		
❏ F-2109H (W-3071H) • 576,000		
❏ F-2109H★ (W-3071H★)		
❏ F-2109J (W-3071J) • 1,008,000		
❏ F-2109J★ (W-3071J★)		
❏ F-2109K (W-3071K) • 1,008,000		
❏ F-2109K★ (W-3071K★)		
❏ F-2109L (W-3071L) • 1,872,000		
❏ F-2109L★ (W-3071L★)		
❏ F-2110A (W-3072A) • 720,000		
❏ F-2110A★ (W-3072A★)		
❏ F-2110B (W-3072B) • 5,328,000		

F-No. (W-No.) • Printage *(rarity)*	Grade	Comments
Series of 1950–1950-E *(continued)*		
❑ F-2110B★ (W-3072B★)		
❑ F-2110C (W-3072C) • 1,296,000		
❑ F-2110C★ (W-3072C★)		
❑ F-2110D (W-3072D) • 1,296,000		
❑ F-2110D★ (W-3072D★)		
❑ F-2110E (W-3072E) • 1,296,000		
❑ F-2110E★ (W-3072E★)		
❑ F-2110G (W-3072G) • 1,728,000		
❑ F-2110G★ (W-3072G★)		
❑ F-2110H (W-3072H) • 576,000		
❑ F-2110H★ (W-3072H★)		
❑ F-2110I (W-3072I) • 144,000		
❑ F-2110I★ (W-3072I★)		
❑ F-2110J (W-3072J) • 432,000		
❑ F-2110J★ (W-3072J★)		
❑ F-2110K (W-3072K) • 720,000		
❑ F-2110K★ (W-3072K★)		
❑ F-2110L (W-3072L) • 1,152,000		
❑ F-2110L★ (W-3072L★)		
❑ F-2111A (W-3073A) • 1,728,000		
❑ F-2111A★ (W-3073A★)		
❑ F-2111B (W-3073B) • 7,200,000		
❑ F-2111B★ (W-3073B★)		
❑ F-2111C (W-3073C) • 2,736,000		
❑ F-2111C★ (W-3073C★)		
❑ F-2111D (W-3073D) • 2,880,000		
❑ F-2111D★ (W-3073D★)		
❑ F-2111E (W-3073E) • 2,616,000		
❑ F-2111E★ (W-3073E★)		
❑ F-2111F (W-3073F) • 576,000		
❑ F-2111F★ (W-3073F★)		
❑ F-2111G (W-3073G) • 4,176,000		
❑ F-2111G★ (W-3073G★)		

F-No. (W-No.) • Printage *(rarity)*	Grade	Comments
❏ F-2111H (W-3073H) • 1,440,000		
❏ F-2111H★ (W-3073H★)		
❏ F-2111I (W-3073I) • 288,000		
❏ F-2111I★ (W-3073I★)		
❏ F-2111J (W-3073J) • 720,000		
❏ F-2111J★ (W-3073J★)		
❏ F-2111K (W-3073K) • 1,296,000		
❏ F-2111K★ (W-3073K★)		
❏ F-2111L (W-3073L) • 2,160,000		
❏ F-2111L★ (W-3073L★)		
❏ F-2112B (W-3074B) • 3,024,000		
❏ F-2112B★ (W-3074B★)		
❏ F-2112G (W-3074G) • 1,008,000		
❏ F-2112G★ (W-3074G★)		
❏ F-2112L (W-3074L) • 1,296,000		
❏ F-2112L★ (W-3074L★)		
Series of 1963-A		
❏ F-2113A (W-3075A) • 1,536,000		
❏ F-2113A★ (W-3075A★) • 320,000		
❏ F-2113B (W-3075B) • 11,008,000		
❏ F-2113B★ (W-3075B★) • 1,408,000		
❏ F-2113C (W-3075C) • 3,328,000		
❏ F-2113C★ (W-3075C★) • 704,000		
❏ F-2113D (W-3075D) • 3,584,000		
❏ F-2113D★ (W-3075D★) • 256,000		
❏ F-2113E (W-3075E) • 3,072,000		
❏ F-2113E★ (W-3075E★) • 704,000		
❏ F-2113F (W-3075F) • 768,000		
❏ F-2113F★ (W-3075F★) • 384,000		
❏ F-2113G (W-3075G) • 6,912,000		
❏ F-2113G★ (W-3075G★) • 768,000		
❏ F-2113H (W-3075H) • 512,000		
❏ F-2113H★ (W-3075H★) • 128,000		
❏ F-2113I (W-3075I) • 512,000		

F-No. (W-No.) • Printage *(rarity)*	Grade	Comments
Series of 1963-A *(continued)*		
❏ F-2113I★ (W-3075I★) • 128,000		
❏ F-2113J (W-3075J) • 512,000		
❏ F-2113J★ (W-3075J★) • 64,000		
❏ F-2113K (W-3075K) • 1,536,000		
❏ F-2113K★ (W-3075K★) • 128,000		
❏ F-2113L (W-3075L) • 4,352,000		
❏ F-2113L★ (W-3075L★) • 704,000		
Series of 1969–1969-C		
❏ F-2114A (W-3076A) • 2,048,000		
❏ F-2114B (W-3076B) • 12,032,000		
❏ F-2114B★ (W-3076B★) • 384,000		
❏ F-2114C (W-3076C) • 3,584,000		
❏ F-2114C★ (W-3076C★) • 128,000		
❏ F-2114D (W-3076D) • 3,584,000		
❏ F-2114D★ (W-3076D★) • 192,000		
❏ F-2114E (W-3076E) • 2,560,000		
❏ F-2114E★ (W-3076E★) • 64,000		
❏ F-2114F (W-3076F) • 256,000		
❏ F-2114G (W-3076G) • 9,728,000		
❏ F-2114G★ (W-3076G★) • 256,000		
❏ F-2114H (W-3076H) • 256,000		
❏ F-2114I (W-3076I) • 512,000		
❏ F-2114J (W-3076J) • 1,280,000		
❏ F-2114J★ (W-3076J★) • 64,000		
❏ F-2114K (W-3076K) • 1,536,000		
❏ F-2114K★ (W-3076K★) • 64,000		
❏ F-2114L (W-3076L) • 6,912,000		
❏ F-2114L★ (W-3076L★) • 256,000		
❏ F-2115A (W-3077A) • 1,536,000		
❏ F-2115A★ (W-3077A★) • 128,000		
❏ F-2115B (W-3077B) • 9,728,000		
❏ F-2115B★ (W-3077B★) • 704,000		
❏ F-2115C (W-3077C) • 2,560,000		
❏ F-2115D (W-3077D) • 2,816,000		

F-No. (W-No.) • Printage *(rarity)*	Grade	Comments
❏ F-2115E (W-3077E) • 2,304,000		
❏ F-2115E★ (W-3077E★) • 64,000		
❏ F-2115F (W-3077F) • 256,000		
❏ F-2115F★ (W-3077F★) • 64,000		
❏ F-2115G (W-3077G) • 3,584,000		
❏ F-2115G★ (W-3077G★) • 192,000		
❏ F-2115H (W-3077H) • 256,000		
❏ F-2115I (W-3077I) • 512,000		
❏ F-2115J (W-3077J) • 256,000		
❏ F-2115K (W-3077K) • 1,024,000		
❏ F-2115K★ (W-3077K★) • 64,000		
❏ F-2115L (W-3077L) • 5,120,000		
❏ F-2115L★ (W-3077L★) • 256,000		
❏ F-2116A (W-3078A) • 1,024,000		
❏ F-2116B (W-3078B) • 2,560,000		
❏ F-2116C (W-3078C) • 2,048,000		
❏ F-2116E (W-3078E) • 1,536,000		
❏ F-2116F (W-3078F) • 512,000		
❏ F-2116G (W-3078G) • 1,024,000		
❏ F-2116K (W-3078K) • 1,024,000		
❏ F-2116K★ (W-3078K★) • 128,000		
❏ F-2117A (W-3079A) • 1,792,000		
❏ F-2117A★ (W-3079A★) • 64,000		
❏ F-2117B (W-3079B) • 7,040,000		
❏ F-2117B★ (W-3079B★) • 192,000		
❏ F-2117C (W-3079C) • 3,584,000		
❏ F-2117C★ (W-3079C★) • 256,000		
❏ F-2117D (W-3079D) • 5,120,000		
❏ F-2117D★ (W-3079D★) • 192,000		
❏ F-2117E (W-3079E) • 2,304,000		
❏ F-2117E★ (W-3079E★) • 64,000		
❏ F-2117F (W-3079F) • 256,000		
❏ F-2117F★ (W-3079F★) • 64,000		
❏ F-2117G (W-3079G) • 6,784,000		

F-No. (W-No.) • Printage *(rarity)*	Grade	Comments
Series of 1969–1969-C *(continued)*		
❏ F-2117G★ (W-3079G★) • 576,000		
❏ F-2117H (W-3079H) • 2,688,000		
❏ F-2117H★ (W-3079H★) • 64,000		
❏ F-2117I (W-3079I) • 256,000		
❏ F-2117I★ (W-3079I★) • 64,000		
❏ F-2117J (W-3079J) • 1,280,000		
❏ F-2117J★ (W-3079J★) • 128,000		
❏ F-2117K (W-3079K) • 3,456,000		
❏ F-2117K★ (W-3079K★) • 64,000		
❏ F-2117L (W-3079L) • 4,608,000		
❏ F-2117L★ (W-3079L★) • 256,000		
Series of 1974		
❏ F-2118A (W-3080A) • 3,840,000		
❏ F-2118A★ (W-3080A★) • 256,000		
❏ F-2118B (W-3080B) • 38,400,000		
❏ F-2118B★ (W-3080B★) • 768,000		
❏ F-2118C (W-3080C) • 7,040,000		
❏ F-2118C★ (W-3080C★) • 192,000		
❏ F-2118D (W-3080D) • 21,200,000		
❏ F-2118D★ (W-3080D★) • 640,000		
❏ F-2118E (W-3080E) • 14,080,000		
❏ F-2118E★ (W-3080E★) • 576,000		
❏ F-2118F (W-3080F) • 1,280,000		
❏ F-2118F★ (W-3080F★) • 640,000		
❏ F-2118G (W-3080G) • 30,720,000		
❏ F-2118G★ (W-3080G★) • 1,536,000		
❏ F-2118H (W-3080H) • 1,920,000		
❏ F-2118H★ (W-3080H★) • 128,000		
❏ F-2118I (W-3080I) • 3,200,000		
❏ F-2118I★ (W-3080I★) • 192,000		
❏ F-2118J (W-3080J) • 4,480,000		
❏ F-2118J★ (W-3080J★) • 192,000		
❏ F-2118K (W-3080K) • 8,320,000		

F-No. (W-No.) • Printage *(rarity)*	Grade	Comments
❑ F-2118K★ (W-3080K★) • 128,000		
❑ F-2118L (W-3080L) • 7,378,000		
❑ F-2118L★ (W-3080L★) • 64,000		
Series of 1977		
❑ F-2119A (W-3081A) • 16,400,000		
❑ F-2119A★ (W-3081A★) • 1,088,000		
❑ F-2119B (W-3081B) • 49,920,000		
❑ F-2119B★ (W-3081B★) • 2,112,000		
❑ F-2119C (W-3081C) • 5,120,000		
❑ F-2119C★ (W-3081C★) • 128,000		
❑ F-2119D (W-3081D) • 23,040,000		
❑ F-2119D★ (W-3081D★) • 1,024,000		
❑ F-2119E (W-3081E) • 19,200,000		
❑ F-2119E★ (W-3081E★) • 896,000		
❑ F-2119F (W-3081F) • 2,560,000		
❑ F-2119F★ (W-3081F★) • 128,000		
❑ F-2119G (W-3081G) • 47,360,000		
❑ F-2119G★ (W-3081G★) • 2,304,000		
❑ F-2119H (W-3081H) • 3,840,000		
❑ F-2119H★ (W-3081H★) • 512,000		
❑ F-2119I (W-3081I) • 3,840,000		
❑ F-2119I★ (W-3081I★) • 128,000		
❑ F-2119J (W-3081J) • 7,680,000		
❑ F-2119J★ (W-3081J★) • 256,000		
❑ F-2119K (W-3081K) • 14,080,000		
❑ F-2119K★ (W-3081K★) • 576,000		
❑ F-2119L (W-3081L) • 19,200,000		
❑ F-2119L★ (W-3081L★) • 768,000		
Series of 1981 and 1981-A		
❑ F-2120A (W-3082A) • 18,560,000		
❑ F-2120B (W-3082B) • 78,080,000		
❑ F-2120B★ (W-3082B★) • 768,000		
❑ F-2120C (W-3082C) • 1,280,000		
❑ F-2120D (W-3082D) • 28,160,000		

F-No. (W-No.) • Printage *(rarity)*	Grade	Comments
Series of 1981 and 1981-A *(continued)*		
❑ F-2120D★ (W-3082D★) • 256,000		
❑ F-2120E (W-3082E) • 25,600,000		
❑ F-2120F (W-3082F) • 4,480,000		
❑ F-2120F★ (W-3082F★) • 768,000		
❑ F-2120G (W-3082G) • 67,200,000		
❑ F-2120G★ (W-3082G★) • 128,000		
❑ F-2120H (W-3082H) • 4,480,000		
❑ F-2120I (W-3082I) • 5,760,000		
❑ F-2120I★ (W-3082I★) • 128,000		
❑ F-2120J (W-3082J) • 18,560,000		
❑ F-2120J★ (W-3082J★) • 128,000		
❑ F-2120K (W-3082K) • 19,840,000		
❑ F-2120L (W-3082L) • 35,200,000		
❑ F-2120L★ (W-3082L★) • 256,000		
❑ F-2121A (W-3083A) • 9,600,000		
❑ F-2121B (W-3083B) • 28,800,000		
❑ F-2121B★ (W-3083B★) • 3,200,000		
❑ F-2121D (W-3083D) • 12,800,000		
❑ F-2121E (W-3083E) • 704,000		
❑ F-2121E★ (W-3083E★) • 704,000		
❑ F-2121F (W-3083F) • 3,200,000		
❑ F-2121G (W-3083G) • 28,800,000		
❑ F-2121H (W-3083H) • 3,200,000		
❑ F-2121I (W-3083I) • 3,200,000		
❑ F-2121J (W-3083J) • 6,400,000		
❑ F-2121K (W-3083K) • 6,400,000		
❑ F-2121L (W-3083L) • 22,400,000		
❑ F-2121L★ (W-3083L★) • 640,000		
Series of 1985		
❑ F-2122A (W-3084A) • 51,200,000		
❑ F-2122A★ (W-3084A★) • 64,000		
❑ F-2122B (W-3084B) • 182,400,000		
❑ F-2122B★ (W-3084B★) • 1,408,000		

F-No. (W-No.) • Printage *(rarity)*	Grade	Comments
❑ F-2122C (W-3084C) • 3,200,000		
❑ F-2122D (W-3084D) • 57,600,000		
❑ F-2122D★ (W-3084D★) • 64,000		
❑ F-2122E (W-3084E) • 54,400,000		
❑ F-2122F (W-3084F) • 9,600,000		
❑ F-2122G (W-3084G) • 112,000,000		
❑ F-2122G★ (W-3084G★) • 1,280,000		
❑ F-2122H (W-3084H) • 6,400,000		
❑ F-2122I (W-3084I) • 12,800,000		
❑ F-2122J (W-3084J) • 9,600,000		
❑ F-2122K (W-3084K) • 25,600,000		
❑ F-2122L (W-3084L) • 57,600,000		
Series of 1988		
❑ F-2123A (W-3085A) • 9,600,000		
❑ F-2123B (W-3085B) • 214,400,000		
❑ F-2123B★ (W-3085B★) • 1,408,000		
❑ F-2123D (W-3085D) • 32,000,000		
❑ F-2123E (W-3085E) • 12,800,000		
❑ F-2123G (W-3085G) • 80,000,000		
❑ F-2123J (W-3085J) • 6,400,000		
❑ F-2123L (W-3085L) • 12,800,000		
Series of 1990		
❑ F-2124A (W-3086A) • 28,800,000		
❑ F-2124B (W-3086B) • 232,000,000		
❑ F-2124B★ (W-3086B★) • 3,116,000		
❑ F-2124C (W-3086C) • 41,600,000		
❑ F-2124C★ (W-3086C★) • 1,280,000		
❑ F-2124D (W-3086D) • 92,800,000		
❑ F-2124E (W-3086E) • 76,800,000		
❑ F-2124G (W-3086G) • 108,800,000		
❑ F-2124G★ (W-3086G★) • 1,032,000		
❑ F-2124H (W-3086H) • 16,000,000		
❑ F-2124I (W-3086I) • 22,400,000		
❑ F-2124J (W-3086J) • 35,200,000		
❑ F-2124J★ (W-3086J★) • 640,000		

$50

F-No. (W-No.) • Printage *(rarity)*	Grade	Comments
Series of 1990 *(continued)*		
❏ F-2124K (W-3086K) • 16,000,000		
❏ F-2124L (W-3086L) • 119,200,000		
Series of 1993		
❏ F-2125A (W-3087A) • 41,600,000		
❏ F-2125B (W-3087B) • 544,000,000		
❏ F-2125B★ (W-3087B★) • 4,224,000		
❏ F-2125D (W-3087D) • 60,800,000		
❏ F-2125D★ (W-3087D★) • 1,280,000		
❏ F-2125E (W-3087E) • 35,200,000		
❏ F-2125G (W-3087G) • 144,000,000		
❏ F-2125G★ (W-3087G★) • 1,280,000		
❏ F-2125H (W-3087H) • 3,200,000		
❏ F-2125J (W-3087J) • 12,800,000		
❏ F-2125K (W-3087K) • 9,600,000		
Series of 1996		
❏ F-2126A (W-3088A) • 54,400,000		
❏ F-2126B (W-3088B) • 560,800,000		
❏ F-2126B★ (W-3088B★) • 5,120,000		
❏ F-2126C (W-3088C) • 76,800,000		
❏ F-2126D (W-3088D) • 119,200,000		
❏ F-2126E (W-3088E) • 106,400,000		
❏ F-2126F (W-3088F) • 119,200,000		
❏ F-2126G (W-3088G) • 241,600,000		
❏ F-2126G★ (W-3088G★) • 1,280,000		
❏ F-2126H (W-3088H) • 28,800,000		
❏ F-2126I (W-3088I) • 35,200,000		
❏ F-2126J (W-3088J) • 57,600,000		
❏ F-2126J★ (W-3088J★) • 1,920,000		
❏ F-2126K (W-3088K) • 92,800,000		
❏ F-2126L (W-3088L) • 219,200,000		
❏ F-2126L★ (W-3088L★) • 3,200,000		
Series of 2001		
❏ F-2127A (W-3089A) • 6,400,000		
❏ F-2127B (W-3089B) • 54,400,000		

F-No. (W-No.) • Printage *(rarity)*	Grade	Comments
❏ F-2127B★ (W-3089B★) • 320,000		
❏ F-2127C (W-3089C) • 19,200,000		
❏ F-2127D (W-3089D) • 16,000,000		
❏ F-2127E (W-3089E) • 32,000,000		
❏ F-2127E★ (W-3089E★) • 640,000		
❏ F-2127F (W-3089F) • 22,800,000		
❏ F-2127G (W-3089G) • 35,200,000		
❏ F-2127H (W-3089H) • 3,200,000		
❏ F-2127I (W-3089I) • 3,200,000		
❏ F-2127J (W-3089J) • 3,200,000		
❏ F-2127K (W-3089K) • 6,400,000		
❏ F-2127L (W-3089L) • 32,000,000		
Series of 2004 and 2004-A		
❏ F-2128A (W-3090A) • 9,600,000		
❏ F-2128B (W-3090B) • 41,600,000		
❏ F-2128C (W-3090C) • 22,400,000		
❏ F-2128D (W-3090D) • 32,000,000		
❏ F-2128E (W-3090E) • 3,200,000		
❏ F-2128E★ (W-3090E★) • 800,000		
❏ F-2128F (W-3090F) • 44,800,000		
❏ F-2128G (W-3090G) • 115,200,000		
❏ F-2128G★ (W-3090G★) • 3,200,000		
❏ F-2128H (W-3090H) • 9,600,000		
❏ F-2128I (W-3090I) • 12,800,000		
❏ F-2128J (W-3090J) • 22,400,000		
❏ F-2128K (W-3090K) • 32,000,000		
❏ F-2128K★ (W-3090K★) • 3,200,000		
❏ F-2128L (W-3090L) • 51,200,000		
❏ F-2129A (W-3091A) • 16,000,000		
❏ F-2129B (W-3091B) • 38,400,000		
❏ F-2129B★ (W-3091B★) • 64,000		
❏ F-2129E (W-3091E) • 32,000,000		
❏ F-2129E★ (W-3091E★) • 2,560,000		
❏ F-2129F (W-3091F) • 51,200,000		

F-No. (W-No.) • Printage *(rarity)*	Grade	Comments
Series of 2004 and 2004-A *(continued)*		
❏ F-2129G (W-3091G) • 54,400,000		
❏ F-2129J (W-3091J) • 19,200,000		
❏ F-2129L (W-3091L) • 6,400,000		
Series of 2006		
❏ F-2130A (W-3092A) • 48,000,000		
❏ F-2130A★ (W-3092A★) • 640,000		
❏ F-2130B (W-3092B) • 185,600,000		
❏ F-2130C (W-3092C) • 38,400,000		
❏ F-2130D (W-3092D) • 70,400,000		
❏ F-2130E (W-3092E) • 41,600,000		
❏ F-2130F (W-3092F) • 32,000,000		
❏ F-2130G (W-3092G) • 48,000,000		
❏ F-2130G★ (W-3092G★) • 512,000		
❏ F-2130H (W-3092H) • 6,400,000		
❏ F-2130I (W-3092I) • 28,800,000		
❏ F-2130J (W-3092J) • 12,800,000		
❏ F-2130K (W-3092K) • 44,800,000		
❏ F-2130L (W-3092L) • 92,800,000		
Series of 2009		
❏ F-2131A • 25,600,000		
❏ F-2131A★ • 640,000		
❏ F-2131B • 153,600,000		
❏ F-2131C • 25,600,000		
❏ F-2131D • 86,400,000		
❏ F-2131E • 51,200,000		
❏ F-2131F • 70,400,000		
❏ F-2131G • 76,800,000		
❏ F-2131G★ • 3,200,000		
❏ F-2131H • 6,400,000		
❏ F-2131I • 19,200,000		
❏ F-2131J • 28,800,000		
❏ F-2131K • 44,800,000		
❏ F-2131K★ • 640,000		
❏ F-2131L • 76,800,000		

F-No. (W-No.) • Printage *(rarity)*	Grade	Comments
Series of 2013		
❏ F-2132A		
❏ F-2132B		
❏ F-2132C		
❏ F-2132D		
❏ F-2132E		
❏ F-2132E★		
❏ F-2132F		
❏ F-2132G		
❏ F-2132H		
❏ F-2132I		
❏ F-2132J		
❏ F-2132K		
❏ F-2132K★		
❏ F-2132L		
❏		
❏		
Series of 2017		
❏		
❏		
❏		
❏		
❏		
❏		
❏		
❏		
❏		
❏		
❏		
❏		
❏		
❏		
❏		
❏		

LARGE-SIZE

$100 Interest-Bearing Notes

F-No. (W-No.) • Printage *(rarity)*	Grade	Comments
March 3, 1863, 5%, 1 Year		
❑ F-199 (W-3245) • 136,400 *(3 known)*		
March 3, 1863, 5%, 2 Years		
❑ F-204 (W-3260) • 96,800 *(2 known)*		
June 30, 1864, 7.3%, 3 Years		
❑ F-212a (W-3280) • 566,039 *(4 known)*		
March 3, 1865, 7.3%, 3 Years		
❑ F-212e (W-3300) • 338,227 *(1 known)*		
❑ F-212e (W-3310) • 472,080 *(2 known)*		

$100 Legal Tender Notes

F-No. (W-No.) • Printage *(rarity)*	Grade	Comments
Series of 1862, First Obligation		
❑ F-165 (W-3430) • est. 100,000 *(15–17)*		
❑ F-165a (W-3432) • est. 35,000 *(12–14)*		
❑ F-165a (W-3433) • est. 155,000 *(12–14)*		
Series of 1862 and 1863, Second Obligation		
❑ F-167 (W-3435) • 29,440 *(2 known)*		
❑ F-167a (W-3436) • 56,560 *(27–30)*		
❑ F-167b (W-3434) • 24,000 *(2 known)*		
Series of 1869		
❑ F-168 (W-3480) • 364,000 *(30–33)*		
Series of 1875		
❑ F-169 (W-3481) • 122,000 *(13–15)*		

F-No. (W-No.) • Printage *(rarity)*	Grade	Comments
❑ F-170 (W-3482) • 40,000 *(6 known)*		
Series of 1878		
❑ F-171 (W-3483) • 202,000 *(22–25)*		
Series of 1880		
❑ F-172 (W-3484) • 60,000 *(12–14)*		
❑ F-173 (W-3485) • 80,000 *(10–12)*		
❑ F-174 (W-3486) • 80,000 *(20–23)*		
❑ F-175 (W-3487) • 20,000 *(2 known)*		
❑ F-176 (W-3488) • 80,000 *(12–14)*		
❑ F-177 (W-3489) • 80,000 *(23–26)*		
❑ F-178 (W-3490) • 60,000 *(18–20)*		
❑ F-179 (W-3491) • 172,000 *(30–35)*		
❑ F-180 (W-3492) • 28,000 *(7 known)*		
❑ F-181 (W-3493) • 176,000 *(60–70)*		

$100 Compound Interest Treasury Notes

F-No. (W-No.) • Printage *(rarity)*	Grade	Comments
Series of 1863 and 1864		
❑ F-193 (W-3350) • 450,944 *(2 known)*		
❑ F-193a (W-3370) • incl. above *(1 known)*		
❑ F-193b (W-3390) • incl. above *(12–14)*		

$100 National Bank Notes

F-No. (W-No.) • Printage *(rarity)*	Grade	Comments
Original Series ("First Charter Period")		
❑ F-452 (W-3500) • *(4 known)*		
❑ F-454 (W-3501) • *(16–18)*		
❑ F-455 (W-3502) • *(3 known)*		
Series of 1875 ("First Charter Period")		
❑ F-456 (W-3530) • *(16–18)*		
❑ F-457 (W-3531) • *(7 known)*		
❑ F-458 (W-3532) • *(4 known)*		
❑ F-459 (W-3533) • *(9–10)*		
❑ F-460 (W-3534) • *(7 known)*		
❑ F-461 (W-3535) • *(3 known)*		
❑ F-462 (W-3536) • *(1 known)*		
❑ F-462a (W-3537) • *(1 known)*		

F-No. (W-No.) • Printage *(rarity)*	Grade	Comments
Series of 1875 ("First Charter Period") *(continued)*		
❑ F-463 (W-3538) • *(4 known)*		
Series of 1882, Brown Back ("Second Charter Period")		
❑ F-519 (W-3544) • *(19–22)*		
❑ F-520 (W-3545) • *(52–56)*		
❑ F-521 (W-3546) • *(6 known)*		
❑ F-522 (W-3547) • *(32–35)*		
❑ F-523 (W-3548) • *(10–12)*		
❑ F-524 (W-3549) • *(32–35)*		
❑ F-525 (W-3550) • *(20–23)*		
❑ F-526 (W-3551) • *(7 known)*		
❑ F-527 (W-3552) • *(35–40)*		
❑ F-528 (W-3553) • *(7 known)*		
❑ F-529 (W-3554) • *(16–18)*		
❑ F-530 (W-3555) • *(55–60)*		
❑ F-531 (W-3556) • *(10–12)*		
Series of 1882, Date Back ("Second Charter Period")		
❑ F-566 (W-3560) • *(9–10)*		
❑ F-567 (W-3561) • *(13–15)*		
❑ F-568 (W-3562) • *(30–35)*		
❑ F-569 (W-3563) • *(12–14)*		
❑ F-570 (W-3564) • *(3 known)*		
❑ F-571 (W-3565) • *(60–70)*		
❑ F-572 (W-3566) • *(3 known)*		
❑ F-572a (W-3567) • *(6 known)*		
Series of 1882, Value Back ("Second Charter Period")		
❑ F-586a (W-3569) • 2,857 *(5 known)*		
Series of 1902, Red Seal ("Third Charter Period")		
❑ F-686 (W-3570) • *(95–105)*		
❑ F-687 (W-3571) • *(9–10)*		
❑ F-688 (W-3572) • *(6 known)*		
Series of 1902, Blue Seal, Date Back ("Third Charter Period")		
❑ F-689 (W-3573) • *(260–275)*		
❑ F-690 (W-3574) • *(48–54)*		
❑ F-691 (W-3575) • *(110–120)*		
❑ F-692 (W-3576) • *(90–100)*		

F-No. (W-No.) • Printage *(rarity)*	Grade	Comments
❑ F-693 (W-3577) • *(60–65)*		
❑ F-694 (W-3578) • *(8 known)*		
❑ F-695 (W-3579) • *(15–17)*		
❑ F-696 (W-3580) • *(18–20)*		
❑ F-697 (W-3581) • *(12–14)*		
Series of 1902, Blue Seal, Plain Back ("Third Charter Period")		
❑ F-698 (W-3582) • *(120–130)*		
❑ F-699 (W-3583) • *(22–25)*		
❑ F-700 (W-3584) • *(48–54)*		
❑ F-701 (W-3585) • *(70–80)*		
❑ F-702 (W-3586) • *(35–40)*		
❑ F-702a (W-3587) • *(19–22)*		
❑ F-703 (W-3589) • *(15–17)*		
❑ F-704 (W-3590) • *(75–85)*		
❑ F-705 (W-3591) • *(60–70)*		
❑ F-706 (W-3592) • *(60–70)*		
❑ F-707 (W-3593) • *(38–47)*		
❑ F-707a (W-3594) • *(2 known)*		

$100 National Gold Bank Notes

F-No. (W-No.) • Printage *(rarity)*	Grade	Comments
Original Series		
❑ F-1162 (W-3510) • 2,000 *(3 known)*		
❑ F-1164 (W-3516) • 200 *(1 known)*		
❑ F-1165 (W-3520) • 400 *(2 known)*		
❑ F-1166 (W-3524) • 100 *(1 known)*		
Series of 1875		
❑ F-1163 (W-3540) • 620 *(2 known)*		

$100 Silver Certificates

F-No. (W-No.) • Printage *(rarity)*	Grade	Comments
Series of 1878		
❑ F-336 (W-3600) • est. 1,500 *(1 known)*		
❑ F-337 (W-3612) • est. 4,000 *(1 known)*		
❑ F-337b (W-3616) • est. 36,000 *(4 known)*		

F-No. (W-No.) • Printage (rarity)	Grade	Comments
Series of 1880		
❏ F-339 (W-3621) • est. 40,000 (4 known)		
❏ F-340 (W-3622) • 80,000 (12–14)		
❏ F-341 (W-3623) • 100,000 (30–35)		
❏ F-342 (W-3624) • 40,000 (13–15)		
Series of 1891		
❏ F-343 (W-3625) • est. 120,000 (23–26)		
❏ F-344 (W-3626) • est. 384,000 (33–36)		

$100 Treasury or Coin Notes

F-No. (W-No.) • Printage (rarity)	Grade	Comments
Series of 1890		
❏ F-377 (W-3630) • 120,000 (37–39)		
Series of 1891		
❏ F-378 (W-3634) • 80,000 (13–15)		

$100 Gold Certificates

F-No. (W-No.) • Printage (rarity)	Grade	Comments
Act of March 3, 1863		
❏ F-1166c (W-3639) • est. 48,000 (2 known)		
❏ F-1166c (W-3640) • est. 72,000 (1 known)		
Series of 1875		
❏ F-1166m (W-3652) • 50,000 (2 known)		
❏ F-unlisted (W-3656) • 20,000 (1 known)		
Series of 1882		
❏ F-1201 (W-3664) • 80,000 (7 known)		
❏ F-1202 (W-3660) • 9,000 (2 known)		
❏ F-1202a (W-3662) • 71,000 (3 known)		
❏ F-1203 (W-3666) • 40,000 (3 known)		
❏ F-1204 (W-3668) • 40,000 (4 known)		
❏ F-1205 (W-3670) • 60,000 (8 known)		
❏ F-1206 (W-3672) • 1,160,000 (47–53)		
❏ F-1207 (W-3674) • 296,000 (21–24)		
❏ F-1208 (W-3676) • 320,000 (30–35)		
❏ F-1209 (W-3678) • 402,000 (52–60)		
❏ F-1210 (W-3680) • 202,000 (32–35)		
❏ F-1211 (W-3682) • 198,000 (54–58)		
❏ F-1212 (W-3684) • 200,000 (47–53)		

F-No. (W-No.) • Printage (rarity)	Grade	Comments
❑ F-1213 (W-3686) • 200,000 (44–48)		
❑ F-1214 (W-3688) • 1,020,000 (320–340)		
Series of 1922		
❑ F-1215 (W-3690) • 2,444,000 (750–850)		
❑ F-1215★ (W-3690★) • (29–32)		

$100 Federal Reserve Notes

F-No. (W-No.) • Printage (rarity)	Grade	Comments
Series of 1914, Red Seal		
❑ F-1072A (W-3700A-a) • 16,000 (25–28)		
❑ F-1072B (W-3700A-b) • 28,000 (18–20)		
❑ F-1073A (W-3700B-a) • 60,000 (16–18)		
❑ F-1073B (W-3700B-b) • 20,000 (6 known)		
❑ F-1074A (W-3700C-a) • 12,000 (16–18)		
❑ F-1074B (W-3700C-b) • 40,000 (25–28)		
❑ F-1075A (W-3700D-a) • 8,000 (6 known)		
❑ F-1075B (W-3700D-b) • 40,000 (25–28)		
❑ F-1076A (W-3700E-a) • 16,000 (15–17)		
❑ F-1076B (W-3700E-b) • 8,000 (6 known)		
❑ F-1077A (W-3700F-a) • 16,000 (8 known)		
❑ F-1077B (W-3700F-b) • 4,000 (2 known)		
❑ F-1078A (W-3700G-a) • 16,000 (11–13)		
❑ F-1078B (W-3700G-b) • 44,000 (32–35)		
❑ F-1079A (W-3700H-a) • 12,000 (11–13)		
❑ F-1079B (W-3700H-b) • 20,000 (10–12)		
❑ F-1080A (W-3700I-a) • 8,000 (3 known)		
❑ F-1080B (W-3700I-b) • 12,000 (9–10)		
❑ F-1081A (W-3700J-a) • 8,000 (9–10)		
❑ F-1081B (W-3700J-b) • 12,000 (18–20)		
❑ F-1082A (W-3700K-a) • 8,000 (6 known)		
❑ F-1082B (W-3700K-b) • 8,000 (5 known)		
❑ F-1083A (W-3700L-a) • 8,000 (8 known)		
❑ F-1083B (W-3700L-b) • 28,000 (24–27)		
Series of 1914, Blue Seal		
❑ F-1084 (W-3710A) • est. 296,000 (30–35)		

F-No. (W-No.) • Printage *(rarity)*	Grade	Comments
Series of 1914, Blue Seal *(continued)*		
❑ F-1085 (W-3711A) • est. 216,000 *(35–40)*		
❑ F-1087 (W-3713A) • est. 172,000 *(32–35)*		
❑ F-1088 (W-3714B) • est. 2,000,000 *(160–170)*		
❑ F-1088★ (W-3714B★) • *(1 known)*		
❑ F-1089 (W-3715B) • est. 288,000 *(58–63)*		
❑ F-1090 (W-3716B) • est. 368,000 *(105–115)*		
❑ F-1090★ (W-3716B★) • *(3 known)*		
❑ F-1091 (W-3717B) • est. 348,000 *(36–42)*		
❑ F-1092 (W-3718C) • est. 548,000 *(110–120)*		
❑ F-1095 (W-3721C) • est. 60,000 *(5 known)*		
❑ F-1096 (W-3722D) • est. 188,000 *(25–28)*		
❑ F-1097 (W-3723D) • est. 68,000 *(16–18)*		
❑ F-1098 (W-3724D) • est. 232,000 *(45–50)*		
❑ F-1098★ (W-3724D★) • *(1 known)*		
❑ F-1099 (W-3725D) • est. 132,000 *(36–42)*		
❑ F-1100 (W-3726E) • est. 272,000 *(48–54)*		
❑ F-1100★ (W-3726E★) • *(1 known)*		
❑ F-1101 (W-3727E) • est. 208,000 *(13–15)*		
❑ F-1104 (W-3730F) • est. 408,000 *(215–230)*		
❑ F-1104★ (W-3730F★) • *(1 known)*		
❑ F-1106 (W-3732F) • est. 12,000 *(7 known)*		
❑ F-1107 (W-3733F) • est. 100,000 *(12–14)*		
❑ F-1108 (W-3734G) • est. 596,000 *(110–120)*		
❑ F-1108★ (W-3734G★) • *(2 known)*		
❑ F-1110 (W-3736G) • est. 228,000 *(75–85)*		
❑ F-1112 (W-3738H) • est. 156,000 *(70–80)*		
❑ F-1116 (W-3742I) • est. 64,000 *(45–50)*		
❑ F-1119 (W-3745I) • est. 40,000 *(13–15)*		
❑ F-1120 (W-3746J) • est. 164,000 *(36–42)*		
❑ F-1120★ (W-3746J★) • *(4 known)*		
❑ F-1123 (W-3749J) • est. 72,000 *(32–35)*		
❑ F-1124 (W-3750K) • est. 96,000 *(40–45)*		
❑ F-1124★ (W-3750K★) • *(1 known)*		

F-No. (W-No.) • Printage *(rarity)*	Grade	Comments
❏ F-1127 (W-3753K) • est. 28,000 *(4 known)*		
❏ F-1128 (W-3754L) • est. 592,000 *(95–105)*		
❏ F-1128★ (W-3754L★) • *(1 known)*		
❏ F-1130 (W-3756L) • est. 196,000 *(60–65)*		
❏ F-1131 (W-3757L) • est. 240,000 *(40–45)*		

SMALL-SIZE

$100 National Bank Notes

F-No. (W-No.) • Printage *(rarity)*	Grade	Comments
Series of 1929, Type 1		
❏ F-1804-1 (W-3803) • *(2,700–2,900)*		
Series of 1929, Type 2		
❏ F-1804-2 (W-3805) • *(300–320)*		

$100 Gold Certificates

F-No. (W-No.) • Printage *(rarity)*	Grade	Comments
Series of 1928		
❏ F-2405 (W-3818) • 3,240,000		
❏ F-2405★ (W-3818★) • 12,000		

$100 Federal Reserve Bank Notes

F-No. (W-No.) • Printage *(rarity)*	Grade	Comments
Series of 1929		
❏ F-1890B (W-3810B) • 480,000		
❏ F-1890B★ (W-3810B★)		
❏ F-1890D (W-3811D) • 276,000		
❏ F-1890D★ (W-3811D★)		
❏ F-1890E (W-3812E) • 192,000		

F-No. (W-No.) • Printage *(rarity)*	Grade	Comments
Series of 1929 *(continued)*		
❏ F-1890E★ (W-3812E★)		
❏ F-1890G (W-3813G) • 384,000		
❏ F-1890G★ (W-3813G★)		
❏ F-1890I (W-3814I) • 144,000		
❏ F-1890I★ (W-3814I★)		
❏ F-1890J (W-3815J) • 96,000		
❏ F-1890J★ (W-3815J★)		
❏ F-1890K (W-3816K) • 36,000		
❏ F-1890K★ (W-3815K★)		

$100 Legal Tender Notes

F-No. (W-No.) • Printage *(rarity)*	Grade	Comments
Series of 1966 and 1966-A		
❏ F-1550 (W-3800) • 768,000		
❏ F-1550★ (W-3800★) • 128,000		
❏ F-1551 (W-3801) • 512,000		

$100 Federal Reserve Notes

F-No. (W-No.) • Printage *(rarity)*	Grade	Comments
Series of 1928		
❏ F-2150A (W-3820A) • 376,000		
❏ F-2150A★ (W-3820A★)		
❏ F-2150B (W-3820B) • 755,400		
❏ F-2150B★ (W-3820B★)		
❏ F-2150C (W-3820C) • 389,100		
❏ F-2150C★ (W-3820C★)		
❏ F-2150D (W-3820D) • 542,400		
❏ F-2150D★ (W-3820D★)		
❏ F-2150E (W-3820E) • 364,416		
❏ F-2150E★ (W-3820E★)		
❏ F-2150F (W-3820F) • 357,000		
❏ F-2150F★ (W-3820F★)		
❏ F-2150G (W-3820G) • 783,300		
❏ F-2150G★ (W-3820G★)		
❏ F-2150H (W-3820H) • 187,200		

F-No. (W-No.) • Printage *(rarity)*	Grade	Comments
❏ F-2150H★ (W-3820H★)		
❏ F-2150I (W-3820I) • 102,000		
❏ F-2150I★ (W-3820I★)		
❏ F-2150J (W-3820J) • 234,612		
❏ F-2150J★ (W-3820J★)		
❏ F-2150K (W-3820K) • 80,140		
❏ F-2150K★ (W-3820K★)		
❏ F-2150L (W-3820L) • 486,000		
❏ F-2150L★ (W-3820L★)		
Series of 1928-A, Green Seal		
❏ F-2151A (W-3821A) • 890,400		
❏ F-2151B (W-3821B) • 2,938,176		
❏ F-2151C (W-3821C) • 1,496,844		
❏ F-2151D (W-3821D) • 992,436		
❏ F-2151E (W-3821E) • 621,364		
❏ F-2151F (W-3821F) • 371,400		
❏ F-2151G (W-3821G) • 4,010,424		
❏ F-2151H (W-3821H) • 749,544		
❏ F-2151I (W-3821I) • 503,040		
❏ F-2151J (W-3821J) • 681,804		
❏ F-2151K (W-3821K) • 594,456		
❏ F-2151L (W-3821L) • 1,228,032		
Series of 1928-A, Light Yellow-Green Seal		
❏ F-2151B (W-3822B) • incl. in F-2151B/W-3821B		
❏ F-2151B★ (W-3822B★)		
❏ F-2151G (W-3822G) • incl. in F-2151G/W-3821G		
❏ F-2151H (W-3822H) • incl. in F-2151H/W-3821H		
❏ F-2151H★ (W-3822H★)		
❏ F-2151I (W-3822I) • incl. in F-2151I/W-3821I		
❏ F-2151J (W-3822J) • incl. in F-2151J/W-3821J		
❏ F-2151L (W-3822L) • incl. in F-2151L/W-3821L		
Series of 1934, Light Yellow-Green Seal		
❏ F-2152A (W-3823A) • 3,710,000		
❏ F-2152A★ (W-3823A★)		
❏ F-2152B (W-3823B) • 3,086,000		

F-No. (W-No.) • Printage *(rarity)*	Grade	Comments
Series of 1934, Light Yellow-Green Seal *(continued)*		
❑ F-2152B★ (W-3823B★)		
❑ F-2152C (W-3823C) • 2,776,800		
❑ F-2152C★ (W-3823C★)		
❑ F-2152D (W-3823D) • 3,447,108		
❑ F-2152D★ (W-3823D★)		
❑ F-2152E (W-3823E) • 4,317,600		
❑ F-2152E★ (W-3823E★)		
❑ F-2152F (W-3823F) • 3,264,420		
❑ F-2152F★ (W-3823F★)		
❑ F-2152G (W-3823G) • 7,075,000		
❑ F-2152G★ (W-3823G★)		
❑ F-2152H (W-3823H) • 2,106,192		
❑ F-2152H★ (W-3823H★)		
❑ F-2152I (W-3823I) • 852,600		
❑ F-2152I★ (W-3823I★)		
❑ F-2152J (W-3823J) • 1,932,900		
❑ F-2152J★ (W-3823J★)		
❑ F-2152K (W-3823K) • 1,506,516		
❑ F-2152K★ (W-3823K★)		
❑ F-2152L (W-3823L) • 6,521,940		
❑ F-2152L★ (W-3823L★)		
Series of 1934, Green Seal		
❑ F-2152A (W-3824A) • incl. in F-2152A/W-3823A		
❑ F-2152A★ (W-3824A★)		
❑ F-2152A (W-3824A Mule)		
❑ F-2152B (W-3824B) • incl. in F-2152B/W-3823B		
❑ F-2152B★ (W-3824B★)		
❑ F-2152C (W-3824C) • incl. in F-2152C/W-3823C		
❑ F-2152C★ (W-3824C★)		
❑ F-2152C (W-3824C Mule)		
❑ F-2152D (W-3824D) • incl. in F-2152D/W-3823D		
❑ F-2152D★ (W-3824D★)		
❑ F-2152D (W-3824D Mule)		

F-No. (W-No.) • Printage *(rarity)*	Grade	Comments
❏ F-2152E (W-3824E) • incl. in F-2152E/W-3823E		
❏ F-2152E★ (W-3824E★)		
❏ F-2152E★ (W-3824E★ Mule)		
❏ F-2152F (W-3824F) • incl. in F-2152F/W-3823F		
❏ F-2152F★ (W-3824F★)		
❏ F-2152F (W-3824F Mule)		
❏ F-2152G (W-3824G) • incl. in F-2152G/W-3823G		
❏ F-2152G★ (W-3824G★)		
❏ F-2152G (W-3824G Mule)		
❏ F-2152G★ (W-3824G Mule★)		
❏ F-2152H (W-3824H) • incl. in F-2152H/W-3823H		
❏ F-2152H★ (W-3824H★)		
❏ F-2152H (W-3824H Mule)		
❏ F-2152I (W-3824I) • incl. in F-2152I/W-3823I		
❏ F-2152I★ (W-3824I★)		
❏ F-2152I (W-3824I Mule)		
❏ F-2152J (W-3824J) • incl. in F-2152J/W-3823J		
❏ F-2152J★ (W-3824J★)		
❏ F-2152J (W-3824J Mule)		
❏ F-2152J★ (W-3824J Mule★)		
❏ F-2152K (W-3824K) • incl. in F-2152K/W-3823K		
❏ F-2152K★ (W-3824K★)		
❏ F-2152K (W-3824K Mule)		
❏ F-2152L (W-3824L) • incl. in F-2152L/W-3823L		
❏ F-2152L★ (W-3824L★)		
❏ F-2152 (W-3824L Mule)		
Series of 1934-A–1934-D		
❏ F-2153A (W-3825A) • 102,000		
❏ F-2153A (W-3825A Mule)		
❏ F-2153A★ (W-3825A Mule★)		
❏ F-2153B (W-3825B) • 15,278,892		
❏ F-2153B (W-3825B Mule)		
❏ F-2153B★ (W-3825B Mule★)		
❏ F-2153C (W-3825C) • 588,000		

F-No. (W-No.) • Printage *(rarity)*	Grade	Comments
Series of 1934-A–1934-D *(continued)*		
❏ F-2153C (W-3825C Mule)		
❏ F-2153C★ (W-3825C Mule★)		
❏ F-2153D (W-3825D) • 645,300		
❏ F-2153D (W-3825D Mule)		
❏ F-2153E (W-3825E) • 770,000		
❏ F-2153E (W-3825E Mule)		
❏ F-2153E★ (W-3825E Mule★)		
❏ F-2153F (W-3825F) • 589,886		
❏ F-2153F (W-3825F Mule)		
❏ F-2153F★ (W-3825F Mule★)		
❏ F-2153G (W-3825G) • 3,328,800		
❏ F-2153G (W-3825G Mule)		
❏ F-2153G★ (W-3825G Mule★)		
❏ F-2153H (W-3825H) • 434,208		
❏ F-2153H (W-3825H Mule)		
❏ F-2153I (W-3825I Mule) • 153,000		
❏ F-2153J (W-3825J) • 455,000		
❏ F-2153J (W-3825J Mule)		
❏ F-2153J★ (W-3825J Mule★)		
❏ F-2153K (W-3825K) • 226,164		
❏ F-2153K (W-3825K Mule)		
❏ F-2153L (W-3825L) • 1,130,400		
❏ F-2153L (W-3825L Mule)		
❏ F-2153L★ (W-3825L Mule★)		
❏ F-2154A (W-3826A) • 41,400		
❏ F-2154C (W-3826C) • 39,600		
❏ F-2154D (W-3826D) • 61,200		
❏ F-2154E (W-3826E) • 977,400		
❏ F-2154E★ (W-3826E★)		
❏ F-2154F (W-3826F) • 645,000		
❏ F-2154G (W-3826G) • 396,000		
❏ F-2154H (W-3826H) • 676,200		
❏ F-2154H★ (W-3826H★)		

F-No. (W-No.) • Printage *(rarity)*	Grade	Comments
❏ F-2154I (W-3826I) • 377,000		
❏ F-2154I★ (W-3826I★)		
❏ F-2154J (W-3826J) • 364,500		
❏ F-2154J★ (W-3826J★)		
❏ F-2154K (W-3826K) • 392,700		
❏ F-2154K★ (W-3826K★)		
❏ F-2155A (W-3827A) • 13,800		
❏ F-2155C (W-3827C) • 13,200		
❏ F-2155D (W-3827D) • 1,473,200		
❏ F-2155D★ (W-3827D★)		
❏ F-2155E (W-3827E) • 1,440,000		
❏ F-2155E★ (W-3827E★)		
❏ F-2155F (W-3827F) • 493,900		
❏ F-2155F★ (W-3827F★)		
❏ F-2155G (W-3827G) • 612,000		
❏ F-2155G★ (W-3827G★)		
❏ F-2155H (W-3827H) • 957,000		
❏ F-2155H★ (W-3827H★)		
❏ F-2155I (W-3827I) • 392,904		
❏ F-2155I★ (W-3827I★)		
❏ F-2155J (W-3827J) • 401,100		
❏ F-2155K (W-3827K) • 280,700		
❏ F-2155L (W-3827L) • 432,600		
❏ F-2155L★ (W-3827L★)		
❏ F-2156B (W-3828B) • 156		
❏ F-2156C (W-3828C) • 308,400		
❏ F-2156C★ (W-3828C★)		
❏ F-2156F (W-3828F) • 260,400		
❏ F-2156F★ (W-3828F★)		
❏ F-2156G (W-3828G) • 78,000		
❏ F-2156G★ (W-3828G★)		
❏ F-2156H (W-3828H) • 166,800		
❏ F-2156K (W-3828K) • 66,000		

F-No. (W-No.) • Printage *(rarity)*	Grade	Comments
Series of 1950–1950-E		
❑ F-2157A (W-3829A) • 768,000		
❑ F-2157A★ (W-3829A★)		
❑ F-2157A (W-3829A Mule)		
❑ F-2157B (W-3829B) • 3,908,000		
❑ F-2157B★ (W-3829B★)		
❑ F-2157B (W-3829B Mule)		
❑ F-2157B★ (W-3829B Mule★)		
❑ F-2157C (W-3829C) • 1,332,000		
❑ F-2157C★ (W-3829C★)		
❑ F-2157C (W-3829C Mule)		
❑ F-2157C★ (W-3829C Mule★)		
❑ F-2157D (W-3829D) • 1,632,000		
❑ F-2157D★ (W-3829D★)		
❑ F-2157D (W-3829D Mule)		
❑ F-2157D★ (W-3829D Mule★)		
❑ F-2157E (W-3829E) • 4,076,000		
❑ F-2157E★ (W-3829E★)		
❑ F-2157E (W-3829E Mule)		
❑ F-2157E★ (W-3829E Mule★)		
❑ F-2157F (W-3829F) • 1,824,000		
❑ F-2157F (W-3829F Mule)		
❑ F-2157G (W-3829G) • 4,428,000		
❑ F-2157G (W-3829G Mule)		
❑ F-2157G★ (W-3829G Mule★)		
❑ F-2157H (W-3829H) • 1,284,000		
❑ F-2157H★ (W-3829H★)		
❑ F-2157H (W-3829H Mule)		
❑ F-2157H★ (W-3829H Mule★)		
❑ F-2157I (W-3829I) • 564,000		
❑ F-2157I (W-3829I Mule)		
❑ F-2157J (W-3829J) • 864,000		
❑ F-2157J★ (W-3829J★)		
❑ F-2157J (W-3829J Mule)		

F-No. (W-No.) • Printage *(rarity)*	Grade	Comments
❑ F-2157J★ (W-3829J Mule★)		
❑ F-2157K (W-3829K) • 1,216,000		
❑ F-2157K (W-3829K Mule)		
❑ F-2157L (W-3829L) • 2,524,000		
❑ F-2157L★ (W-3829L★)		
❑ F-2157L (W-3829L Mule)		
❑ F-2157L★ (W-3829L Mule★)		
❑ F-2158A (W-3830A) • 1,008,000		
❑ F-2158A★ (W-3830A★)		
❑ F-2158B (W-3830B) • 2,880,000		
❑ F-2158B★ (W-3830B★)		
❑ F-2158C (W-3830C) • 576,000		
❑ F-2158C★ (W-3830C★)		
❑ F-2158D (W-3830D) • 288,000		
❑ F-2158D★ (W-3830D★)		
❑ F-2158E (W-3830E) • 2,160,000		
❑ F-2158E★ (W-3830E★)		
❑ F-2158F (W-3830F) • 288,000		
❑ F-2158F★ (W-3830F★)		
❑ F-2158G (W-3830G) • 864,000		
❑ F-2158G★ (W-3830G★)		
❑ F-2158H (W-3830H) • 432,000		
❑ F-2158H★ (W-3830H★)		
❑ F-2158I (W-3830I) • 144,000		
❑ F-2158I★ (W-3830I★)		
❑ F-2158J (W-3830J) • 288,000		
❑ F-2158J★ (W-3830J★)		
❑ F-2158K (W-3830K) • 432,000		
❑ F-2158K★ (W-3830K★)		
❑ F-2158L (W-3830L) • 720,000		
❑ F-2158L★ (W-3830L★)		
❑ F-2159A (W-3831A) • 720,000		
❑ F-2159B (W-3831B) • 6,636,000		
❑ F-2159B★ (W-3831B★)		

F-No. (W-No.) • Printage *(rarity)*	Grade	Comments
Series of 1950–1950-E *(continued)*		
❑ F-2159C (W-3831C) • 720,000		
❑ F-2159C★ (W-3831C★)		
❑ F-2159D (W-3831D) • 432,000		
❑ F-2159D★ (W-3831D★)		
❑ F-2159E (W-3831E) • 1,008,000		
❑ F-2159F (W-3831F) • 576,000		
❑ F-2159F★ (W-3831F★)		
❑ F-2159G (W-3831G) • 2,592,000		
❑ F-2159G★ (W-3831G★)		
❑ F-2159H (W-3831H) • 1,152,000		
❑ F-2159H★ (W-3831H★)		
❑ F-2159I (W-3831I) • 288,000		
❑ F-2159I★ (W-3831I★)		
❑ F-2159J (W-3831J) • 720,000		
❑ F-2159J★ (W-3831J★)		
❑ F-2159K (W-3831K) • 1,728,000		
❑ F-2159K★ (W-3831K★)		
❑ F-2159L (W-3831L) • 2,880,000		
❑ F-2159L★ (W-3831L★)		
❑ F-2160A (W-3832A) • 864,000		
❑ F-2160A★ (W-3832A★)		
❑ F-2160B (W-3832B) • 2,448,000		
❑ F-2160B★ (W-3832B★)		
❑ F-2160C (W-3832C) • 576,000		
❑ F-2160C★ (W-3832C★)		
❑ F-2160D (W-3832D) • 576,000		
❑ F-2160D★ (W-3832D★)		
❑ F-2160E (W-3832E) • 1,440,000		
❑ F-2160E★ (W-3832E★)		
❑ F-2160F (W-3832F) • 1,296,000		
❑ F-2160F★ (W-3832F★)		
❑ F-2160G (W-3832G) • 1,584,000		
❑ F-2160G★ (W-3832G★)		

F-No. (W-No.) • Printage *(rarity)*	Grade	Comments
❑ F-2160H (W-3832H) • 720,000		
❑ F-2160H★ (W-3832H★)		
❑ F-2160I (W-3832I) • 288,000		
❑ F-2160J (W-3832J) • 432,000		
❑ F-2160K (W-3832K) • 720,000		
❑ F-2160K★ (W-3832K★)		
❑ F-2160L (W-3832L) • 2,160,000		
❑ F-2160L★ (W-3832L★)		
❑ F-2161A (W-3833A) • 1,872,000		
❑ F-2161A★ (W-3833A★)		
❑ F-2161B (W-3833B) • 7,632,000		
❑ F-2161B★ (W-3833B★)		
❑ F-2161C (W-3833C) • 1,872,000		
❑ F-2161C★ (W-3833C★)		
❑ F-2161D (W-3833D) • 1,584,000		
❑ F-2161D★ (W-3833D★)		
❑ F-2161E (W-3833E) • 2,880,000		
❑ F-2161E★ (W-3833E★)		
❑ F-2161F (W-3833F) • 1,872,000		
❑ F-2161F★ (W-3833F★)		
❑ F-2161G (W-3833G) • 4,608,000		
❑ F-2161G★ (W-3833G★)		
❑ F-2161H (W-3833H) • 1,440,000		
❑ F-2161H★ (W-3833H★)		
❑ F-2161I (W-3833I) • 432,000		
❑ F-2161I★ (W-3833I★)		
❑ F-2161J (W-3833J) • 864,000		
❑ F-2161J★ (W-3833J★)		
❑ F-2161K (W-3833K) • 1,728,000		
❑ F-2161K★ (W-3833K★)		
❑ F-2161L (W-3833L) • 3,312,000		
❑ F-2161L★ (W-3833L★)		
❑ F-2162B (W-3834B) • 3,024,000		
❑ F-2162B★ (W-3834B★)		

F-No. (W-No.) • Printage *(rarity)*	Grade	Comments
Series of 1950–1950-E *(continued)*		
❑ F-2162G (W-3834G) • 576,000		
❑ F-2162L (W-3834L) • 2,736,000		
❑ F-2162L★ (W-3834L★)		
Series of 1963-A		
❑ F-2163A (W-3835A) • 1,536,000		
❑ F-2163A★ (W-3835A★) • 128,000		
❑ F-2163B (W-3835B) • 12,544,000		
❑ F-2163B★ (W-3835B★) • 1,536,000		
❑ F-2163C (W-3835C) • 1,792,000		
❑ F-2163C★ (W-3835C★) • 192,000		
❑ F-2163D (W-3835D) • 2,304,000		
❑ F-2163D★ (W-3835D★) • 192,000		
❑ F-2163E (W-3835E) • 2,816,000		
❑ F-2163E★ (W-3835E★) • 192,000		
❑ F-2163F (W-3835F) • 1,280,000		
❑ F-2163F★ (W-3835F★) • 128,000		
❑ F-2163G (W-3835G) • 4,352,000		
❑ F-2163G★ (W-3835G★) • 512,000		
❑ F-2163H (W-3835H) • 1,536,000		
❑ F-2163H★ (W-3835H★) • 256,000		
❑ F-2163I (W-3835I) • 512,000		
❑ F-2163I★ (W-3835I★) • 128,000		
❑ F-2163J (W-3835J) • 1,024,000		
❑ F-2163J★ (W-3835J★) • 128,000		
❑ F-2163K (W-3835K) • 1,536,000		
❑ F-2163K★ (W-3835K★) • 192,000		
❑ F-2163L (W-3835L) • 6,400,000		
❑ F-2163L★ (W-3835L★) • 832,000		
Series of 1969–1969-A, 1969-C		
❑ F-2164A (W-3836A) • 2,048,000		
❑ F-2164A★ (W-3836A★) • 128,000		
❑ F-2164B (W-3836B) • 11,520,000		
❑ F-2164B★ (W-3836B★) • 128,000		
❑ F-2164C (W-3836C) • 2,560,000		

F-No. (W-No.) • Printage (rarity)	Grade	Comments
❏ F-2164C★ (W-3836C★) • 128,000		
❏ F-2164D (W-3836D) • 768,000		
❏ F-2164D★ (W-3836D★) • 64,000		
❏ F-2164E (W-3836E) • 2,560,000		
❏ F-2164E★ (W-3836E★) • 192,000		
❏ F-2164F (W-3836F) • 2,304,000		
❏ F-2164F★ (W-3836F★) • 128,000		
❏ F-2164G (W-3836G) • 5,888,000		
❏ F-2164G★ (W-3836G★) • 256,000		
❏ F-2164H (W-3836H) • 1,280,000		
❏ F-2164H★ (W-3836H★) • 64,000		
❏ F-2164I (W-3836I) • 512,000		
❏ F-2164I★ (W-3836I★) • 64,000		
❏ F-2164J (W-3836J) • 1,792,000		
❏ F-2164J★ (W-3836J★) • 384,000		
❏ F-2164K (W-3836K) • 2,048,000		
❏ F-2164K★ (W-3836K★) • 128,000		
❏ F-2164L (W-3836L) • 7,168,000		
❏ F-2164L★ (W-3836L★) • 320,000		
❏ F-2165A (W-3837A) • 1,280,000		
❏ F-2165A★ (W-3837A★) • 320,000		
❏ F-2165B (W-3837B) • 11,264,000		
❏ F-2165B★ (W-3837B★) • 640,000		
❏ F-2165C (W-3837C) • 2,048,000		
❏ F-2165C★ (W-3837C★) • 448,000		
❏ F-2165D (W-3837D) • 1,280,000		
❏ F-2165D★ (W-3837D★) • 192,000		
❏ F-2165E (W-3837E) • 2,304,000		
❏ F-2165E★ (W-3837E★) • 192,000		
❏ F-2165F (W-3837F) • 2,304,000		
❏ F-2165F★ (W-3837F★) • 64,000		
❏ F-2165G (W-3837G) • 5,376,000		
❏ F-2165G★ (W-3837G★) • 320,000		
❏ F-2165H (W-3837H) • 1,024,000		

F-No. (W-No.) • Printage *(rarity)*	Grade	Comments
Series of 1969–1969-A, 1969-C *(continued)*		
❑ F-2165H★ (W-3837H★) • 64,000		
❑ F-2165I (W-3837I) • 1,024,000		
❑ F-2165J (W-3837J) • 512,000		
❑ F-2165K (W-3837K) • 3,328,000		
❑ F-2165K★ (W-3837K★) • 128,000		
❑ F-2165L (W-3837L) • 4,352,000		
❑ F-2165L★ (W-3837L★) • 640,000		
❑ F-2166A (W-3838A) • 2,048,000		
❑ F-2166A★ (W-3838A★) • 64,000		
❑ F-2166B (W-3838B) • 15,616,000		
❑ F-2166B★ (W-3838B★) • 256,000		
❑ F-2166C (W-3838C) • 2,816,000		
❑ F-2166C★ (W-3838C★) • 64,000		
❑ F-2166D (W-3838D) • 3,456,000		
❑ F-2166D★ (W-3838D★) • 64,000		
❑ F-2166E (W-3838E) • 7,296,000		
❑ F-2166E★ (W-3838E★) • 128,000		
❑ F-2166F (W-3838F) • 2,432,000		
❑ F-2166F★ (W-3838F★) • 64,000		
❑ F-2166G (W-3838G) • 6,016,000		
❑ F-2166G★ (W-3838G★) • 320,000		
❑ F-2166H (W-3838H) • 5,376,000		
❑ F-2166H★ (W-3838H★) • 64,000		
❑ F-2166I (W-3838I) • 512,000		
❑ F-2166I★ (W-3838I★) • 64,000		
❑ F-2166J (W-3838J) • 4,736,000		
❑ F-2166J★ (W-3838J★) • 192,000		
❑ F-2166K (W-3838K) • 2,944,000		
❑ F-2166K★ (W-3838K★) • 64,000		
❑ F-2166L (W-3838L) • 10,240,000		
❑ F-2166L★ (W-3838L★) • 512,000		
Series of 1974		
❑ F-2167A (W-3839A) • 11,520,000		

F-No. (W-No.) • Printage (rarity)	Grade	Comments
❑ F-2167A★ (W-3839A★) • 320,000		
❑ F-2167B (W-3839B) • 62,720,000		
❑ F-2167B★ (W-3839B★) • 1,728,000		
❑ F-2167C (W-3839C) • 7,680,000		
❑ F-2167C★ (W-3839C★) • 192,000		
❑ F-2167D (W-3839D) • 8,320,000		
❑ F-2167D★ (W-3839D★) • 256,000		
❑ F-2167E (W-3839E) • 11,520,000		
❑ F-2167E★ (W-3839E★) • 256,000		
❑ F-2167F (W-3839F) • 4,480,000		
❑ F-2167F★ (W-3839F★) • 128,000		
❑ F-2167G (W-3839G) • 26,880,000		
❑ F-2167G★ (W-3839G★) • 1,216,000		
❑ F-2167H (W-3839H) • 5,760,000		
❑ F-2167H★ (W-3839H★) • 192,000		
❑ F-2167I (W-3839I) • 4,480,000		
❑ F-2167I★ (W-3839I★) • 256,000		
❑ F-2167J (W-3839J) • 5,760,000		
❑ F-2167J★ (W-3839J★) • 448,000		
❑ F-2167K (W-3839K) • 10,240,000		
❑ F-2167K★ (W-3839K★) • 192,000		
❑ F-2167L (W-3839L) • 29,440,000		
❑ F-2167L★ (W-3839L★) • 896,000		
Series of 1977		
❑ F-2168A (W-3840A) • 19,200,000		
❑ F-2168A★ (W-3840A★) • 320,000		
❑ F-2168B (W-3840B) • 166,400,000		
❑ F-2168B★ (W-3840B★) • 1,664,000		
❑ F-2168C (W-3840C) • 5,195,000		
❑ F-2168C★ (W-3840C★) • 128,000		
❑ F-2168D (W-3840D) • 16,640,000		
❑ F-2168D★ (W-3840D★) • 192,000		
❑ F-2168E (W-3840E) • 24,320,000		
❑ F-2168E★ (W-3840E★) • 384,000		

F-No. (W-No.) • Printage *(rarity)*	Grade	Comments
Series of 1977 *(continued)*		
❑ F-2168F (W-3840F) • 3,840,000		
❑ F-2168F★ (W-3840F★) • 64,000		
❑ F-2168G (W-3840G) • 39,680,000		
❑ F-2168G★ (W-3840G★) • 960,000		
❑ F-2168H (W-3840H) • 15,360,000		
❑ F-2168H★ (W-3840H★) • 448,000		
❑ F-2168I (W-3840I) • 5,195,000		
❑ F-2168I★ (W-3840I★) • 192,000		
❑ F-2168J (W-3840J) • 38,400,000		
❑ F-2168J★ (W-3840J★) • 640,000		
❑ F-2168K (W-3840K) • 38,400,000		
❑ F-2168K★ (W-3840K★) • 640,000		
❑ F-2168L (W-3840L) • 39,680,000		
❑ F-2168L★ (W-3840L★) • 576,000		
Series of 1981 and 1981-A		
❑ F-2169A (W-3841A) • 8,960,000		
❑ F-2169B (W-3841B) • 105,600,000		
❑ F-2169C (W-3841C) • 12,800,000		
❑ F-2169D (W-3841D) • 5,760,000		
❑ F-2169E (W-3841E) • 23,680,000		
❑ F-2169E★ (W-3841E★) • 640,000		
❑ F-2169F (W-3841F) • 6,400,000		
❑ F-2169G (W-3841G) • 33,280,000		
❑ F-2169H (W-3841H) • 5,760,000		
❑ F-2169I (W-3841I) • 3,200,000		
❑ F-2169J (W-3841J) • 23,680,000		
❑ F-2169K (W-3841K) • 23,680,000		
❑ F-2169L (W-3841L) • 24,960,000		
❑ F-2170A (W-3842A) • 16,000,000		
❑ F-2170B (W-3842B) • 64,000,000		
❑ F-2170C (W-3842C) • 3,200,000		
❑ F-2170D (W-3842D) • 6,400,000		
❑ F-2170E (W-3842E) • 12,800,000		

F-No. (W-No.) • Printage (rarity)	Grade	Comments
❑ F-2170F (W-3842F) • 12,800,000		
❑ F-2170G (W-3842G) • 22,400,000		
❑ F-2170H (W-3842H) • 12,800,000		
❑ F-2170I (W-3842I) • 3,200,000		
❑ F-2170K (W-3842K) • 3,200,000		
❑ F-2170L (W-3842L) • 19,200,000		
❑ F-2170L★ (W-3842L★) • 3,200,000		
Series of 1985		
❑ F-2171A (W-3843A) • 32,000,000		
❑ F-2171B (W-3843B) • 259,200,000		
❑ F-2171C (W-3843C) • 19,200,000		
❑ F-2171D (W-3843D) • 28,800,000		
❑ F-2171D★ (W-3843D★) • 1,280,000		
❑ F-2171E (W-3843E) • 54,400,000		
❑ F-2171F (W-3843F) • 16,000,000		
❑ F-2171G (W-3843G) • 64,000,000		
❑ F-2171H (W-3843H) • 12,800,000		
❑ F-2171I (W-3843I) • 12,800,000		
❑ F-2171J (W-3843J) • 12,800,000		
❑ F-2171J★ (W-3843J★) • 1,280,000		
❑ F-2171K (W-3843K) • 48,000,000		
❑ F-2171K★ (W-3843K★) • 3,200,000		
❑ F-2171L (W-3843L) • 38,400,000		
Series of 1988		
❑ F-2172A (W-3844A) • 9,600,000		
❑ F-2172B (W-3844B) • 448,000,000		
❑ F-2172B★ (W-3844B★) • 4,480,000		
❑ F-2172C (W-3844C) • 9,600,000		
❑ F-2172D (W-3844D) • 35,200,000		
❑ F-2172E (W-3844E) • 19,200,000		
❑ F-2172G (W-3844G) • 51,200,000		
❑ F-2172H (W-3844H) • 9,600,000		
❑ F-2172J (W-3844J) • 9,600,000		
❑ F-2172L (W-3844L) • 10,200,000		

F-No. (W-No.) • Printage *(rarity)*	Grade	Comments
Series of 1990		
❏ F-2173A (W-3845A) • 76,800,000		
❏ F-2173B (W-3845B) • 595,200,000		
❏ F-2173B★ (W-3845B★) • 1,880,000		
❏ F-2173C (W-3845C) • 112,000,000		
❏ F-2173C★ (W-3845C★) • 1,280,000		
❏ F-2173D (W-3845D) • 115,200,000		
❏ F-2173E (W-3845E) • 108,800,000		
❏ F-2173F (W-3845F) • 64,000,000		
❏ F-2173G (W-3845G) • 134,400,000		
❏ F-2173G★ (W-3845G★) • 640,000		
❏ F-2173H (W-3845H) • 121,600,000		
❏ F-2173I (W-3845I) • 48,000,000		
❏ F-2173J (W-3845J) • 76,800,000		
❏ F-2173J★ (W-3845J★) • 3,200,000		
❏ F-2173K (W-3845K) • 165,400,000		
❏ F-2173K★ (W-3845K★) • 1,920,000		
❏ F-2173L (W-3845L) • 147,200,000		
❏ F-2173L★ (W-3845L★) • 3,200,000		
Series of 1993		
❏ F-2174A (W-3846A) • 83,200,000		
❏ F-2174B (W-3846B) • 288,000,000		
❏ F-2174B★ (W-3846B★) • 2,560,000		
❏ F-2174C (W-3846C) • 41,600,000		
❏ F-2174C★ (W-3846C★) • 1,280,000		
❏ F-2174D (W-3846D) • 9,600,000		
❏ F-2174D★ (W-3846D★) • 1,024,000		
❏ F-2174E (W-3846E) • 64,000,000		
❏ F-2174F (W-3846F) • 150,400,000		
❏ F-2174G (W-3846G) • 44,800,000		
❏ F-2174H (W-3846H) • 16,000,000		
❏ F-2174H★ (W-3846H★) • 640,000		
❏ F-2174I (W-3846I) • 9,600,000		
❏ F-2174J (W-3846J) • 9,600,000		

F-No. (W-No.) • Printage (rarity)	Grade	Comments
❑ F-2174K (W-3846K) • 51,200,000		
❑ F-2174L (W-3846L) • 19,200,000		
Series of 1996		
❑ F-2175A (W-3847A) • 125,600,000		
❑ F-2175A★ (W-3847A★) • 2,560,000		
❑ F-2175B (W-3847B) • 2,325,600,000		
❑ F-2175B★ (W-3847B★) • 17,920,000		
❑ F-2175C (W-3847C) • 86,400,000		
❑ F- 2175D (W-3847D) • 176,800,000		
❑ F-2175D★ (W-3847D★) • 160,000		
❑ F-2175E (W-3847E) • 276,800,000		
❑ F-2175E★ (W-3847E★) • 3,200,000		
❑ F-2175F (W-3847F) • 222,400,000		
❑ F-2175F★ (W-3847F★) • 2,560,000		
❑ F-2175G (W-3847G) • 244,800,000		
❑ F-2175G★ (W-3847G★) • 1,920,000		
❑ F-2175H (W-3847H) • 112,800,000		
❑ F-2175I (W-3847I) • 32,000,000		
❑ F-2175J (W-3847J) • 83,200,000		
❑ F-2175K (W-3847K) • 144,800,000		
❑ F-2175K★ (W-3847K★) • 1,920,000		
❑ F-2175L (W-3847L) • 406,400,000		
❑ F-2175L★ (W-3847L★) • 2,560,000		
Series of 1999		
❑ F-2176A (W-3848A) • 48,000,000		
❑ F-2176A★ (W-3848A★) • 3,520,000		
❑ F-2176B (W-3848B) • 172,800,000		
❑ F-2176B★ (W-3848B★) • 3,840,000		
❑ F-2176C (W-3848C) • 3,200,000		
❑ F-2176D (W-3848D) • 19,200,000		
❑ F-2176E (W-3848E) • 60,800,000		
❑ F-2176F (W-3848F) • 16,000,000		
❑ F-2176G (W-3848G) • 52,400,000		
❑ F-2176H (W-3848H) • 22,400,000		

F-No. (W-No.) • Printage *(rarity)*	Grade	Comments
Series of 1999 *(continued)*		
❏ F-2176I (W-3848I) • 70,400,000		
❏ F-2176J (W-3848J) • 25,600,000		
❏ F-2176K (W-3848K) • 19,200,000		
Series of 2001		
❏ F-2177A (W-3849A) • 32,000,000		
❏ F-2177B (W-3849B) • 579,200,000		
❏ F-2177B★ (W-3849B★) • 320,000		
❏ F-2177C (W-3849C) • 32,000,000		
❏ F-2177D (W-3849D) • 19,200,000		
❏ F-2177D★ (W-3849D★) • 1,920,000		
❏ F-2177E (W-3849E) • 64,000,000		
❏ F-2177E★ (W-3849E★) • 1,920,000		
❏ F-2177F (W-3849F) • 99,200,000		
❏ F-2177F★ (W-3849F★) • 1,600,000		
❏ F-2177G (W-3849G) • 57,600,000		
❏ F-2177H (W-3849H) • 25,600,000		
❏ F-2177I (W-3849I) • 9,600,000		
❏ F-2177J (W-3849J) • 22,400,000		
❏ F-2177K (W-3849K) • 60,800,000		
❏ F-2177L (W-3849L) • 147,200,000		
Series of 2003 and 2003-A		
❏ F-2178A (W-3850A) • 35,200,000		
❏ F-2178B (W-3850B) • 364,800,000		
❏ F-2178B★ (W-3850B★) • 2,240,000		
❏ F-2178C (W-3850C) • 41,600,000		
❏ F-2178D (W-3850D) • 32,000,000		
❏ F-2178E (W-3850E) • 86,400,000		
❏ F-2178F (W-3850F) • 166,400,000		
❏ F-2178F★ (W-3850F★) • 1,280,000		
❏ F-2178G (W-3850G) • 80,000,000		
❏ F-2178H (W-3850H) • 38,400,000		
❏ F-2178I (W-3850I) • 16,000,000		
❏ F-2178J (W-3850J) • 38,400,000		
❏ F-2178K (W-3850K) • 32,000,000		

F-No. (W-No.) • Printage *(rarity)*	Grade	Comments
❑ F-2178K★ (W-3850K★) • 2,688,000		
❑ F-2178L (W-3850L) • 89,600,000		
❑ F-2178L★ (W-3850L★) • 320,000		
❑ F-2179A (W-3851A) • 12,800,000		
❑ F-2179B (W-3851B) • 316,800,000		
❑ F-2179B★ (W-3851B★) • 1,280,000		
❑ F-2179C (W-3851C) • 28,800,000		
❑ F-2179D (W-3851D) • 12,800,000		
❑ F-2179E (W-3851E) • 86,400,000		
❑ F-2179F (W-3851F) • 140,800,000		
❑ F-2179G (W-3851G) • 67,200,000		
❑ F-2179G★ (W-3851G★) • 1,920,000		
❑ F-2179H (W-3851H) • 32,000,000		
❑ F-2179H★ (W-3851H★)		
❑ F-2179I (W-3851I) • 6,400,000		
❑ F-2179J (W-3851J) • 28,800,000		
❑ F-2179K (W-3851K) • 105,600,000		
❑ F-2179L (W-3851L) • 249,600,000		
❑ F-2179L★ (W-3851L★) • 1,280,000		
Series of 2006 and 2006-A		
❑ F-2180A (W-3852A) • 128,000,000		
❑ F-2180A★ (W-3852A★) • 4,000,000		
❑ F-2180B (W-3852B) • 1,628,800,000		
❑ F-2180B★ (W-3852B★) • 11,520,000		
❑ F-2180C (W-3852C) • 153,600,000		
❑ F-2180D (W-3852D) • 163,200,000		
❑ F-2180E (W-3852E) • 361,800,000		
❑ F-2180E★ (W-3852E★) • 1,920,000		
❑ F-2180F (W-3852F) • 540,800,000		
❑ F-2180F★ (W-3852F★) • 1,280,000		
❑ F-2180G (W-3852G) • 214,400,000		
❑ F-2180H (W-3852H) • 115,200,000		
❑ F-2180I (W-3852I) • 54,400,000		
❑ F-2180J (W-3852J) • 92,800,000		

$100

F-No. (W-No.) • Printage *(rarity)*	Grade	Comments
Series of 2006 and 2006-A *(continued)*		
❑ F-2180K (W-3852K) • 252,800,000		
❑ F-2180K★ (W-3852K★) • 128,000		
❑ F-2180L (W-3852L) • 355,200,000		
❑ F-2180L★ (W-3852L★) • 8,000,000		
❑ F-2181B • 35,200,000		
❑ F-2181J • 6,400,000		
❑ F-2181K • 92,800,000		
❑ F-2181K★ • 1,280,000		
❑ F-2181L • 326,400,000		
❑ F-2181L★ • 2,560,000		
❑ F-2182A • 70,400,000		
❑ F-2182B • 1,660,800,000		
❑ F-2182B★ • 4,160,000		
❑ F-2182C • 57,600,000		
❑ F-2182D • 134,400,000		
❑ F-2182E • 144,000,000		
❑ F-2182E★ • 320,000		
❑ F-2182F • 361,600,000		
❑ F-2182G • 150,400,000		
❑ F-2182H • 67,200,000		
❑ F-2182I • 38,400,000		
❑ F-2182J • 64,000,000		
❑ F-2182K • 329,600,000		
❑ F-2182K★ • 6,144,000		
❑ F-2182L • 464,000,000		
❑ F-2182L★ • 4,160,000		
Series of 2009		
❑ F-2184A		
❑ F-2184A★		
❑ F-2184B		
❑ F-2184B★		
❑ F-2184C		
❑ F-2184D		
❑ F-2184E		

F-No. (W-No.) • Printage *(rarity)*	Grade	Comments
❏ F-2184E★		
❏ F-2185B		
❏ F-2185B★		
❏ F-2185F		
❏ F-2185F★		
❏ F-2185G		
❏ F-2185H		
❏ F-2185H★		
❏ F-2185I		
❏ F-2185J		
❏ F-2185J★		
❏ F-2185K		
❏ F-2185K★		
❏ F-2185L		
❏ F-2185L★		
❏ F-2186B		
❏ F-2186D		
❏ F-2186G		
❏ F-2186H		
❏ F-2186L		
❏ F-2187A		
❏ F-2187A★		
❏ F-2187B		
❏ F-2187B★		
❏ F-2187C		
❏ F-2187C★		
❏ F-2187D		
❏ F-2187D★		
❏ F-2187E		
❏ F-2187E★		
❏ F-2187F		
❏ F-2187F★		
❏ F-2187G		
❏ F-2187G★		

F-No. (W-No.) • Printage *(rarity)*	Grade	Comments
Series of 2009 *(continued)*		
❑ F-2187H		
❑ F-2187H★		
❑ F-2187I		
❑ F-2187I★		
❑ F-2187J		
❑ F-2187K		
❑ F-2187K★		
❑ F-2187L		
❑ F-2187L★		
Series of 2013		
❑ F-2188B		
❑ F-2188B★		
❑		
❑		
❑		
❑		
❑		
❑		
❑		
❑		
❑		
❑		
Series of 2017		
❑		
❑		
❑		
❑		
❑		
❑		
❑		
❑		
❑		
❑		
❑		

LARGE-SIZE

$500 Interest-Bearing Notes

F-No. (W-No.) • Printage *(rarity)*	Grade	Comments
March 2, 1861, 6%, 2 Years		
❑ F-202c (W-3920) • 13,665 *(1 known)*		
❑ F-202c (W-3930) • incl. above		
July 17, 1861, 7.3%, 3 Years		
❑ F-209 (W-3950) • *(2 known)*		
June 30, 1864, 7.3%, 3 Years		
❑ F-212b (W-3975) • 171,666 *(1 known)*		
March 3, 1865, 7.3%, 3 Years		
❑ F-212f (W-3980) • 175,682 *(1 known)*		

$500 Legal Tender Notes

F-No. (W-No.) • Printage *(rarity)*	Grade	Comments
Series of 1862, First Obligation		
❑ F-183a (W-4001) • 26,000 *(1 known)*		
Series of 1862 and 1863, Second Obligation		
❑ F-183c (W-4005) • 22,000 *(3 known)*		
❑ F-183c (W-4006) • 8,000 *(1 known)*		
❑ F-183d (W-4007) • 20,000 *(1 known)*		
Series of 1869		
❑ F-184 (W-4060) • 89,360 *(4 known)*		
Series of 1874		
❑ F- unlisted (W-4062) • 56,000 *(5 known)*		
Series of 1875		
❑ F-185b (W-4064) • 32,000 *(1 known)*		
❑ F-185c (W-4066) • 24,800 *(1 known)*		

F-No. (W-No.) • Printage *(rarity)*	Grade	Comments
Series of 1878		
❏ F- unlisted (W-4070) • 24,000 *(6 known)*		
Series of 1880		
❏ F-185f (W-4074) • 12,000 *(2 known)*		
❏ F-185i (W-4080) • 16,000 *(3 known)*		
❏ F-185j (W-4082) • 16,000 *(2 known)*		
❏ F-185k (W-4084) • 20,000 *(6 known)*		
❏ F-185l (W-4086) • 12,000 *(5 known)*		
❏ F-185m (W-4088) • 20,000 *(5 known)*		

$500 National Bank Notes

F-No. (W-No.) • Printage *(rarity)*	Grade	Comments
Original Series ("First Charter Period")		
❏ F-unlisted (W-4100) • *(2 known)*		
❏ F-464 (W-4102) • *(1 known)*		
Series of 1875 ("First Charter Period")		
❏ F-unlisted (W-4133) • *(1 known)*		

$500 Silver Certificates

F-No. (W-No.) • Printage *(rarity)*	Grade	Comments
Series of 1878		
■ F-345a (W-4165) • est. 4,000 *(1 known)*		
Series of 1880		
❏ F-345c (W-4173) • 16,000 *(5 known)*		
❏ F-345d (W-4174) • 8,000 *(7 known)*		

$500 Gold Certificates

F-No. (W-No.) • Printage *(rarity)*	Grade	Comments
Series of 1870		
■ F-1166i (W-4194) • 40,000 *(1 known)*		
Series of 1882		
❏ F-1215a (W-4202) • 8,000 *(1 known)*		
■ F-1215c (W-4204) • 20,000 *(1 known)*		
■ F-1215d (W-4206) • 16,000 *(1 known)*		
❏ F-1216 (W-4210) • 128,000 *(28–32)*		
❏ F-1216a (W-4214) • 40,000 *(38–43)*		
❏ F-1216b (W-4216) • 40,000 *(52–56)*		
Series of 1922		
❏ F-1217 (W-4220) • 84,000 *(60–65)*		

$500 Federal Reserve Notes

F-No. (W-No.) • Printage *(rarity)*	Grade	Comments
Series of 1918		
❑ F-1132A (W-4240A) • 17,600 *(4 known)*		
❑ F-1132B (W-4243B) • est. 108,000 *(47–52)*		
❑ F-1132bB (W-4246B) • est. 17,600 *(5 known)*		
❑ F-1132C (W-4249C) • 24,000 *(5 known)*		
❑ F-1132D (W-4252D) • 15,600 *(16–18)*		
❑ F-1132F (W-4258F) • 30,400 *(9–10)*		
❑ F-1132G (W-4264G) • 38,000 *(44–48)*		
❑ F-1132H (W-4267H) • 14,400 *(5 known)*		
❑ F-1132I (W-4270I) • 7,200 *(1 known)*		
❑ F-1132J (W-4273J) • 15,600 *(15–17)*		
❑ F-1132K (W-4279K) • 6,000 *(4 known)*		
❑ F-1132L (W-4282L) • 16,000 *(21–24)*		
❑ F-1132aL (W-4285L) • 8,000 *(3 known)*		

SMALL-SIZE

$500 Gold Certificates

F-No. (W-No.) • Printage *(rarity)*	Grade	Comments
Series of 1928		
❑ F-2407 (W-4300) • 420,000		

$500 Federal Reserve Notes

F-No. (W-No.) • Printage *(rarity)*	Grade	Comments
Series of 1928, Green Seal		
❑ F-2200A (W-4350A) • 69,120		
❑ F-2200B (W-4350B) • 299,400		

F-No. (W-No.) • Printage *(rarity)*	Grade	Comments
Series of 1928, Green Seal *(continued)*		
❑ F-2200C (W-4350C) • 135,120		
❑ F-2200C★ (W-4350C★) • *(1 known)*		
❑ F-2200D (W-4350D) • 166,440		
❑ F-2200D★ (W-4350D★) • *(1 known)*		
❑ F-2200E (W-4350E) • 84,720		
❑ F-2200F (W-4350F) • 69,360		
❑ F-2200G (W-4350G) • 573,600		
❑ F-2200G★ (W-4350G★) • *(2 known)*		
❑ F-2200H (W-4350H) • 66,180		
❑ F-2200I (W-4350I) • 34,680		
❑ F-2200J (W-4350J) • 510,720		
❑ F-2200K (W-4350K) • 70,560		
❑ F-2200L (W-4350L) • 64,080		
Series of 1928, Light Yellow-Green Seal		
❑ F-2200B (W-4360B) • incl. in F-2200B/W-4350B		
❑ F-2200G (W-4360G) • incl. in F-2200G/W-4350G		
❑ F-2200J (W-4360J) • incl. in F-2200J/W-4350J		
Series of 1934, Light Yellow-Green Seal		
❑ F-2201A (W-4365A) • incl. in F-2201A/W-4370A		
❑ F-2201B (W-4365B) • incl. in F-2201B/W-4370B		
❑ F-2201C (W-4365C) • incl. in F-2201C/W-4370C		
❑ F-2201D (W-4365D) • incl. in F-2201D/W-4370D		
❑ F-2201E (W-4365E) • incl. in F-2201E/W-4370E		
❑ F-2201F (W-4365F) • incl. in F-2201F/W-4370F		
❑ F-2201G (W-4365G) • incl. in F-2201G/W-4370G		
❑ F-2201H (W-4365H) • incl. in F-2201H/W-4370H		
❑ F-2201I (W-4365I) • incl. in F-2201I/W-4370I		
❑ F-2201J (W-4365J) • incl. in F-2201J/W-4370J		
❑ F-2201K (W-4365K) • incl. in F-2201K/W-4370K		
❑ F-2201L (W-4365L) • incl. in F-2201L/W-4370L		
Series of 1934, Green Seal		
❑ F-2201A (W-4370A) • 56,628		
❑ F-2201A★ (W-4370A★)		
❑ F-2201B (W-4370B) • 288,000		

F-No. (W-No.) • Printage *(rarity)*	Grade	Comments
❑ F-2201B★ (W-4370B★)		
❑ F-2201C (W-4370C) • 31,200		
❑ F-2201C★ (W-4370C★)		
❑ F-2201D (W-4370D) • 39,000		
❑ F-2201D★ (W-4370D★)		
❑ F-2201E (W-4370E) • 40,800		
❑ F-2201E★ (W-4370E★)		
❑ F-2201F (W-4370F) • 46,200		
❑ F-2201F★ (W-4370F★)		
❑ F-2201G (W-4370G) • 212,400		
❑ F-2201G★ (W-4370G★)		
❑ F-2201H (W-4370H) • 24,000		
❑ F-2201H★ (W-4370H★) • *(3 known)*		
❑ F-2201I (W-4370I) • 24,000		
❑ F-2201I★ (W-4370I★) • *(2 known)*		
❑ F-2201J (W-4370J) • 40,800		
❑ F-2201J★ (W-4370J★) • *(1 known)*		
❑ F-2201K (W-4370K) • 31,200		
❑ F-2201K★ (W-4370K★) • *(4 known)*		
❑ F-2201L (W-4370L) • 83,400		
❑ F-2201L★ (W-4370L★)		
Series of 1934-A		
❑ F-2202B (W-4375B) • 276,000		
❑ F-2202B★ (W-4375B★) • *(6 known)*		
❑ F-2202C (W-4375C) • 45,300		
❑ F-2202D (W-4375D) • 28,800		
❑ F-2202E (W-4375E) • 36,000		
❑ F-2202E★ (W-4375E★) • *(3 known)*		
❑ F-2202F (W-4375F) • incl. in F-2201F/W-4370F		
❑ F-2202G (W-4375G) • 214,800		
❑ F-2202G★ (W-4375G★) • *(7 known)*		
❑ F-2202H (W-4375H) • 57,600		
❑ F-2202H★ (W-4375H★) • *(1 known)*		
❑ F-2202I (W-4375I) • 14,400		

F-No. (W-No.) • Printage *(rarity)*	Grade	Comments
Series of 1934-A *(continued)*		
❑ F-2202J (W-4375J) • 55,200		
❑ F-2202J★ (W-4375J★) • *(4 known)*		
❑ F-2202K (W-4375K) • 34,800		
❑ F-2202L (W-4375L) • 93,000		
❑ F-2202L★ (W-4375L★)		

LARGE-SIZE

$1,000 Interest-Bearing Notes

F-No. (W-No.) • Printage *(rarity)*	Grade	Comments
March 3, 1865, 7.3% Interest, 3 Years		
■ F-212g (W-4465) • 118,528 *(2 known)*		
■ F-212g (W-4467) • 71,879 *(1 known)*		

$1,000 Legal Tender Notes

F-No. (W-No.) • Printage *(rarity)*	Grade	Comments
Series of 1863		
❑ F-186c (W-4494) • 24,904 *(1 known)*		
❑ F-186d (W-4496) • 64,000 *(2 known)*		
■ F-186e (W-4497) • 20,000 *(1 known)*		
Series of 1869		
❑ F-186f (W-4510) • 74,400 *(2 known)*		
Series of 1878		
■ F-187a (W-4512) • 24,000 *(2 known)*		
Series of 1880		
❑ F-187b (W-4513) • 12,000 *(2 known)*		
■ F-187c (W-4514) • 24,000 *(1 known)*		
■ F-187d (W-4515) • 4,000 *(1 known)*		
■ F-187e (W-4516) • 8,000 *(1 known)*		
■ F-187g (W-4518) • 56,000 *(1 known)*		
❑ F-187j (W-4521) • 56,000 *(13–15)*		
❑ F-187k (W-4522) • 20,000 *(4 known)*		

$1,000 Silver Certificates

F-No. (W-No.) • Printage (rarity)	Grade	Comments
Series of 1880		
❑ F-346d (W-4567) • 8,000 (5 known)		
Series of 1891		
❑ F-346e (W-4570) • 8,000 (2 known)		

$1,000 Treasury or Coin Notes

F-No. (W-No.) • Printage (rarity)	Grade	Comments
Series of 1890		
❑ F-379a (W-4580) • 16,000 (5 known)		
❑ F-379b (W-4581) • 12,000 (2 known)		
Series of 1891		
■ F-379c (W-4586) • 24,000 (2 known)		

$1,000 Gold Certificates

F-No. (W-No.) • Printage (rarity)	Grade	Comments
Act of March 3, 1863		
■ F-1166e (W-4590) • 117,000 (1 known)		
Series of 1870		
■ F-1166j (W-4600) • 50,000 (1 known)		
Series of 1882		
■ F-1218a (W-4610) • 12,000 (2 known)		
■ F-1218b (W-4614) • 20,000 (1 known)		
■ F-1218c (W-4616) • 16,000 (1 known)		
❑ F-1218d (W-4618) • 8,000 (3 known)		
❑ F-1218e (W-4620) • 8,000 (3 known)		
❑ F-1218f (W-4622) • 96,000 (9–10)		
❑ F-1218g (W-4624) • 16,000 (4 known)		
Series of 1907		
❑ F-1219 (W-4626) • 32,000 (6 known)		
❑ F-1219b (W-4630) • 12,000 (1 known)		
❑ F-1219c (W-4632) • 12,000 (4 known)		
❑ F-1219d (W-4634) • 48,000 (9–10)		
❑ F-1219e (W-4636) • 112,000 (45–50)		
Series of 1922		
❑ F-1220 (W-4640) • 80,000 (44–48)		

$1,000 Federal Reserve Notes

F-No. (W-No.) • Printage (rarity)	Grade	Comments
Series of 1918		
❏ F-1133A (W-4650A) • 39,600 (3 known)		
❏ F-1133B (W-4653B) • est. 100,000 (21–24)		
❏ F-1133aB (W-4656B) • est. 24,800 (8–9)		
❏ F-1133C (W-4659C) • 16,400 (13–15)		
❏ F-1133D (W-4662D) • 8,800 (12–14)		
❏ F-1133F (W-4668F) • 26,800 (8–9)		
❏ F-1133bF (W-4671F) • 16,400 (5 known)		
❏ F-1133G (W-4674G) • 23,600 (30–35)		
❏ F-1133H (W-4677H) • 8,400 (7 known)		
❏ F-1133I (W-4680I) • 7,600 (2 known)		
❏ F-1133J (W-4683J) • 13,200 (4 known)		
❏ F-1133K (W-4689K) • 6,000 (3 known)		
❏ F-1133L (W-4692L) • 19,600 (56–60)		
❏ F-1133bL (W-4695L) • 2,800 (4 known)		

SMALL-SIZE

$1,000 Gold Certificates

F-No. (W-No.) • Printage (rarity)	Grade	Comments
Series of 1928		
❏ F-2408 (W-4800) • 28,800		
❏ F-2408★ (W-4800★)		

$1,000 Federal Reserve Notes

F-No. (W-No.) • Printage (rarity)	Grade	Comments
Series of 1928, Green Seal		
❏ F-2210A (W-4810A) • 58,320		

F-No. (W-No.) • Printage *(rarity)*	Grade	Comments
Series of 1928, Green Seal *(continued)*		
❑ F-2210A★ (W-4810A★)		
❑ F-2210B (W-4810B) • 139,200		
❑ F-2210B★ (W-4810B★)		
❑ F-2210C (W-4810C) • 96,708		
❑ F-2210C★ (W-4810C★)		
❑ F-2210D (W-4810D) • 79,680		
❑ F-2210D★ (W-4810D★)		
❑ F-2210E (W-4810E) • 66,840		
❑ F-2210E★ (W-4810E★)		
❑ F-2210F (W-4810F) • 47,400		
❑ F-2210F★ (W-4810F★)		
❑ F-2210G (W-4810G) • 355,800		
❑ F-2210G★ (W-4810G★)		
❑ F-2210H (W-4810H) • 60,000		
❑ F-2210H★ (W-4810H★)		
❑ F-2210I (W-4810I) • 26,640		
❑ F-2210I★ (W-4810I★)		
❑ F-2210J (W-4810J) • 62,172		
❑ F-2210J★ (W-4810J★)		
❑ F-2210K (W-4810K) • 42,960		
❑ F-2210K★ (W-4810K★)		
❑ F-2210L (W-4810L) • 67,920		
❑ F-2210L★ (W-4810L★)		
Series 1928, Light Yellow-Green Seal		
❑ F-2210E (W-4815E) • incl. in F-2210E/W-4810E		
❑ F-2210G (W-4815G) • incl. in F-2210G/W-4810G		
❑ F-2210H (W-4815H) • incl. in F-2210H/W-4810H		
❑ F-2210J (W-4815J) • incl. in F-2210J/W-4810J		
❑ F-2210L (W-4815L) • incl. in F-2210L/W-4810L		
Series 1934, Light Yellow-Green Seal		
❑ F-2211A (W-4820A) • incl. in F-2211A/W-4830A		
❑ F-2211B (W-4820B) • incl. in F-2211B/W-4830B		
❑ F-2211C (W-4820C) • incl. in F-2211C/W-4830C		

F-No. (W-No.) • Printage *(rarity)*	Grade	Comments
❑ F-2211D (W-4820D) • incl. in F-2211D/W-4830D		
❑ F-2211E (W-4820E) • incl. in F-2211E/W-4830E		
❑ F-2211F (W-4820F) • incl. in F-2211F/W-4830F		
❑ F-2211G (W-4820G) • incl. in F-2211G/W-4830G		
❑ F-2211H (W-4820H) • incl. in F-2211H/W-4830H		
❑ F-2211I (W-4820I) • incl. in F-2211I/W-4830I		
❑ F-2211J (W-4820J) • incl. in F-2211J/W-4830J		
❑ F-2211K (W-4820K) • incl. in F-2211K/W-4830K		
❑ F-2211L (W-4820L) • incl. in F-2211L/W-4830L		
Series of 1934, Green Seal		
❑ F-2211A (W-4830A) • 46,200		
❑ F-2211A★ (W-4830A★)		
❑ F-2211B (W-4830B) • 322,784		
❑ F-2211B★ (W-4830B★)		
❑ F-2211C (W-4830C) • 33,000		
❑ F-2211C★ (W-4830C★)		
❑ F-2211D (W-4830D) • 35,400		
❑ F-2211D★ (W-4830D★)		
❑ F-2211E (W-4830E) • 19,560		
❑ F-2211E★ (W-4830E★)		
❑ F-2211F (W-4830F) • 67,800		
❑ F-2211F★ (W-4830F★)		
❑ F-2211G (W-4830G) • 167,040		
❑ F-2211G★ (W-4830G★)		
❑ F-2211H (W-4830H) • 22,400		
❑ F-2211H★ (W-4830H★)		
❑ F-2211I (W-4830I) • 12,000		
❑ F-2211I★ (W-4830I★)		
❑ F-2211J (W-4830J) • 51,840		
❑ F-2211J★ (W-4830J★)		
❑ F-2211K (W-4830K) • 46,800		
❑ F-2211K★ (W-4830K★)		
❑ F-2211L (W-4830L) • 90,600		
❑ F-2211L★ (W-4830L★)		

F-No. (W-No.) • Printage *(rarity)*	Grade	Comments
Series of 1934-A		
❏ F-2212A (W-4835A) • 30,000		
❏ F-2212A★ (W-4835A★)		
❏ F-2212B (W-4835B) • 174,348		
❏ F-2212B★ (W-4835B★)		
❏ F-2212C (W-4835C) • 78,000		
❏ F-2212C★ (W-4835C★)		
❏ F-2212D (W-4835D) • 28,800		
❏ F-2212D★ (W-4835D★)		
❏ F-2212E (W-4835E) • 16,800		
❏ F-2212E★ (W-4835E★)		
❏ F-2212F (W-4835F) • 80,964		
❏ F-2212F★ (W-4835F★)		
❏ F-2212G (W-4835G) • 134,400		
❏ F-2212G★ (W-4835G★)		
❏ F-2212H (W-4835H) • 39,600		
❏ F-2212H★ (W-4835H★)		
❏ F-2212I (W-4835I) • 4,800		
❏ F-2212I★ (W-4835I★)		
❏ F-2212J (W-4835J) • 21,600		
❏ F-2212J★ (W-4835J★)		
❏ F-2212L (W-4835L) • 36,600		
❏ F-2212L★ (W-4835L★)		

LARGE-SIZE

$5,000 Gold Certificates

F-No (W-No.) • Printage *(rarity)*	Grade	Comments
Act of March 3, 1863		
■ F-1166f (W-4980) • 93,400 *(1 known)*		
Series of 1882		
■ F-1221j (W-5036) • 32,000 *(2 known)*		

$5,000 Federal Reserve Notes

F-No (W-No.) • Printage *(rarity)*	Grade	Comments
Series of 1918		
■ F-1134 (W-5065B) • 5,200 *(2 known)*		
■ F-1134 (W-5075D) • 800 *(1 known)*		
■ F-1134 (W-5090G) • 2,800 *(1 known)*		
■ F-1134 (W-5105L) • 3,200 *(1 known)*		

SMALL-SIZE

$5,000 Gold Certificates

F-No. (W-No.) • Printage *(rarity)*	Grade	Comments
Series of 1928		
■ F-2410 (W-5150) • 24,000 *(1 known)*		

$5,000 Federal Reserve Notes

F-No. (W-No.) • Printage *(rarity)*	Grade	Comments
Series of 1928		
❏ F-2220A (W-5204A) • 1,320		
❏ F-2220E (W-5204E) • 3,984		
❏ F-2220F (W-5204F) • 1,440		
❏ F-2220G (W-5204G) • 3,480		
❏ F-2220J (W-5204J) • 720		
Series of 1934		
❏ F-2221A (W-5206A) • 9,480		
❏ F-2221B (W-5206B) • 11,520		
❏ F-2221C (W-5206C) • 3,000		
❏ F-2221E (W-5206E) • 2,400		
❏ F-2221F (W-5206F) • 3,600		
❏ F-2221G (W-5206G) • 6,600		
❏ F-2221H (W-5206H) • 2,400		
❏ F-2221J (W-5206J) • 2,400		
❏ F-2221K (W-5206K) • 2,400		
❏ F-2221L (W-5206L) • 6,000		

LARGE-SIZE

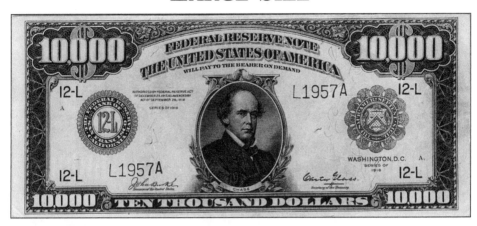

$10,000 Gold Certificates

F-No. (W-No.) • Printage *(rarity)*	Grade	Comments
Series of 1875		
■ F-1166q (W-5330) • 5,000 *(1 known)*		
Series of 1882		
❑ F-1223g (W-5370) • 108,000 *(2 known)*		
Series of 1900		
❑ F-1225a (W-5400) • 36,000 *(4 known)*		
❑ F-1225b (W-5420) • 6,000 *(7 known)*		
❑ F-1225c (W-5440) • 36,000 *(28–32)*		
❑ F-1225d (W-5460) • 18,000 *(3 known)*		
❑ F-1225e (W-5480) • 18,000 *(27–32)*		
❑ F-1225g (W-5520) • 30,000 *(8 known)*		
❑ F-1225h (W-5540) • 213,000 *(325–375)*		

$10,000 Federal Reserve Notes

F-No. (W-No.) • Printage *(rarity)*	Grade	Comments
Series of 1918		
■ F-1135B (W-5555B) • 5,600 *(2 known)*		
■ F-1135D (W-5565D) • 800 *(1 known)*		
■ F-1135L (W-5595L) • 2,800 *(2 known)*		

SMALL-SIZE

$10,000 Federal Reserve Notes

F-No. (W-No.) • Printage *(rarity)*	Grade	Comments
Series of 1928		
■ F-2230B (W-5670B) • 4,680 *(1 known)*		
❑ F-2230D (W-5670D) • 960		
❑ F-2230E (W-5670E) • 3,024		
❑ F-2230F (W-5670F) • 1,440		
Series of 1934		
❑ F-2231A (W-5676A) • 9,720		
❑ F-2231B (W-5676B) • 11,520		
❑ F-2231C (W-5676C) • 6,000		
❑ F-2231E (W-5676E) • 1,200		
❑ F-2231F (W-5676F) • 2,400		
❑ F-2231G (W-5676G) • 3,840		
❑ F-2231H (W-5676H) • 2,040		
❑ F-2231J (W-5676J) • 1,200		
❑ F-2231K (W-5676K) • 1,200		
❑ F-2231L (W-5676L) • 3,600		

	Grade	Comments
❑		
❑		
❑		
❑		
❑		
❑		
❑		
❑		
❑		
❑		
❑		
❑		
❑		
❑		
❑		
❑		
❑		
❑		
❑		
❑		
❑		
❑		
❑		
❑		
❑		
❑		
❑		
❑		
❑		
❑		
❑		
❑		
❑		

POSTAGE AND FRACTIONAL CURRENCY

POSTAGE CURRENCY

F-No. (W-No.)	Grade	Comments
First Issue, 5¢ • 44,857,780 printed		
❑ F-1228 (W-6103)		
❑ F-1229 (W-6101)		
❑ F-1230 (W-6107)		
❑ F-1231 (W-6105)		
First Issue, 10¢ • 41,153,780 printed		
❑ F-1240 (W-6123)		
❑ F-1241 (W-6121)		
❑ F-1242 (W-6127)		
❑ F-1243 (W-6125)		
First Issue, 25¢ • 20,902,768 printed		
❑ F-1279 (W-6143)		
❑ F-1280 (W-6141)		
❑ F-1281 (W-6147)		
❑ F-1282 (W-6145)		
First Issue, 50¢ • 17,263,344 printed		
❑ F-1310 (W-6162)		
❑ F-1310a (W-6163)		
❑ F-1311 (W-6161)		
❑ F-1312 (W-6167)		
❑ F-1313 (W-6165)		

FRACTIONAL CURRENCY

F-No. (W-No.)	Grade	Comments
Second Issue, 5¢ • 56,708,296 printed		
❏ F-1232 (W-6201)		
❏ F-1233 (W-6203)		
❏ F-1234 (W-6205)		
❏ F-1235 (W-6207)		
Second Issue, 10¢ • 63,012,579 printed		
❏ F-1244 (W-6221)		
❏ F-1245 (W-6223)		
❏ F-1246 (W-6225)		
❏ F-1247 (W-6227)		
❏ F-1248 (W-6229)		
❏ F-1249 (W-6231)		
Second Issue, 25¢ • 32,143,653 printed		
❏ F-1283 (W-6251)		
❏ F-1284 (W-6253)		
❏ F-1285 (W-6255)		
❏ F-1286 (W-6257)		
❏ F-1288 (W-6259)		
❏ F-1289 (W-6261)		
❏ F-1290 (W-6263)		
Second Issue, 50¢ • 13,524,002 printed		
❏ F-1316 (W-6271)		
❏ F-1317 (W-6273)		
❏ F-1318 (W-6275)		
❏ F-1320 (W-6277)		
❏ F-1321 (W-6279)		
❏ F-1322 (W-6281)		

F-No. (W-No.)	Grade	Comments
Third Issue, 3¢ • 20,064,130 printed		
❏ F-1226 (W-6301)		
❏ F-1227 (W-6303)		
Third Issue, 5¢ • 13,140,055 printed		
❏ F-1236 (W-6315)		
❏ F-1237 (W-6317)		
❏ F-1238 (W-6311)		
❏ F-1239 (W-6313)		
Third Issue, 10¢ • 169,761,345 printed		
❏ F-1251 (W-6337)		
❏ F-1252 (W-6343)		
❏ F-1253 (W-6339)		
❏ F-1254 (W-6341)		
❏ F-1255 (W-6331)		
❏ F-1255a (W-6333)		
❏ F-1256 (W-6335)		
Third Issue, 25¢ • 124,572,755 printed		
❏ F-1291 (W-6365)		
❏ F-1292 (W-6366)		
❏ F-1294 (W-6351)		
❏ F-1295 (W-6353)		
❏ F-1296 (W-6355)		
❏ F-1297 (W-6357)		
❏ F-1298 (W-6359)		
❏ F-1299 (W-6361)		
❏ F-1300 (W-6363)		
Third Issue, 50¢ • 73,470,853 printed		
❏ F-1324 (W-6371)		
❏ F-1325 (W-6383)		

F-No. (W-No.)	Grade	Comments
❑ F-1326 (W-6381)		
❑ F-1327 (W-6379)		
❑ F-1328 (W-6373)		
❑ F-1329 (W-6375)		
❑ F-1330 (W-6377)		
❑ F-1331 (W-6391)		
❑ F-1332 (W-6397)		
❑ F-1333 (W-6395)		
❑ F-1334 (W-6393)		
❑ F-1335 (W-6399)		
❑ F-1336 (W-6405)		
❑ F-1337 (W-6403)		
❑ F-1338 (W-6401)		
❑ F-1339 (W-6407)		
❑ F-1340 (W-6413)		
❑ F-1341 (W-6411)		
❑ F-1342 (W-6409)		
❑ F-1343 (W-6415)		
❑ F-1344 (W-6423)		
❑ F-1345 (W-6421)		
❑ F-1346 (W-6419)		
❑ F-1347 (W-6425)		
❑ F-1348 (W-6433)		
❑ F-1349 (W-6431)		
❑ F-1350 (W-6429)		
❑ F-1351 (W-6435)		
❑ F-1352 (W-6443)		
❑ F-1353 (W-6441)		
❑ F-1354 (W-6439)		
❑ F-1355 (W-6417)		
❑ F-1356 (W-6427)		
❑ F-1357 (W-6437)		
❑ F-1358 (W-6445)		
❑ F-1359 (W-6451)		

F-No. (W-No.)	Grade	Comments
Third Issue, 50¢ *(continued)*		
❏ F-1360 (W-6449)		
❏ F-1361 (W-6447)		
❏ F-1362 (W-6471)		
❏ F-1363 (W-6477)		
❏ F-1364 (W-6475)		
❏ F-1365 (W-6473)		
❏ F-1366 (W-6453)		
❏ F-1367 (W-6459)		
❏ F-1368 (W-6457)		
❏ F-1369 (W-6455)		
❏ F-1370 (W-6461)		
❏ F-1371 (W-6467)		
❏ F-1372 (W-6465)		
❏ F-1373 (W-6463)		
❏ F-1373a (W-6469)		

F-No. (W-No.)	Grade	Comments
Fourth Issue, 10¢ • 349,409,600 printed		
❏ F-1257 (W-6601)		
❏ F-1258 (W-6603)		
❏ F-1259 (W-6605)		
❏ F-1261 (W-6607)		
Fourth Issue, 15¢ • 35,361,440 printed		
❏ F-1267 (W-6611)		
❏ F-1268 (W-6613)		
❏ F-1269 (W-6615)		
❏ F-1271 (W-6617)		
Fourth Issue, 25¢ • 235,689,024 printed		
❏ F-1301 (W-6621)		

F-No. (W-No.) • *(rarity)*	Grade	Comments
❑ F-1302 (W-6623)		
❑ F-1303 (W-6625)		
❑ F-1307 (W-6627)		
Fourth Issue, 50¢ • 154,799,200 printed		
❑ F-1374 (W-6631)		
❑ F-1376 (W-6635)		
❑ F-1379 (W-6639)		

F-No. (W-No.) • *(rarity)*	Grade	Comments
Fifth Issue, 10¢ • 199,899,000 printed		
❑ F-1264 (W-6651)		
❑ F-1265 (W-6653)		
❑ F-1266 (W-6655)		
Fifth Issue, 25¢ • 144,368,000 printed		
❑ F-1308 (W-6661)		
❑ F-1309 (W-6663)		
Fifth Issue, 50¢ • 13,160,000 printed		
❑ F-1381 (W-6667)		

FRACTIONAL CURRENCY SHIELDS

F-No. (W-No.) • *(rarity)*	Grade	Comments
❑ F-1382 (W-6801) • *(300–400)*		
❑ F-1383 (W-6803) • *(20 known)*		
❑ F-1383a (W-6805) • *(10 known)*		

SPECIMENS AND PROOFS

F-No. (W-No.)	Grade	Comments
First Issue, Postage Currency, 5¢ • 43,560 printed		
❏ F-1231-SP (W-7001)		
❏ F-1231-SP (W-7003)		
❏ F-1231-SP (W-7005)		
❏ F-1231-SP (W-7008)		
First Issue, Postage Currency, 10¢ • 67,560 printed		
❏ F-1243-SP (W-7011)		
❏ F-1243-SP (W-7013)		
❏ F-1243-SP (W-7015)		
❏ F-1243-SP (W-7018)		
First Issue, Postage Currency, 25¢ • 62,688 printed		
❏ F-1282-SP (W-7021)		
❏ F-1282-SP (W-7023)		
❏ F-1282-SP (W-7025)		
❏ F-1282-SP (W-7028)		
First Issue, Postage Currency, 50¢ • 43,488 printed		
❏ F-1313-SP (W-7031)		
❏ F-1313-SP (W-7033)		
❏ F-1313-SP (W-7035)		
❏ F-1313-SP (W-7038)		
Second Issue, Fractional Currency, 5¢ • 18,000 printed		
❏ F-1232-SP (W-7101)		
❏ F-1232-SP (W-7103)		
❏ F-1232-SP (W-7105)		
❏ F-1232-SP (W-7107)		
Second Issue, Fractional Currency, 10¢ • 18,000 printed		
❏ F-1244-SP (W-7111)		
❏ F-1244-SP (W-7113)		
❏ F-1244-SP (W-7115)		
❏ F-1244-SP (W-7117)		
Second Issue, Fractional Currency, 25¢ • 18,000 printed		
❏ F-1283-SP (W-7121)		
❏ F-1283-SP (W-7123)		

FRACTIONAL CURRENCY

F-No. (W-No.)	Grade	Comments
❏ F-1283-SP (W-7125)		
❏ F-1283-SP (W-7127)		
Second Issue, Fractional Currency, 50¢ • 18,000 printed		
❏ F-1314-SP (W-7131)		
❏ F-1314-SP (W-7133)		
❏ F-1314-SP (W-7135)		
❏ F-1314-SP (W-7137)		
Third Issue, Fractional Currency, 3¢ • 21,000 printed		
❏ F-1226-SP (W-7201)		
❏ F-1226-SP (W-7203)		
❏ F-1227-SP (W-7205)		
❏ F-1227-SP (W-7207)		
❏ F-1227-SP (W-7209)		
❏ F-1227-SP (W-7211)		
Third Issue, Fractional Currency, 5¢ • 31,500 printed		
❏ F-1236-SP (W-7239)		
❏ F-1236-SP (W-7241)		
❏ F-1238-SP (W-7231)		
❏ F-1238-SP (W-7233)		
❏ F-1238-SP (W-7235)		
❏ F-1238-SP (W-7237)		
Third Issue, Fractional Currency, 10¢ • 54,250 printed		
❏ F-1251-SP (W-7251)		
❏ F-1251-SP (W-7253)		
❏ F-1251-SP (W-7267)		
❏ F-1251-SP (W-7269)		
❏ F-1253-SP (W-7255)		
❏ F-1253-SP (W-7257)		
❏ F-1254-SP (W-7259)		
❏ F-1254-SP (W-7261)		
❏ F-1255-SP (W-7263)		
❏ F-1255-SP (W-7265)		

FRACTIONAL CURRENCY Specimens

F-No. (W-No.)	Grade	Comments
Third Issue, Fractional Currency, 15¢ • 25,800 printed		
❑ F-1272-SP (W-7285)		
❑ F-1272-SP (W-7287)		
❑ F-1272-SP (W-7301)		
❑ F-1272-SP (W-7303)		
❑ F-1273-SP (W-7289)		
❑ F-1274-SP (W-7293)		
❑ F-1274-SP (W-7295)		
❑ F-1274-SP (W-7305)		
❑ F-1274-SP (W-7307)		
❑ F-1275-SP (W-7297)		
❑ F-1275-SP (W-7299)		
❑ F-1276-SP (W-7281) • *(1 known)*		
Third Issue, Fractional Currency, 25¢ • est. 50,000 printed		
❑ F-1291-SP (W-7329)		
❑ F-1291-SP (W-7331)		
❑ F-1294-SP (W-7321)		
❑ F-1294-SP (W-7323)		
❑ F-1294-SP (W-7325)		
❑ F-1294-SP (W-7327)		
Third Issue, Fractional Currency, 50¢ • 50,584 printed		
❑ F-1324-SP (W-7351)		
❑ F-1324-SP (W-7353)		
❑ F-1324-SP (W-7387)		
❑ F-1324-SP (W-7389)		
❑ F-1328-SP (W-7355)		
❑ F-1328-SP (W-7357)		
❑ F-1329-SP (W-7363)		
❑ F-1329-SP (W-7365)		
❑ F-1330a-SP (W-7359)		
❑ F-1330a-SP (W-7361)		
❑ F-1331-SP (W-7379)		
❑ F-1331-SP (W-7381)		
❑ F-1339-SP (W-7383)		
❑ F-1339-SP (W-7385)		

FRACTIONAL CURRENCY

F-No. (W-No.)	Grade	Comments
❏ F-1343-SP (W-7367)		
❏ F-1343-SP (W-7369)		
❏ F-1355-SP (W-7371)		
❏ F-1355-SP (W-7373)		
❏ F-1357a-SP (W-7375)		
❏ F-1357a-SP (W-7377)		

MISCELLANEOUS

	Grade	Comments
❑		
❑		
❑		
❑		
❑		
❑		
❑		
❑		
❑		
❑		
❑		
❑		
❑		
❑		
❑		
❑		
❑		
❑		
❑		
❑		
❑		
❑		
❑		
❑		
❑		
❑		
❑		
❑		
❑		
❑		
❑		
❑		